Tourism, Travel, and Blogging

Travel often inspires the creation of narratives about journeys and destinations, more so with the increasing availability of online platforms, applications for smartphones and tablets, and various other social media technologies. This book examines travel blogs and their associated social media as a form of self-presentation that negotiates the tensions between discourses of travel and tourism. As such, it addresses how contemporary travellers use online platforms to communicate their experiences of journeys and destinations, and how the traveller/tourist dichotomy finds expression in these narratives. Addressing the need for more in-depth analysis through a study of blogs, this exploration of networked narratives of an individual's travel experience considers personal motivations, self-promotion, and self-presentation as key factors in the creation of both personal and commercial travel blogs. As this text applies concepts such as self-presentation and heteroglossia, it will be of interest to both students and scholars of tourism, new media, sociology, cultural studies, and discourse studies.

Deepti Ruth Azariah teaches professional writing and publishing, creative writing, and web communication in the School of Media, Culture, and Creative Arts, Curtin University, Perth, Western Australia. Her research interests include discourse analysis, travel writing, and digital publishing. She has also taught mass communication at the University of Mumbai and has published a number of short stories for children with *The Hindu*, an Indian national daily.

New Directions in Tourism Analysis

Series Editor: Dimitri Ioannides

E-TOUR, Mid Sweden University, Sweden

Although tourism is becoming increasingly popular both as a taught subject and an area for empirical investigation, the theoretical underpinnings of many approaches have tended to be eclectic and somewhat underdeveloped. However, recent developments indicate that the field of tourism studies is beginning to develop in a more theoretically informed manner, but this has not yet been matched by current publications.

The aim of this series is to fill this gap with high quality monographs or edited collections that seek to develop tourism analysis at both theoretical and substantive levels using approaches which are broadly derived from allied social science disciplines such as Sociology, Social Anthropology, Human and Social Geography, and Cultural Studies. As Tourism Studies covers a wide range of activities and sub fields, certain areas such as Hospitality Management and Business, which are already well provided for, would be excluded. The series will therefore fill a gap in the current overall pattern of publication.

Suggested themes to be covered by the series, either singly or in combination, include consumption, cultural change, development, gender, globalisation, political economy, social theory, and sustainability.

For a full list of titles in this series, please visit www.routledge.com/New-Directions-in-Tourism-Analysis/book-series/ASHSER1207

37 Being and Dwelling through Tourism
Catherine Palmer

38 Dark Tourism
Practice and interpretation
Edited by Glenn Hooper and John J. Lennon

39 Tourism Destination Evolution
Edited by Patrick Brouder, Salvador Anton Clavé, Alison Gill and Dimitri Ioannides

40 Tourism, Travel, and Blogging
A discursive analysis of online travel narratives
Deepti Ruth Azariah

Tourism, Travel, and Blogging

A discursive analysis of online travel narratives

Deepti Ruth Azariah

Routledge
Taylor & Francis Group
LONDON AND NEW YORK

First published 2017
by Routledge
2 Park Square, Milton Park, Abingdon, Oxon OX14 4RN

and by Routledge
711 Third Avenue, New York, NY 10017

Routledge is an imprint of the Taylor & Francis Group, an informa business

British Library Cataloguing in Publication Data
A catalogue record for this book is available from the British Library

Library of Congress Cataloging in Publication Data
A catalog record for this book has been requested

ISBN: 978-1-4724-5981-7 (hbk)
ISBN: 978-1-315-55068-8 (ebk)

Typeset in Times New Roman
by Saxon Graphics Ltd, Derby

For Miguel

Contents

Figures

Acknowledgements

This book owes its completion to the support and encouragement of many people. It is a pleasure to thank all those who made this possible.

The editorial team at Taylor and Francis have been of immense help and their guidance has been instrumental in the writing of this research monograph. In particular, I would like to thank Philippa Mullins and Emma Travis for believing in my proposal and for supporting me.

My family has been a constant source of inspiration during the long and sometimes difficult journey that has been the writing of this text. As always, they have been the best of travel companions. I would like to thank my parents, Chandran and Rani, and my brother, Rubik, for their faith in me, for their patience, for impromptu proofreading, and for simply being there when I needed them.

I have been fortunate to have two excellent colleagues and doctoral supervisors in Deborah Hunn and Tama Leaver of Curtin University. They have been my pathfinders when I lost my sense of direction. Their guidance and constructive criticism of my writing has been invaluable and I appreciate their keen interest and enthusiastic support. I would also like to thank Tim Dolin for his contribution to the writing of my thesis.

I would like to thank all the friends I have met along the way, whose help and advice has been invaluable. In particular, I am grateful to Robyn Creagh, Alana Arcus, Jane Armstrong, and Joey Wu for coffee and conversation and especially for listening and offering a shoulder to lean on when the going got rough. I also thank my other friends at St Martin-in-the-Fields, especially Bill and Judy Mackintosh and Ken Bennett, and others who are too many to name, but whose care and support is not too little to be forgotten. Finally, Miguel, for you were there at the journey's end and have made all this worthwhile.

Because of you, I have reached my destination.

1 Introduction

Tourism, travel, and blogging

More often than not, it is preferable to be perceived as a traveller than a tourist, or so researchers and writers of travel narratives would have us believe (Fussell 1980; Galani-Moutafi 2000; McCabe 2005; O'Reilly 2005). Travel is associated with authenticity, adventure, and spontaneity. Tourism, on the other hand, has the less desirable connotations of being planned and superficial. This view is emphatically encapsulated in American historian Daniel J. Boorstin's observation that: 'The traveller was active; he went strenuously in search of people, of adventure, of experience. The tourist is passive; he expects interesting things to happen to him. He goes "sight-seeing"….' (1992, p. 85).

These associations are not particularly new – the question of a distinction between travel and tourism and whether such a dichotomy does indeed exist has long engaged academic debate in tourist studies (Franklin and Crang 2001). Following the rise of mass tourism, this has found expression in many works of travel literature. Writers such as G. K. Chesterton and William Wordsworth have denigrated the tourist and deplored the decline of real travel. Other more contemporary theorists have suggested that that the traveller no longer exists, but has been supplanted by the mass tourist (Fussell 1980; Urry 2002). This book adds to this longstanding discussion with its exploration of how the tensions between travel and tourism are discursively expressed and negotiated in a relatively new form of travel-related communication – the travel blog.

Travel has long inspired writing. Over the centuries, it has generated texts both fictional and promotional, ranging from the travel books, diaries and photographs that recount personal holiday experiences or record journeys of exploration to the brochures, guidebooks, postcards, and posters that are integral to commercial tourism. More recently, social media platforms such as blogs, social networks, microblogs and photo-sharing services, and applications for mobile phones and tablets have made it easier for those who travel to publish and publicise personal narratives of their travel experiences. This has introduced a variety of new discursive forms to an already extensive body of travel-related communication. Blogs have proved particularly popular. Generic platforms such as *Blogger* and *Wordpress* and travel-specific blogging sites such as *TravelBlog, TravelPod, BootsnAll, MyTripJournal* and *OffExploring* have enabled individuals to capture their travel experiences in words and images and share these with a large and diverse online audience. These online narratives incorporate various narrative techniques and discourses, the examination of which is the central purpose of this book.

In order to understand how discourses of travel and tourism inform travel blogs, it is first necessary to understand these texts as a narrative form. Blogs, otherwise known as weblogs, evolve from the traditions of diary writing and like their forerunners are usually serialised topical and personal narratives (McNeill 2003; Serfaty 2004a; Sorapure 2003; Van Dijck 2004; Walker Rettberg 2014). Interestingly, there is an allusion to travel in the terms 'blog' and 'weblog', which originate from the word 'log', referring to the nautical record of a journey (Walker Rettberg 2014, p. 30). Travel blogs resemble early travel diaries in that they are usually written as public documents intended for others to read. Yet, some significant differences also exist. The authors of the latter were, in general, renowned individuals whose travel narratives were usually sanctioned by the state. Moreover, unlike diaries, entries in a blog appear in reverse-chronological order, usually contain hyperlinks to other online resources and generally allow readers to comment on the content (Bruns and Jacobs 2006; Walker Rettberg 2014). In comparison with personal diaries and early travel diaries, blogs are, for the most part, participatory rather than exclusive and democratised rather than elitist. As such, they are personal narratives, yet they are also public by nature.

Given their personal yet public quality, it is hardly surprising that blogs are often interpreted from the symbolic interactionist perspective, which stresses the importance of social context to the concept of self. Erving Goffman's conceptualisation in *The Presentation of Self in Everyday Life* (1969) of social interaction as a stage performance has proved an appropriate metaphor for understanding how individuals position themselves online and interact with their audiences (see, for example, Bullingham and Vasconcelos 2013; McCullagh 2008; Papacharissi 2009; Pinch 2010; Reed 2005; Robinson 2007; Sanderson 2008; Schmidt 2007; Trammell and Keshelashvili 2005). Within this context, blogs may be described as a narrative form of self-presentation. Blogging in this sense is a 'performative act' (Baumer *et al.* 2011). Blogs themselves are 'straightforward indexes of self' available to a wide audience (Reed 2005, p. 27). As Jan Schmidt notes, 'publishing a blog is a way of self-presentation that has to meet certain expectations about personal authenticity while maintaining a balance between staying private and being public' (2007, p. 1413), which conclusion succinctly articulates both the social aspects of these texts and the needs of their audiences while also emphasising the centrality of the self in the narrative.

Extending this view to travel blogs, this book examines these narratives principally as forms of self-presentation since the description of travel experiences often involves the presentation of a traveller self. However, this is but one of many other roles that travel bloggers may occupy – other examples discussed in this book include adventurer, explorer, foodie, travel writer, tour guide, travel advisor, technology expert, teacher, and so on. It is necessary, therefore, to acknowledge that this self-presentation comprises multiple voices and many discourses including those of travel and tourism. This 'presentation of multiple personas', as Holland and Huggan (1998, p. 16) term it, through the interchange of narrative positions is characteristic of most travel narratives. Such an online self has often been described as being multifaceted or 'threaded' (Hevern 2004, p. 322). The possibly disparate positions it occupies are indicated by the different narrative voices in which the self speaks, sometimes within the space of a single blog entry.

This book proposes that the multifaceted online self of a travel blogger can be critically interpreted through juxtaposing Goffman's self-presentation and Russian discourse theorist Mikhail Bakhtin's heteroglossia (the presence of multiple discourses) and polyphony (multiple narrative voices). The combination of these two concepts in the academic interrogation of online self-presentation is little used but hardly innovative (for examples, see Hermans 2004; Hevern 2004; Sanderson 2008; Serfaty 2004b). In Goffman's terms, individuals adopt several faces, each a different aspect of the same self, to meet the needs of the particular social situation they are in and the audience they interact with. From a Bakhtinian point of view, such an online self is polyphonic for speaking in multiple voices, each corresponding with the narrative roles it occupies. Travel blogs are polyphonic when the voices of the author, readers, advertisers, and web hosts interact with each other. They are heteroglossic for incorporating narrative forms and styles associated with various social spheres particularly those associated with travel as opposed to tourism. Approaching travel blogs from the combined theoretical perspectives of Goffmanian self-presentation and Bakhtinian discourse thus facilitates a deeper and meaningful interrogation of an online self that plays multiple narrative roles.

Often, the features of the online platform, in this case the blog, facilitate the performance of the different narrative roles online. In saying this, the book subscribes to Trevor Pinch's conclusion that in the presentation of self in any social situation 'the *staging* of the interaction, the *mediation* of the interaction and its *performance* depend crucially on the detailed material and technological arrangements in place' (Pinch 2010, p. 414). In other words, a considered employment of the formal features of a travel blog in the staging of a narrative role, such as that of a traveller, and interacting with the audience witnessing this performance are both fundamental to the presentation of the online self. These features include discursive elements such as the title banner, the home page, the 'About Me' section, and the entries, all of which are usually created and customised by the bloggers themselves. These indicate the various aspects of a travel blogger's online self, such as the itinerant adventurer implied by *Wandering Earl* (Baron 2016) or the culinary tourist in *Forks and Jets* (Rees and Rees 2008). Other elements such as the comments box below each entry, widgets that distribute content to linked platforms such as a *Facebook* page or a *Twitter* stream as well as hyperlinks to other similar websites and blogs facilitate the performance of various roles through social interaction. Hyperlinks to other travel-related blogs, in particular, enable the display of a network of connections to like-minded individuals, a technique that Donath and boyd have observed to be characteristic of online self-presentation (2004). Accordingly, this book examines how individuals use such online tools and features, the affordances[1] of various blogging platforms, arguing that these are integral to the presentation of the travel experience and a traveller self in an online narrative.

A matter of discourse

Although the travel blogs examined in this book generally present multiple personas to a single online self, from a discursive point of view, the presentation of the self as a traveller rather than a tourist is of particular interest; first, as this distinction has been repeatedly questioned by tourism academics, and second, because it introduces tensions in the narrative (Franklin and Crang 2001). The traveller is generally defined, against the tourist, as being a more sophisticated individual who seeks unique off-the-beaten-path experiences instead of the destinations marketed by the tourism industry. Likewise, while contemporary research often uses 'travel' and 'tourism' interchangeably, the two terms suggest very different contexts. Travel is generally regarded as more authentic for being adventurous, spontaneous, and involving some degree of hardship and therefore being more worthy of admiration than tourism, which is perceived as being superficial, passive, devoid of any real risk and commercially motivated (Fussell 1980; O'Reilly 2005).

These differences are generally expressed through specific narrative techniques. Several analyses of forms of travel-related communication indicate that individuals use a certain language to present the self as a traveller and associate their experiences with travel as opposed to tourism (Dann 1999; O'Reilly 2005; McCabe 2005). Conversely, tourist discourse has clearly identifiable narrative features that reflect its commercial associations and promotional purpose (Dann 1996). Both discursive styles are manifest in a number of travel blogs, which position the blogger as a traveller but are also featured on tourism website *Lonely Planet* (2016) or are commercialised in other ways.

It seems reasonable therefore to argue that in order to understand how individuals present themselves in travel blogs and how these texts negotiate discursive tensions, it is necessary to identify and establish specific narrative techniques, social contexts, and themes associated with discourses of travel and tourism. By subscribing to Jaworski and Coupland's interpretation of discourse as 'language reflecting social order' (1999, p. 3), it is possible to demonstrate how blogs about travel can provide a broader picture of some of the practices or views associated with travel and tourism. Specific activities related to tourism or travel shape the narrative that is the travel blog. For example, taking an iconic photograph of a popular destination signifies that one is a tourist just as going off the beaten path communicates the idea that one is a traveller. Similarly, Jaworski and Coupland's broad view of discourse as consisting not only of written and spoken words but also of 'non-linguistic semiotic systems' (1999, p. 7) such as performance art, painting, photography, sculpture, etc. facilitates the examination of travel blogs as narratives incorporating many forms – diary-like entries, photographs, advertisements, and a range of paratextual elements such as titles, title banners, and a variety of other visual elements. Each of these corresponds with social contexts relevant to the practice of either travel or tourism via which an audience may recognise the figure of the travel writer, the touristic photographer, or the promoter of commercial tourism. Several existing studies of backpacker narratives, travel writing, and other forms of travel-related communication outline the narrative forms and techniques used to distinguish travel from tourism (Elsrud 2001; Noy 2004; O'Reilly 2005). Extrapolating from these, it is possible to arrive at a general framework for travel discourse that can be applied to the study of travel blogs. Similarly, a significant body of research stems from Graham Dann's work on the 'language of tourism' and John Urry and Jonas Larsen's investigation of a 'tourist gaze' as exhibited in advertisements, brochures, photographs, posters, and a variety of other similar travel-related texts that organise touristic consumption of place. These studies provide a useful starting point for identifying tourist discourse in both the words and images of travel blogs (Dann 1996; Urry and Larsen 2011).

The language of travel

Several critical discussions of travel-related communication demonstrate how those who describe their journeys often disassociate themselves from the figure of the tourist and the commercial tourism industry, preferring instead to position themselves as travellers. A study of discussions between backpackers by Greg Richards and Julie Wilson finds that the obvious strategy of identifying one's self as a traveller is a predominant theme (2004). An excellent point of reference is Graham Dann's demonstration of how three authors of travel books – Paul Theroux, Ted Simon and Nick Danziger – manipulate space and time in their narratives to 'write out' the tourist and present their experiences as travel (Dann 1999). They do this by describing travel as being timeless, solitary, and focused on the journey rather than the destination.

Several other studies of descriptions of travel, as opposed to touristic, experiences validate these observations. For instance, David Dunn finds that the impression of travel as a solitary experience is also explicit in the way some television programmes position their presenters as lone travellers (Dunn 2005). This sense of solitude is created in travel narratives by employing such techniques as a personal tone, an emphasis on the self and an absence of references to fellow travellers (Blanton 2002; Dann 1999; Robinson 2004). Visiting a place where time appears to pass quicker or slower than one is accustomed to, also associates an experience with travel (Molz 2010). The impression that an individual is a traveller is also generally achieved by toning down references to iconic destinations while highlighting 'unique experiences off the beaten track' and associating these with values such as adventurousness, spontaneity, and heroism, as expressed by writers like Ernest Hemingway, Jack Kerouac and Bruce Chatwin (Richards and Wilson 2004, pp. 60–61). The narration of a journey as a difficult or risky undertaking and as an accomplishment to be admired is a recurring element of backpacker narratives (Noy 2004; O'Reilly 2005). Often, what emerges from studies such as these is a sense that much travel writing is gendered, masculine, privileging a male gaze, and centred around the white European male (Galani-Moutafi 2000; Pritchard and Morgan 2000). This book presents a working definition of the discourse of travel based on these findings.

The presence of the language of travel in a text is, therefore, largely determined by its narrative voice, theme, tone, the organisation of and reference to space and time, and the positioning of its narrator. First of all, the travel experience is generally presented as a solitary activity, which heightens the impression that it is both personal and focused on the self. This emphasis on the personal, often manifest in the use of a first person voice in most texts concerned with narrating travel as opposed to tourism, imbues these texts with a sense of aloneness. This effect is also achieved by 'writing out' fellow travellers and tourists (Dann 1999). In this sense, travel is about isolation and frequently uses the metaphor of an inner journey (Noy 2004). A second quality of the travel experience is that it is a difficult one, accompanied by hardship rather than ease. It is described as an adventure, an exploration, and often a nomadic encounter of that which is previously undiscovered or unrecognised, accomplished at some cost to the traveller. Third, travel is distinguished by its lack of reference to destination, emphasising the journey rather than the place. Destinations are thus only mentioned for being unique or off the beaten track. Indeed, travel is characterised by its uniqueness, for being an escape from routine, and so being something out of the ordinary. A fourth feature of travel is its sense of timelessness, and this is usually conveyed by narrating the experience as if it is happening at the present time – an effect generally achieved by the use of the present tense. The spontaneity of travel also contributes to this sense of a lack of preoccupation with time. Consequently, the self as a traveller is generally perceived to be a lone adventurer, indicatively if not actually male, headed for places unknown or hitherto unexplored, and more concerned with the hardships encountered during a journey than with following any itinerary. This working definition is useful as a basis for identifying the narrative techniques of travel discourse; however, it is necessary to recognise that a text that describes an experience as travel can also have elements of touristic discourse.

The language of tourism

As with travel discourse, particular themes, narrative techniques, and a certain treatment of time and space characterise the discourse of tourism. There have been a number of efforts to analyse how discourse represents place and directs its consumption by tourists. Of these, a particularly relevant point of reference is Graham Dann's extensive and in-depth examination of various travel-related texts such as brochures, advertisements, and posters which concludes that there is a 'language of tourism', incorporating specific narrative techniques that address tourists and stimulate tourist activities (1996). The study considers many different forms of travel-related communication but does not distinguish between discourses of travel and tourism. However, it is worth noting that the majority of these have a commercial or promotional purpose. Also, while Dann's original purpose is to demonstrate how language constructs and directs a tourist's consumption of destinations, it also reveals the existence of a discourse of tourism, which though not diametrically opposed to travel discourse has, nonetheless, several qualities that mirror the traveller/tourist dichotomy.

A second point of reference is John Urry's work on the tourist gaze, which outlines how the representation of tourist destinations in various media directs the consumption of these same places. This is a process that reiterates the same touristic messages, ultimately resulting in a hermeneutic circle of representation, a concept first described by Heidegger, subsequently applied by Albers and James in their study of travel photography in postcards, and popularised by Urry (Albers and James 1988). This forms the basis of several studies that examine how tourists photograph sites they visit (Baerenholdt *et al.* 2003; Garrod 2009; Jenkins 2003). It is possible to extrapolate from these and identify narrative techniques characteristic of travel blog photographs or title banner images that are touristic.

If travel discourse emphasises the personal and is largely concerned with positioning the self as traveller, it does not necessarily follow that tourist discourse presents the self as tourist. Dann's framework for tourist discourse indicates that it is largely impersonal for several reasons (1996). While travel discourse generally looks inward to the self and is reflective, tourist discourse tends to look outward. First, there is often a lack of identification of the sender of the message. Second, texts in tourist discourse generally address an anonymous audience, an implied and occasionally explicit 'you' who is often positioned as a potential tourist and consumer, in a second person voice that is both knowledgeable and authoritarian. This is the voice Dann identifies in texts such as brochures and guidebooks, whose implicit narrators are usually positioned as guides or experts and use techniques such as 'ego-targeting' to promote destinations and direct individuals to consume places in a particular way. The style of address in touristic discourse is consequently often monologic. Third, the discourse of tourism essentially focuses on destination and reflects a commercial purpose in its promotion of place, usually through euphoric adjective-filled descriptions and tautology. Finally, in contrast with the timelessness of travel, tourist discourse is inextricably caught up in time, and this is what makes it superficial according to critics such as Paul Fussell. Where travel is fluid, spontaneous, and unfettered to itineraries, an organising principle of tourism is that a certain number of sites must be consumed within a particular period of time. The preoccupation with time is evident in techniques such as temporal contrast, indicated by a change of tense, to suggest that individuals can exchange a past state of dissatisfaction for a pleasant experience at some future destination (Dann 1996, pp. 200–201). The tourist experience is therefore characterised by its passivity – it is organised and planned rather than impulsive, it is guided rather than exploratory or adventurous, and it is perceived as commercially motivated.

The interpretation of the photographs in travel blogs requires a different set of critical tools. This book applies Mike Robinson and David Picard's findings (2009) on the distinctive style of tourist photographs in conjunction with concepts drawn from Susan Sontag's work on photography (1977) and tourism and Roland

Barthes' theories of the connotative meaning of images (1977, 1993) to the study of photographs in travel blogs. Also, John Urry's work (2002) on the hermeneutic circle of representation offers a means of understanding how photographic techniques associated with the promotion of tourism may be employed in the presentation of a travel experience and vice versa. A more elaborate explanation of how the theoretical framework employed in the examination of travel and tourist discourses in photographs is presented in the chapter dedicated to images in travel blogs.

A negotiation of discursive tensions

There is some implication here that certain forms of travel-related communication may be classified as being travel discourse while others may be termed touristic. For example, it may appear that travel writing is largely travel discourse whereas the guidebook is comprised of tourist discourse. This is perhaps largely because many previous analyses of these discourses tend to focus on a single form of travel-related communication and a single discourse. For example, O'Reilly's study (2005) looks mainly at backpacker narratives and analyses how the authors use travel discourse in their self-presentation. Similarly, Dann (1996) bases his findings on tourist discourse largely on analyses of guidebooks, posters, and brochures, that is to say texts that have clear associations with the tourism industry. There are few studies that look at how both discourses are manifest in a single form. Nevertheless, Dann also sees some aspects of tourist discourse in travel writing, a form of travel-related communication that he returns to in his later analyses of discourse. A classification of travel-related communication as either travel or tourist discourse simply based on genre is too easy and erroneous. A single form of travel-related communication can contain discourses of both travel and tourism and this applies to travel blogs as well.

Although this book draws on the aforementioned studies and applies these findings to reveal the perceived oppositions between discourses of travel and tourism, it does so to demonstrate that the discourses of travel and tourism are by no means mutually exclusive or independent of each other. Instead, they constantly negotiate each other and that which is presented as travel can have touristic implications. It can be argued that travel paves the way for tourism. For example, a narrative describing a destination that offers a unique travel experience by being off the beaten path can potentially prompt others to visit the same place, as a result turning it into a popular tourist site. For authors who intend to distance themselves from touristic activities by seeking out such an experience, this is perhaps an unintentional and unwanted consequence of creating such narratives. Sometimes, travel is subsumed by tourism. Backpackers generally regard themselves as being different from tourists for seeking adventurous and difficult travel experiences, and yet backpacking itself is now easier to do and is increasingly a mainstream touristic activity with the associated commodification that this implies (O'Reilly 2006). Conversely, it may be said that travel grows out of tourism when individuals seek experiences that are off the beaten path in order to avoid overcrowded tourist sites.

There is some suggestion of this in Dean MacCannell's conception of a 'second gaze' that begins by looking at a touristic attraction and then looks beyond it for that which is hidden, unexpected, or real (MacCannell 2001). Ultimately, the principal purpose of the conceptual framework suggested here is to identify courses of travel and tourism in blogs in order to demonstrate how these are perceived to be distinct and oppositional and yet constantly collapsing into each other.

Shifting contours of travel blogs

There have been various attempts to define the blog format, but these descriptions are often inadequate and there are challenges to pinning down the specific characteristics of travel blogs. As Jill Walker Rettberg states, it is difficult to arrive at a 'watertight definition' of blogs, and by extension travel blogs (2014, p. 34). The majority of definitions of blogs are, for the most part, similar in their emphasis on technical features. This is perhaps because, as Walker Rettberg points out, it is easy to define blogs by their formal elements. In general, such definitions refer to the presence of entries, hyperlinks, comments, and other media (see Walker Rettberg 2014, p. 19; Bruns and Jacobs 2006, pp. 2–3; Schmidt 2007, p. 1409). The following chapter discusses some of these definitions in greater depth. There are several drawbacks to basing a study of travel blogs solely on such descriptions. On the one hand, they create a certain expectation of what qualities an online narrative or website should have to be termed a blog. Yet, and this is the argument of the following chapter, the presence of these features in a website does not necessarily make it a blog.

Defining travel blogs as forms of online language may be more suitable from a cultural studies perspective. As such, to quote Nancy Baym, (2010, p. 66) '[they] blend and incorporate styles from conversations and writing with stylistic and formal elements of film, television, music videos and photography and other genres and practices'. This description accommodates the tendency of travel blogs to incorporate a variety of media forms, using both words and images to present individuals and their experiences. Alternatively, given their self-presentational nature, blogs may be approached as online stories of the self. As such, they may be viewed, from the perspective of Nelson and Hull (2008), as narratives that often employ multiple discourses to reflect the authors and to meet the expectations of their audience. In fact, several studies interpret blogs as heteroglossic texts containing multiple discourses and narrative techniques (Andreasen 2006; Hevern 2004; Serfaty 2004a). That is to say they manifest a text's ability, according to Bakhtin, to include diverse forms drawn from different social and professional spheres such as speeches, letters, professional jargon, and everyday conversation (1981). It can be argued along these lines that travel blogs, whose written entries are often accompanied by photographs and videos, creatively combine multiple narrative forms.

Another definitive feature, often regarded as essential to blogs, is the presence of a clearly identifiable author and a distinct authorial voice (Nardi *et al.* 2004; Walker Rettberg 2014). There is some debate as to whether authors do indeed play a central role in their blogs. Nevertheless, despite arguments for the lessening of authorial control in such personal online narratives, there is evidence to suggest that particular formal features of the blog, such as their entries and links, do in fact highlight authorial presence, authorial voice and personal ownership (Chesher 2005; Landow 2006).

Given these inherent discursive qualities that must be acknowledged, an alternative approach is to view blogs as a genre and define them by their thematic content and discursive style (Lomborg 2009; Walker Rettberg 2014). A different set of parameters then comes into play. Stine Lomborg's genre-based typology of blogs overcomes the limitations of a number of existing technical definitions and categorisations of blogs by using three criteria – content, directionality and style, as represented by the three axes as seen in Figure 1.1 – to classify blogs. On the face of it, travel blogs should occupy a position on the upper right-hand quadrant due to their capacity for social interaction as well as their clearly defined theme. However, this is too easy a classification. In actual fact, Lomborg's framework demonstrates the particular challenges to describing travel blogs, which shift from intimacy to objectivity, from monologic description to dialogue with readers and from topical descriptions of place to internal reflections of the author, sometimes within a single entry. While this confounds any attempts to position these texts on a fixed point along these axes, such contradictions indicate the presence of multiple discourses in travel blogs and the somewhat amorphous nature of these texts.

The fact of the matter is that although blogs are often described by structure and function, their constantly changing nature complicates their definition. As Mary Garden observes, any investigation of blogs must use a definition of the format that is appropriate to the parameters of the study and recognises the 'shifting boundaries of the blogosphere' (2011, p. 13). Technical definitions can therefore be only a starting point analysing travel blogs. It is necessary to appreciate their

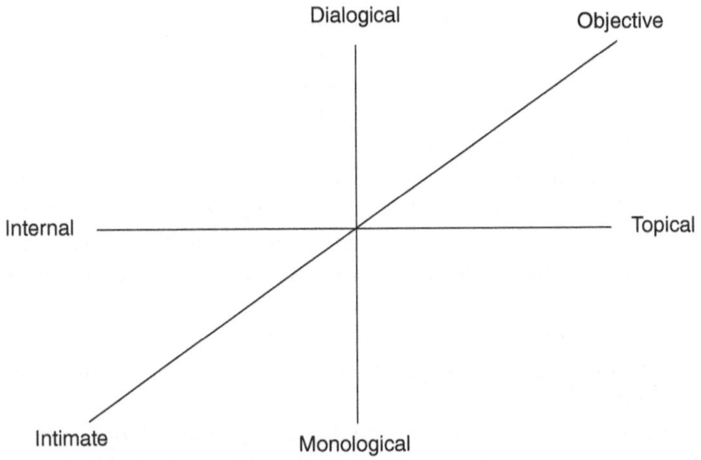

Figure 1.1 Stine Lomborg's typological dimensions for categorising weblogs

usefulness but also to move beyond them and consider the personal, social, heteroglossic and polyphonic nature of travel blogs, all of which are equally significant characteristic elements that influence the tensions between travel and tourism in these texts. Consequently, this book approaches travel blogs as online texts that are usually personal and self-presentational narratives of travel consisting of reverse-chronological entries with the capacity to link to other online platforms and resources and facilitate social interaction. It recognises that these texts, by virtue of being a form of online language, contain multiple discourses and voices.

The structure of the book

While this book's definition of travel blogs is by necessity flexible, it hardly makes it easier to circumscribe this investigation of the format. Given the enormous number of publicly available travel blogs, their increasingly distributed nature and the constant evolution of this platform, the exploration of the travel blogosphere could well be a journey without end. Not all new online content is indexed by search engines (Herring 2010). It is also difficult to access travel blogs that are kept private or created in languages other than English. A single travel blog can have hundreds of posts, not merely within the blog but also on other platforms such as social networks and microblogs, complicating a close textual analysis of all its content. Furthermore, some travel blogs are complete accounts, others are incomplete, and still others are works in progress. There is also the question of whether blogs written as accompaniments to television travel programmes or travel books should be regarded as travel blogs. This book cannot be an exhaustive study of all these narratives; however, it offers a comprehensive look at three principal types of travel blogs and their associated social media platforms.

The chapters are organised around Schmalleger and Carson's categorisation of travel blogs by authorship (2008). These include travel blogs from guidebook publishers, those published on travel-specific web hosts sponsored by commercial advertising and those that are independently hosted travel blogs and generally have a single author. *Lonely Planet*'s reputation as a leading publisher of guidebooks has been a deciding factor in the selection and study of *Tony Wheeler's Travels*. This travel blog was initially hosted on the *Lonely Planet* website but has since evolved into a website in its own right following the British Broadcasting Corporation's (BBC) acquisition of the firm. *TravelBlog*, *TravelPod* and *BootsnAll*, web hosts that figure prominently in the Google search results for 'travel blog', feature in a following chapter. Blogs have been previously chosen from these websites for researching destination image and consumers of touristic products (for examples, see Akehurst 2009; Schmallegger and Carson 2008; Wenger 2008) and by using a different approach, this book adds a new dimension to earlier findings. Here, the focus is on a few blogs that have received special mention on the web hosts' home pages. Finally, independently hosted travel blogs have been located both by using search engines as well as blogrolls and for the most part chosen for their reputation. For example, Gary Arndt's (2015) *Everything Everywhere* has featured in *Time*, and *Nomadic Matt's Travel Site* (Nomadic Matt

2016) is listed on many blogrolls and has since inspired several books by its author. Since independently hosted travel blogs generally have extensive links to content created by their authors on other social media platforms, this book includes a chapter on how travel bloggers use *Facebook* and *Twitter*. Photographs are an integral element in all of these blogs and are discussed not only in each chapter but also in depth in the penultimate chapter. The bloggers themselves are of different ages and social backgrounds and include individuals who identify themselves as backpackers, grey nomads, members of a tour group, and, arguably, a corporate blogger in Tony Wheeler. What follows is a description of the ground that each chapter does cover – an overview of how different travel blogs negotiate the relationship between discourses of travel and tourism.

The chapters

This foray into the travel blogosphere begins in the second chapter with an examination of *Lonely Planet* founder Tony Wheeler's eponymous website with reference to the previously discussed definitive traits of travel blogs. This text has been chosen specifically for its claim to being one of the earliest travel blogs. Although it is positioned as a blog and answers many of the requirements of being a blog, this text only partially resembles one. *Tony Wheeler's Travels* was originally hosted on the *Lonely Planet* website where it was essentially presented as a narrative of the founder's travel experiences. Nonetheless, it also served a promotional purpose and, despite having become a website in its own right, still is in fact inextricably bound up in discourses of tourism. That is to say, travel discourse often collapses into tourist discourse. The inherent discursive tensions point to a need for a more expansive definition of blogs.

The third chapter examines the extent to which blogs hosted on travel-specific web hosts, which are sponsored by tourism advertising, can be said to give a sense of who the author is. At least some of the content in these blogs, depending on the service of choice, comes from the web host and the advertising sponsor. The three web hosts selected for this analysis are *TravelPod*, *TravelBlog* and *BootsnAll* (TravelPod 2016; TravelBlog 2016; BootsnAll 2016, respectively). Here the discourse of travel encapsulated in blog entries forms the basis for advertisements generated by programs such as Google's AdSense. The chapter also illustrates how authors rely on tourist discourse to authenticate their narratives of travel and the self as traveller. It argues that the tensions between travel and tourist discourses can in fact complicate authorship, authorial identity, authorial voice, and the positioning of the blog. The aim here is first, to demonstrate the hybridity of the travel blog, and second, to suggest a broader interpretation of authorship with respect to blogs found on travel-specific web hosts sponsored by advertising.

Chapter 4 discusses the self-presentational aspects of independently hosted travel blogs. As in the previous chapter, the idea that a blog gives a sense of its author is examined here, but with significantly different results. In general, the travel bloggers studied in Chapter 4 are keen to present themselves as travellers and label themselves as adventurers, explorers, and nomads. In these blogs, narrative techniques of both travel and tourism create the impression that the authors are authentic bloggers. The analysis suggests that discursive tensions play a significant part in this self-presentation.

Chapter 5 explores the idea that a blog is a centralising force whose content is distributed across a range of online platforms. It demonstrates how authors of independent travel blogs use *Facebook* and *Twitter* and discusses how the discursive tensions between travel and tourism in their blogs extend to the other platforms they link to. Consequently, any consideration of blogs as being social in nature needs to account for connections and conversations they have with other platforms. The chapter explores the relationship *Lonely Planet* has with several independent travel bloggers. It should be noted here that this publisher uses the idea of travel as opposed to tourism to promote its products and services. Thus, the networked self-presentation has some implications for discursive tension.

Visual elements in a travel blog have considerable significance and accordingly Chapter 6 explores the role of travel-related photographs in some depth. It finds that discursive tensions extend to photographs as well. Here, the meaning of a photograph and the experience it represents is negotiated in the interaction between bloggers and their audiences. The analysis demonstrates travel-related photographs have considerable bearing on the impression of the travel blogger and the places they visit. It reveals further links between bloggers and *Lonely Planet*. The chapter also discusses how tagging influences the meaning of these photographs. It suggests that there cannot be a single fixed meaning for a photograph or the destination it represents.

The concluding chapter reiterates the particular challenges to defining travel blogs and suggests some key factors that must be taken into consideration while attempting to do so. It also suggests that technology has some bearing on how the self is presented in these texts. It goes on to collate various findings on the relationship between *Lonely Planet* and those who create travel-related content and considers the implications this may have. It ends with a summary of the different ways in which travel blogs negotiate the tensions between the discourses of travel and tourism.

New directions

If much contemporary research no longer distinguishes between travel and tourism or between traveller and tourist, this is because over the years the debate has shifted from equating travellers with tourists, to differentiating between the two and then to such a blurring of these distinctions that travellers have ceased to exist and only tourists remain. In the Western tradition, for instance, especially during the eighteenth and nineteenth centuries, travel is described as an enriching experience. Wealthy young aristocrats departed on the Grand Tour, which was considered a form of training, a necessary phase of their preparation for entering society (Buzard 2002, pp. 39–41). The 'traveller' of this period is synonymous with the 'tourist' (Buzard 1993, p. 1). However, the introduction of mass tourism and the package tour soon led to a distinction being made between the traveller and the tourist and the words gained different connotations (Hulme and Youngs 2002, p. 7). Writers of this period such as William Wordsworth denigrate the tourist as a shallow-minded figure while the traveller is portrayed as individualistic, bold, resilient, and someone to be admired (Buzard 1993). For the most part, in the literature of the twentieth century, tourism symbolises the decay of culture, especially for modernist thinkers such as D. H. Lawrence, T. S. Eliot and Samuel Beckett (Buzard 1993, p. 2). For many academics in the latter half of the twentieth century, there is only the tourist. Among the more prominent of these is American historian Daniel Boorstin (1992), who describes all those who travel as mass tourists. Similarly, Paul Fussell's *Abroad*, published in 1982, distinguishes between travel and tourism but deplores the replacement of travel by tourism. More recent scholarship is concerned with the figure of the post-tourist, an individual who is self-deprecatingly aware of his or her position as a tourist, as described by Maxine Feifer and popularised by John Urry.

Thus far, a number of discursive approaches to the study of tourism, such as those inspired by Graham Dann's *The Language of Tourism* (1996) or John Urry's *The Tourist Gaze* (2002), have been concerned with how various media representations of place construct the tourist experience. Alternatively, existing analyses have focused on the significance of discourse in organising the consumption of tourist experiences, and tourism in turn has been regarded as a discourse that shapes globalisation and knowledge of the world (Franklin and Crang 2001; Jaworski and Pritchard 2005; Thurlow and Jaworski 2010; Urry and Larsen 2011). Such studies examine a variety of travel-related texts in print or broadcast media such as brochures, in-flight magazines, photographs, posters, and guidebooks. There has been some application of discourse theory to the study of issues related to identity and the self in online travel narratives such as websites, one example of this being Richard W. Hallet and Judith Kaplan-Weinger's comprehensive critical analysis of official tourism websites (Hallett and Kaplan-Weinger 2010). This investigates how discourse constructs both the tourist and the destination, examining in particular the implications of this for national identity. Academic interest in the narrative structure and content of travel blogs is comparatively scant and tends to have an outward rather than an inward focus, investigating visitors' impressions of a place or how the construction of identity enables them to make sense of their experience of a destination. In fact, destination image is central to several studies of travel blogs (Carson 2008; Pan *et al.* 2007; Schmallegger and Carson 2008; Wenger 2008). As yet, little has been written about the discourses constituting travel blogs, nor has there been a significant exploration of the distinctions between travel and tourism in online narratives on the subject.

Still, a number of recent studies of travel-related communication point to a revival of academic interest in how the traveller/tourist dichotomy is manifest in discourse (Gillespie 2007). For instance, O'Reilly's analysis of backpacker narratives (2005) indicates that these distinctions continue to be expressed by those who travel. Likewise, Scott McCabe observes that it is important to understand how individuals 'construct' themselves as travellers and not tourists, given the negativity associated with the latter and to look more closely at how people talk about their tourist activities (2005). This endorses Franklin and Crang's assertion that there is 'a continual oscillation between the poles of traveller and tourist' in the study of travel and tourism' (2001, p. 8). A substantial body of research that examines tourism as performance has grown out of Boorstin's critique of tourism as a phenomenon based on 'pseudo-events', or false attractions contrived by the industry, and Dean MacCannell's interpretation of tourism as a quest for authenticity as laid out in his seminal book *The Tourist* (1976). These too have some bearing on this investigation of the tensions between travel and tourist discourse. Such studies largely interpret the consumption of tourist experiences and destinations as performances staged for the benefit of visitors (see Rickly-Boyd *et al.* 2014 for a detailed discussion of approaches to place and tourist practices within the theoretical framework of perfomance), focusing mainly on practices employed at tourist destinations. There has been little interest in how similar touristic performances are staged online. Nevertheless, it can be argued, that attributing an illusory quality to tourist experience suggests that it is being defined against something more authentic and that some opposition still exists. Such critical discussions suggest a discursive tension that owes something to the very opposition between traveller and tourist.

The purpose of this book is to contribute to these discussions by examining how travel blogs negotiate these tensions. It approaches travel and tourism as distinct discourses that underpin online performances of the self via travel blogs and their associated media. It draws principally on the works of Bakhtin, Dann, and Goffman and existing research into discourse in travel-related narratives to propose a framework within which to examine the narrative techniques constituting travel and tourist discourses in these blogs. In doing so, it acknowledges the intertwining nature of travel and tourism and the instability of this binary opposition. With this approach, the book takes a road less travelled that makes all the difference to the study of travel and tourism online.

Note

1 The term 'affordance' was first used by James W. Gibson to refer to the possibilities for action offered by any given object. Ian Hutchby has since explored this concept from a sociological perspective. The theory of affordances forms the basis of a number of studies in the social uses of Internet technologies.

References

Akehurst, G. 2009. User generated content: the use of blogs for tourism organisations and tourism consumers. *Service Business* [Online], 3, 51–61. Available: http://link.springer.com/article/10.1007/s11628-008-0054-2 [Accessed 17 Apr. 2012].

Albers, P. C. and James, W. R. 1988. Travel photography: a methodological approach. *Annals of Tourism Research* [Online], 15(1), 134–158. Available: http://dx.doi.org/10.1016/0160-7383(88)90076-X [Accessed 21 Apr. 2011].

Andreasen, L. B. 2006. Weblogs as forums for discussion – an alternative to the computer conference as a Standard in Online Learning. *In:* Buhl, M., Sørensen, B. H. and Meyer,

B. (eds.) *Media and ICT – learning potentials*. Copenhagen: Danish University of Education Press.

Arndt, G. 2015. *Everything everywhere* [Online]. Available: http://www.facebook.com/EverythingEverywhere [Accessed 18 January 2016].

Baerenholdt, J. O., Haldrup, M., Larsen, J. and Urry, J. 2003. *Performing tourist places,* Aldershot, UK: Ashgate.

Bakhtin, M. 1981. *The dialogic imagination: four essays,* Austin, TX, US: University of Texas Press.

Baron, D. E. 2016. *Wandering Earl* [Online]. Available: http://www.wanderingearl.com/ [Accessed 17 January 2016].

Barthes, R. 1977. *Image, music, text,* New York: Noonday.

Barthes, R. 1993. *Camera lucida: reflections on photography,* London: Vintage.

Baumer, E. P., Sueyoshi, M. and Tomlinson, B. 2011. Bloggers and readers blogging together: collaborative co-creation of political blogs. *Computer Supported Cooperative Work (CSCW),* 20, 1–36.

Baym, N. K. 2010. *Personal connections in the digital age,* Cambridge, UK: Polity.

Blanton, C. 2002. *Travel writing: the self and the world,* New York: Routledge.

Boorstin, D. J. 1992. *The image: A guide to pseudo-events in America,* New York: Vintage.

BootsnAll. 2016. BootsnAll Travel Network. *BootsnAll* [Online]. Available: http://www.bootsnall.com/ [Accessed 18 January 2016].

Bruns, A. and Jacobs, J. 2006. *Uses of blogs,* New York: Peter Lang.

Bullingham, L. and Vasconcelos, A. C. 2013. 'The presentation of self in the online world': Goffman and the study of online identities. *Journal of Information Science,* 39, 101–112.

Buzard, J. 1993. *The beaten track: European tourism, literature, and the ways to culture, 1800-1918,* Oxford, UK: Oxford University Press.

Buzard, J. 2002. The Grand Tour and after (1660–1840). *In:* Hulme, P. and Youngs, T. (eds.) *The Cambridge companion to travel writing.* Cambridge, UK: Cambridge University Press.

Carson, D. 2008. The 'blogosphere' as a market research tool for tourism destinations: a case study of Australia's Northern Territory. *Journal of Vacation Marketing* [Online], 14. Available: http://jvm.sagepub.com/cgi/content/abstract/14/2/111 [Accessed 1 Apr. 2009].

Chesher, C. 2005. *Blogs and the crisis of authorship* [Online]. Sydney. Available: http://incsub.org/blogtalk/?page_id=40 [Accessed 14 Mar. 2010].

Dann, G. 1996. *The language of tourism: a sociolinguistic perspective,* Wallingford, UK: CAB International.

Dann, G. 1999. Writing out the tourist in space and time. *Annals of Tourism Research* [Online], 26. Available: http://www.sciencedirect.com/science/article/B6V7Y-3VS7VK0-8/2/644ebe6402ad134ca201678b33b3afc4 [Accessed 30 Mar. 2009].

Donath, J. and boyd, d. 2004. Public displays of connection. *BT Technology Journal* [Online], 22(4), 71–82. Available: http://link.springer.com/article/10.1023/B:BTTJ.0000047585.06264.cc [Accessed 8 Oct. 2010].

Dunn, D. 2005. Venice observed: the traveller, the tourist, the post-tourist and British television. *In:* Jaworski, A. and Pritchard, A. (eds.) *Discourse, communication, and tourism.* Clevedon, UK: Channel View.

Elsrud, T. 2001. Risk creation in traveling: backpacker adventure narration. *Annals of Tourism Research,* 28, 597–617.

Franklin, A. and Crang, M. 2001. The trouble with tourism and travel theory? *Tourist Studies* [Online], 1(1), 5–22. Available: http://tou.sagepub.com/content/1/1/5 [Accessed 29 Apr. 2009].

Fussell, P. 1980. *Abroad: British literary traveling between the wars,* New York: Oxford University Press.

Galani-Moutafi. 2000. The self and the other: traveler, ethnographer, tourist. *Annals of Tourism Research* [Online], 27(1), 203–224, [Accessed 30 Mar. 2009].

Garden, M. 2011. Defining blog: a fool's errand or a necessary undertaking. *Journalism* [Online]. Available: http://jou.sagepub.com/content/early/2011/09/14/1464884911421700.abstract [Accessed 20 Sept. 2011].

Garrod, B. 2009. Understanding the relationship between tourism destination imagery and tourist photography. *Journal of Travel Research* [Online], 47. Available: http://www.scopus.com/inward/record.url?eid=2-s2.0-58149508293&partnerID=40 [Accessed 1 Dec. 2009].

Gillespie, A. 2007. Collapsing self/other positions: identification through differentiation. *British Journal of Social Psychology* [Online], 46. Available: http://dx.doi.org/10.1348/014466606X155439 [Accessed 11 Apr. 2012].

Goffman, E. 1969. *The presentation of self in everyday life,* London: Allen Lane.

Hallett, R. W. and Kaplan-Weinger, J. 2010. *Official tourism websites: a discourse analysis perspective.* Clevedon, UK: Channel View Publications.

Hermans, H. J. M. 2004. Introduction: the dialogical self in a global and digital age. *Identity: An International Journal of Theory and Research* [Online], 4. Available: http://www.informaworld.com/10.1207/s1532706xid0404_1 [Accessed 28 June 2010].

Herring, S. C. 2010. Web content analysis: expanding the paradigm. *In:* Hunsinger, J., Klastrup, L. and Allen, M. (eds.) *International Handbook of Internet Research.* Netherlands: Springer.

Hevern, V. W. 2004. Threaded identity in cyberspace: weblogs and positioning in the dialogical self. *Identity* [Online], 4(4). Available: http://www.tandfonline.com/doi/pdf/10.1207/s1532706xid0404_2 [Accessed 17 Mar. 2009].

Holland, P. and Huggan, G. 1998. *Tourists with typewriters: critical reflections on contemporary travel writing,* Ann Arbor, MI, US: University of Michigan Press.

Hulme, P. and Youngs, T. (eds.) 2002. *The Cambridge companion to travel writing* Cambridge, UK: Cambridge University Press.

Jaworski, A. and Coupland, N. 1999. *The discourse reader,* London: Routledge.

Jaworski, A. and Pritchard, A. 2005. *Discourse, communication, and tourism,* Clevedon, UK: Channel View.

Jenkins, O. 2003. Photography and travel brochures: the circle of representation. *Tourism Geographies: An International Journal of Tourism Space, Place, and Environment* [Online], 5. Available: http://www.informaworld.com/10.1080/14616680309715 [Accessed 1 Dec. 2009].

Landow, G. P. 2006. *Hypertext 3.0: critical theory and new media in an era of globalization,* Baltimore, US: Johns Hopkins University Press.

Lomborg, S. 2009. Navigating the blogosphere: towards a genre-based typology of weblogs. *First Monday* [Online], 14. Available: http://www.uic.edu/htbin/cgiwrap/bin/ojs/index.php/fm/article/view/2329/2178 [Accessed 28 January 2010].

Lonely Planet. 2016. *About us and our authors.* [Online]. Available: http://www.lonelyplanet.com/about/our-authors [Accessed 14 Jan. 2016].

McCabe, S. 2005. 'Who is a tourist?': A critical review. *Tourist Studies*, 5(1), 85–106 [Online] Available: http://tou.sagepub.com/content/5/1/85 [Accessed 13 Nov. 2009].

MacCannell, D. 1976. *The tourist: a new theory of the leisure class,* New York: Schocken.
MacCannell, D. 2001. Tourist agency. *Tourist Studies* [Online], 1. Available: http://tou.sagepub.com/cgi/content/abstract/1/1/23 [Accessed June 1, 2001].
McCullagh, K. 2008. Blogging: self presentation and privacy. *Information and Communications Technology Law* [Online], 17. Available: http://www.informaworld.com/10.1080/13600830801886984 [Accessed 22 June 2010].
McNeill, L. 2003. Teaching an old genre new tricks: the diary on the Internet. *Biography* [Online], 26(1), 24–47. [Accessed 21 May 2009].
Molz, J. G. 2010. Performing global geographies: time, space, place and pace in narratives of round-the-world travel. *Tourism Geographies* [Online], 12. Available: http://dx.doi.org/10.1080/14616688.2010.494684 [Accessed 20 December 2011].
MyTripJournal. 2016. Tours By Locals Canada. *MyTripJournal* [Online]. Available: http://www.mytripjournal.com/ [Accessed 18 January 2016].
Nardi, B. A., Schiano, D. J., Gumbrecht, M. and Swartz, L. 2004. Why we blog. *Communications of the ACM: The Blogosphere* [Online], 47(12), 41–46. Available: http://dl.acm.org/citation.cfm?doid=1035134.1035163 [Accessed 29 Feb. 2011].
Nelson, M. E. and Hull, G. A. 2008. Self-presentation through multimedia: a Bakhtinian perspective on digital storytelling. *In:* Lundby, K. (ed.) *Digital storytelling, mediatized stories: self-representations in new media.* New York: Peter Lang.
Nomadic Matt. 2016. N.p. *Nomadic Matt's Travel Site.* [Online]. Available: http://www.nomadicmatt.com/ [Accessed 14 April 2016].
Noy, C. 2004. This trip really changed me: backpackers' narratives of self-change. *Annals of Tourism Research* [Online], 31(1), 78–102 [Accessed 14 Jan. 2010].
OffExploring. 2016. Tyne and Wear: OffExploring. *OffExploring.* [Online]. Available: http://www.offexploring.com/ [Accessed 18 January 2016].
O'Reilly, C. C. 2005. Tourist or traveller? Narrating backpacker identity. *In:* Jaworski, A. and Pritchard, A. (eds.) *Discourse, communication, and tourism.* Clevedon, UK: Channel View.
O'Reilly, C. C. 2006. From drifter to gap year tourist: mainstreaming backpacker travel. *Annals of Tourism Research*, 33, 998–1017.
Pan, B., Maclaurin, T. and Crotts, J. C. 2007. Travel blogs and the implications for destination marketing. *Journal of Travel Research* [Online], 46. Available: http://jtr.sagepub.com/content/46/1/35.abstract [Accessed 7 Oct. 2009].
Papacharissi, Z. 2009. The virtual geographies of social networks: a comparative analysis of Facebook, LinkedIn and ASmallWorld. *New Media and Society,* 11, 199–220.
Pinch, T. 2010. The invisible technologies of Goffman's sociology from the merry-go-round to the Internet. *Technology and Culture* [Online], 51(2), 409–425r [Accessed 19 July 2010].
Pritchard, A. and Morgan, N. J. 2000. Privileging the male gaze: gendered tourism landscapes. *Annals of Tourism Research* [Online], 27. Available: http://www.sciencedirect.com/science/article/pii/S0160738399001139 [Accessed 2 Mar. 2012].
Reed, A. 2005. 'My blog is me': Texts and persons in UK online journal culture (and anthropology). *Ethnos* [Online], 70. Available: http://dx.doi.org/10.1080/00141840500141311 [Accessed 6 July 2010].
Rees, E. and Rees, J. 2008. *Forks and Jets* [Online]. Available: http://forksandjets.com/ [Accessed 26 February 2016].
Richards, G. and Wilson, J. 2004. Travel writers and writers who travel: nomadic icons for the backpacker subculture? *Journal of Tourism and Cultural Change* [Online], 2. Available: http://dx.doi.org/10.1080/14766820408668168 [Accessed 12 Jan. 2012].

Rickly-Boyd, J. M., Knudsen, D. C., Braverman, L. C. and Metro-Roland, M. M. 2014. *Tourism, performance, and place: a geographic perspective*. Farnham, UK: Ashgate Publishing Company.

Robinson, L. 2007. The cyberself: the self-ing project goes online, symbolic interaction in the digital age. *New Media and Society* [Online], 9, 93–110. Available: http://dx.doi.org/10.1145/1035134 [Accessed 16 Nov. 2010].

Robinson, M. 2004. Narratives of being elsewhere: tourism and travel writing. *In:* Lew, A. A., Williams, A. M. and Hall, C. M. (eds.) *A companion to tourism*. Malden, MA, US: Blackwell.

Robinson, M. and Picard, D. 2009. Moments, magic, and memories: photographing tourists, tourist photographs, and making worlds. *In:* Robinson, M. and Picard, D. (eds.) *The framed world: tourism, tourists, and photography*. Farnham, UK: Ashgate.

Sanderson, J. 2008. The blog is serving its purpose: self-presentation strategies on 38pitches.com. *Journal of Computer-Mediated Communication* [Online], 13. Available: http://dx.doi.org/10.1111/j.1083-6101.2008.00424.x [Accessed 11 Aug. 2010].

Schmallegger, D. and Carson, D. 2008. Blogs in tourism: changing approaches to information exchange. *Journal of Vacation Marketing* [Online], 14. Available: http://jvm.sagepub.com/cgi/content/abstract/14/2/99 [Accessed 15 May 2009].

Schmidt, J. 2007. Blogging practices: an analytical framework. *Journal of Computer-Mediated Communication* [Online], 12. Available: http://dx.doi.org/10.1111/j.1083-6101.2007.00379.x [Accessed 24 Feb. 2011].

Serfaty, V. 2004a. *The mirror and the veil: an overview of American online diaries and blogs*, Amsterdam: Rodopi.

Serfaty, V. 2004b. Online diaries: towards a structural approach. *Journal of American Studies* [Online], 38(3), 457–471. Available: http://ssrn.com/abstract=1607997 [Accessed 9 Oct. 2009].

Sontag, S. 1977. *On photography*, New York: Farrar, Strauss, and Giroux.

Sorapure, M. 2003. Screening moments, scrolling livesdiary writing on the Web. *Biography* [Online], 26(1), 1–23. Available: https://muse.jhu.edu/article/42425 [Accessed 14 Sept. 2009].

Thurlow, C. and Jaworski, A. 2010. *Tourism discourse: language and global mobility*, Houndmills, UK: Palgrave Macmillan.

Trammell, K. D. and Keshelashvili, A. 2005. Examining the new influencers: A self-presentation study of A-list blogs. *Journalism and Mass Communication Quarterly* [Online], 82(4), 968. Available: http://jmq.sagepub.com/content/82/4/968.short [Accessed 11 Sept. 2010].

TravelBlog. 2016. *TravelBlog* [Online]. Available: https://www.travelblog.org [Accessed 18 January 2016].

TravelPod. 2016. Ottawa: Travel Pod. *TravelPod*. [Online]. Available: http://www.travelpod.com/ [Accessed 18 January 2016].

Urry, J. 2002. *The tourist gaze*, London: Sage.

Urry, J. and Larsen, J. 2011. *The tourist gaze 3.0*, Los Angeles, CA, US: Sage.

Van Dijck, J. 2004. Composing the self: of diaries and lifelogs. *The Fibreculture Journal* [Online]. Available: http://three.fibreculturejournal.org/fcj-012-composing-the-self-of-diaries-and-lifelogs/ [Accessed 15 Mar. 2012].

Walker Rettberg, J. 2014. *Blogging*, Cambridge, UK: Polity.

Wenger, A. 2008. Analysis of travel bloggers' characteristics and their communication about Austria as a tourism destination. *Journal of Vacation Marketing* [Online], 14. Available: http://jvm.sagepub.com/cgi/content/abstract/14/2/169 [Accessed 27 Oct. 2010].

2 A pioneer in the blogosphere

Tony Wheeler's Travels

Despite the ubiquity of blogs on travel, the use of this format by guidebook publishers is comparatively rare. A number of well-known publishers including *Lonely Planet*, Frommer Media, Michelin, Rough Guides, and Time Out, among others, have a well-developed online presence that includes websites, *Facebook* pages and *Twitter* streams that complement their print publications. Few have, however, ventured into the blogosphere to either create or host narratives of journeys or travel experiences. The publisher of the Rough Guides series provides forums for travel communities via *Facebook* and *Twitter* whereas Michelin's 'Le Guide Vert', on *Facebook* mainly promotes content published on the Michelin travel websites (Rough Guides 2016a; 2016b). Thus far, however, blogs have been conspicuously absent among the online offerings of both these publishers. Time Out gives a perfunctory nod to blogging by categorising some of its online travel articles as 'blog' posts, but these are really feature articles embedded in the content of its main website and do not necessarily describe a personal travel experience or have a blog-like structure (Time Out 2016). Written in a similar vein, but more like a blog in format, is *Arthur Frommer Online*, a text by the editors and founder of Frommers and hosted on its website (Frommer Media 2016). For the most part, this publicises the best travel deals available and comments on issues pertaining to commercial travel. It presents these as a series of posts in reverse-chronological order. It is not, despite its allusive title, a narrative of the travels of the founder Arthur Frommer, or indeed his own blog in entirety, and cannot in this sense be regarded as a travel blog. In general, the abovementioned publishers have engaged to some degree with social media platforms such as *Facebook* and *Twitter* to gain more visibility. However, as erstwhile Frommers online editor Jason Clampet observes, 'Guidebook companies know that growth will come from digital, but they're all legacy print operations paralysed by fiefdoms and an older skill set.... when they try content, old-school content companies just bumble when it comes to digital' (G.M. 2013). This may account for their reluctance, thus far, to strengthen and extend this online presence to other platforms such as blogs.

Quite appropriately, given its name, *Lonely Planet* has proved an exception in its comparatively deeper foray into the blogosphere (*Lonely Planet* 2016a). It does this in two ways: by hosting a blog with content created by the publisher and by sourcing content from other travel bloggers (*Lonely Planet* 2016b). The website originally hosted *Tony Wheeler's Blog*, which described the travels of the organisation's founder, Tony Wheeler. In this sense, this was quite literally a blog about a guidebook publisher's travels aimed at giving a traveller's face to a touristic corporation. Following the sale of *Lonely Planet* to BBC Worldwide, and subsequently to NC2 Media, this has since been replaced by the *Lonely Planet Blog*, written by a team of staff writers. In addition to this, the website hosts *Lonely Planet Pathfinders*, an initiative that invites individuals to register their travel blogs with *Lonely Planet* and features content sourced from various independent blogs (*Lonely Planet* 2016c).

Lonely Planet is an iconic name in the tourism industry and its guidebooks are perceived as a 'definitive information source' that is indispensable to many travellers (Hanlan and Kelly 2005, p. 169). As a guidebook publisher, *Lonely Planet* has a strong association with the discourse of tourism, and yet through *Tony Wheeler's Blog*, and now through the *Pathfinders* initiative, it also advocates the idea of independent and adventurous travel in order to promote itself. The *Pathfinders* blogs supplement the information the *Lonely Planet* website provides and act as testimonials that validate both the publisher's guidebooks and the website itself. In turn, being registered with, and consequently recognised, by *Lonely Planet* authenticates a *Pathfinders* travel blog. Yet, in the very moment of this authentication, these travel narratives are also subsumed by the discourses of corporate tourism.

The *Lonely Planet Blog* is heavily reliant on *Pathfinder* blogs, often curating content culled from their posts for its own entries. Any additional content created by its authors generally promotes *Lonely Planet* and consists of announcements of its competitions and surveys, advertisements for activities sponsored by the organisation, and interviews of *Lonely Planet* editors who have recently travelled to interesting destinations. To some extent, this blog's dependence on *Pathfinders* content supports the publisher's presentation of itself as an organisation associated with travel, committed to discovering 'little-known facts', whose authors get to the 'heart of the place' they are in. These writers have no commercial interests but are dedicated to identifying that which is new and genuinely local by engaging with 'fellow travellers': '*Lonely Planet* authors know the destination.... They don't take freebies in exchange for positive coverage, so you can be sure the advice you're given is impartial.'

In effect, this dissociation from commercialism and the connection – indeed, a fraternisation – with 'travellers' lends credibility to the publisher's positioning of itself as an advocate of independent travel. *Lonely Planet* displays an awareness of the negative associations of tourism and skilfully harnesses travel discourse as represented by these blogs towards the promotion of destinations via the *Lonely Planet Blog*. As many of the blog's posts consist of the best photographs, entries, or videos found in its *Pathfinder* blogs, it makes sense to analyse the discourses of travel and tourism present in the latter and so determine the significance of their links to *Lonely Planet*. Such an analysis would facilitate an understanding of the discursive tensions between commercial tourism as represented by a publisher of guidebook and 'real' travel as represented by these blogs. However, it would be impossible to do justice to this investigation within the space of this chapter, and so some of the *Pathfinder* blogs are discussed at length in the latter half of this book.

Instead, this chapter concerns itself mainly with *Tony Wheeler's Blog*, now titled *Tony Wheeler's Travels*, both for its claim to be one of the earliest travel blogs and as a travel narrative that exemplifies the evolving nature of the blog and problematises definitions of the same. By describing itself as one of the first travel blogs, *Tony Wheeler's Blog* complemented *Lonely Planet*'s positioning of itself as a pioneer of unexplored destinations and ways of travelling, and extended this to its venture into the blogosphere. Despite its subsequent change of title, the narrative may still be regarded as a blog. *Tony Wheeler's Travels* retains much of its original format and the search function on the website invites readers to explore the 'blog'. As a continuously developing narrative, it provides a means of measuring some of the inadequacies and problems inherent in definitions of blogs on the basis of format and discursive qualities such as heteroglossia, polyphony, and a distinct authorial voice. Its positioning, initially as a guidebook publisher's blog and now as a travel writer's blog that nevertheless continues to promote *Lonely Planet*, sheds light on how some of the consequent tensions between discourses of travel and tourism are negotiated.

Defining travel blogs

What then is this thing we call a travel blog? Some tourism researchers emphasise formal features in their definitions of travel blogs. Wenger, for example, includes features such as layout and visual elements (2008). Bosangit *et al.* rely on Herring *et al.*'s generic description of blogs as consisting of dated entries arranged in reverse-chronological order (Bosangit *et al.* 2009). Others like Pühringer and Taylor lay more emphasis on content and find that travel blogs are online diaries consisting of individual entries on travel-related themes, hosted on 'provider sites' that are 'tourism specific' (2008, p. 129). For the most part, these researchers refer to travel blogs as blogs like any other, but with travel as a central theme. Any attempt to understand what a travel blog is must therefore begin with a general definition of what a blog is.

For Jill Walker Rettberg, a blog is 'a frequently updated Web site consisting of dated entries arranged in reverse chronological order' (2014, p. 32). Likewise, Bruns and Jacobs focus on 'the reverse-chronological posting of individual entries that include the capacity to provide hypertext links and often allow comment-based responses from readers' (2006, pp. 2–3). In a similar vein, Jan Schmidt writes that blogs are 'frequently updated websites where content (text, pictures, sound files, etc.) is posted on a regular basis and displayed in reverse-chronological order' (2007, p. 1409).

As most of these definitions focus on technical aspects of blogs rather than their content, the underlying implication is that such narratives are largely defined by their formal elements. This suggests that any website that refers to itself as a 'blog' or 'travel blog' must contain these elements, and therefore, so must *Tony Wheeler's Travels*. A comparison of these various definitions indicates that a typical blog consists of regularly updated, reverse-chronological posts that are often topical, offering personal anecdotes or commentary. These entries are accompanied by hyperlinks and are open to comments or responses by readers. While such a description seems broad enough to accommodate most travel blogs, researchers also need to recognise that format is continuously evolving – *Tony Wheeler's Travels* demonstrates this fairly effectively. Blogs have acquired many more features than those previously identified as being characteristic of this form. For example, a blog, and by extension a travel blog, may now be viewed not merely as a stand-alone website, as implied by such definitions, but as a 'centralising force', located in a larger network of online platforms such as social networks, microblogs, and photo-sharing websites (Helmond 2010, p. 8). Also, photographs are now an essential element of most travel blogs, whereas many early blogs had few images. Definitions must perforce accommodate the versatility of this form of communication.

Both researchers and potential tourists use blogs as a credible source of information about those who travel and the places they visit. As yet, however, there has been little academic interrogation of the discursive qualities suggested by the term 'travel blog' and the aura of authenticity associated with the term (Akehurst 2009; Carson 2008; Schmallegger and Carson 2008; Wenger 2008). Furthermore, analyses of the content of travel blogs, some of which are referred to at the start of this section, often pertain to consumer research and destination marketing and overlook the possibility of discursive tensions existing within travel blogs (Crotts *et al.* 2009; Pühringer and Taylor 2008; Wenger 2008). Yet, blogs have a number of definitive discursive qualities. The first of these is the presence of multiple discourses or heteroglossia. From a Bakhtinian point of view, a heteroglossic text contains not only various discourses, but also 'incorporated genres' (Bakhtin 1981, p. 320). This may explain how narrative techniques associated with other forms of travel-related communication, such as guidebooks or travel books, may find their way into *Tony Wheeler's Travels*. This would also account for the presence of discourses of both travel and tourism, among other discourses in the text. Robert Glenn Howard's observation that a blog is potentially a site of negotiation for various conflicting discourses is, therefore, applicable to travel blogs (2008).

A second discursive quality evident in most blogs is a tendency towards multivocality or polyphony, which includes the presence of a distinct and identifiable authorial voice. The polyphony arises from both the author's ability to adopt different positions and speak in different voices – traveller, tourist, tour guide, etc. – and from the voices that enter the blog via readers' comments, advertisements, and content created by a web host. These may be heard both throughout the blog and sometimes within the space of a single entry. Tom van Nuenen's definition of travel blogs, which emphasises authorial identity as a principal characteristic along with formal features, deserves a special mention here for its expansiveness, defining the genre as 'a set of personal webpages and entries served from a single web domain created and operated by one or multiple, authors, dedicated to planned, current, or past travel by the same authors.... Furthermore, the blogs all contain an About section detailing the identity of the authors' (2015, p. 5).

The definition goes on to add that frequent updates and hyperlinks are also typical and perhaps desirable for a high visibility in search engine results. It should be noted here that van Nuenen focuses on highly visible independent blogs as opposed to those hosted on commercial travel blog hosts such as *Trip Advisor*, and this has some bearing on his definition. Here, the implication that a clear sense of the author(s) online self is an essential element of a blog is particularly significant. The succeeding chapter explores the implications of the presence of other additional voices, especially those of the readers, webhosts, and advertisers, for this authorial voice.

Labelling a website a 'blog' creates certain expectations in its audience as regards its form and content (Howard 2008, p. 208). The use of the term 'blog' in the original title of *Tony Wheeler's Travels*, its current use of the reverse-chronological format, and its reference to itself as a blog in its search box, all position the text as a blog and imply that it has certain intrinsic qualities. The definitions outlined here and in the previous chapter indicate that there are certain practices and identifiable features associated with blogs. This chapter applies these definitions to *Tony Wheeler's Travels*, in order to ascertain how far the text answers the description of a travel blog, particularly given its original title and subsequent evolution, and to determine whether it can be said to meet the expectations readers may have of a text that positions itself, especially in its early entries, as a blog. This chapter also examines how this website employs various narrative techniques and discourses to position itself as a narrative of a travel experience, and its author as a traveller rather than a promoter of tourism. Despite its efforts to do this, however, this narrative, purportedly of authentic travel, frequently collapses into tourist discourse. These discourses have some bearing on the presentation of the text as a blog and its author as an authentic blogger. However, as *Tony Wheeler's Travels* negotiates these discursive tensions, it takes on certain aspects of a blog while omitting or only imitating others. Finally, the chapter determines the extent to which this text is heteroglossic and polyphonic and considers how far these may be considered definitive qualities of a blog.

The trappings of a travel blog

At first glance, *Tony Wheeler's Travels* is the quintessential travel blog, with reverse-chronological posts on travel-related themes, accompanied by hyperlinks, photographs, and an author profile. However, a closer analysis reveals that the text wears only the shell of a blog, providing the reader with what they expect to see, at least on a superficial level. The earliest entry is dated 25 March 1994. This date is significant given that the mid-1990s are widely accepted as the period when the earliest blogs were first published (Jones 2003; Rosenberg 2009; Walker Rettberg 2014). The introductory paragraph is a note from Wheeler, which begins, 'In 1994

I drove coast-to-coast across the USA (and back again) in an ancient Cadillac and posted a daily blog as we went along' (Wheeler 1994). There is some ambiguity in this statement, and a reader who begins the narrative at this point may be forgiven for thinking that *Tony Wheeler's Travels* was started in that same year or, given his subsequent reference to 'looking back at that blog', that the original blog has evolved into this website.

This preface fails to state that the original text was a travel diary written for a webzine, a fact only mentioned in the author's book about *Lonely Planet* where he writes, 'Today it would be called a blog' (Wheeler and Wheeler 2006, p. 304). This identification with early blogs is reiterated elsewhere in the blog where he writes, 'These days everybody's doing one, but I reckon I did one of the first travel blogs' (Wheeler 2005). This implies that while it was not originally conceived as one, *Tony Wheeler's Travels* originally titled itself as a blog to associate itself with the larger body of discourse that is the blogosphere. It could be argued, that having established itself as such, it subsequently employs the word 'travels' in the more recent title to position the narrative as a text on travel as opposed to tourism, particularly given its commercial and corporate origins. A title that includes the author's name also supports the text's positioning as a personal narrative.

It should be pointed out that there is no rule that a travel blog must have the word 'blog' in its title. Indeed, a change of title does not denote or require a change of format, but is merely indicative of the tendency of such narratives to be in a state of flux. The fact that *Tony Wheeler's Travels* invites readers to 'view posts', has a tag cloud often typical of blogs, and allows visitors to 'search the blog', are all elements that attest to this narrative's blog-like nature, in spite of its dropping the term from its title. Yet, within this context, the unexplained absence of entries between July 1994 and February 2005, glaringly obvious in the list of dates under the website's 'Archive', is a noteworthy anomaly. As a blog generally has frequent and regular updates usually in the form of posts, eleven years is a noticeably significant gap. It is also difficult to verify when the first post appeared, or to determine what happened in the intervening years. In short, the text wears the trappings of a blog with the suggestion that it is as old as the first blogs and that it was purposely written as a blog.

An analysis of other formal elements in *Tony Wheeler's Travels* reinforces the sense that the text may resemble a blog in appearance, but not necessarily in content. This is particularly true of the external hyperlinks accompanying each entry. Blogs usually provide hyperlinks to other blogs, older entries, or to an email address (Serfaty 2004; Sorapure 2003; Walker Rettberg 2014). For Madeleine Sorapure, linking, both within the blog and to other similar blogs, is an important feature that creates 'meaningful connections' and 'conceptual transitions' (2003, p. 14). Links to other similar blogs are usually listed in a blogroll. Such linking results in the creation of a network of blogs with topical affinity, what Lovink describes as the 'enclave culture of blogs' (2008, p. 252). While it is not clear whether such reciprocal linking is mandatory for a text to be considered a blog, it is generally assumed that these links are the author's choice, and are external. Furthermore, such networking emphasises the social nature of blogging. *Tony Wheeler's Travels* does not, at the time of writing, link to other blogs. While it offers a contact form that visitors may fill out to correspond with the author, it does not encourage a personal relationship with the author by permitting visitor feedback via an email address. As *Tony Wheeler's Blog*, each webpage displayed 'My Lists', a list of links that appeared in a column along the right-hand margin, consisting largely of links to older entries. The structure, then, was reminiscent of the blogroll. This feature was later replaced by a list of links at the bottom of each webpage to organisations in which Wheeler has some vested interest: Lonely Planet, The Wheeler Centre for writers, Text Publishing, Planet Wheeler, Global Heritage Fund and Chemical Media. Links to older entries are now embedded in the posts. Ultimately, while the 'blog' can be said to have some 'meaningful connections' in its hyperlinks, it only appears to participate in the 'enclave culture' and readers expecting to find links to similar blogs will be disappointed.

Sorapure observes that most blogs encourage feedback through links and comment boxes. For her, such interactive features point to the social nature of the blog. In fact, blogs are often discussed as social or conversational media, implying that bloggers are part of and engage with a community of authors and readers (Finin *et al.* 2008; Scoble and Israel 2006; Sorapure 2003). For Lars Andreasen (2006), blogs become heteroglossic when readers post comments, while the same feature makes blogs polyphonic for Viviane Serfaty (2004). The comments box is therefore a structural element that supports the existence of heteroglossia and polyphony in the blog. Although this chapter has dismissed *Arthur Frommer Online* as being more of a commentary blog than a personal travel blog, it is worth noting it facilitates the posting of comments by its readers. There is, however, little actual engagement with its audience as most posts receive no response. It could be argued that the commentary of its posts is far too authoritarian, leaving little for a reader to either refute or respond to. Nevertheless, the narrative goes through the motions of being participatory and open to interpretation. By comparison, *Tony Wheeler's Travels* is noticeably lacking in this regard.

The absence of a comments box is particularly significant, as this is considered a 'standard feature of the typical blog' (Rosenberg 2009, p. 149). Howard sees the comments section as a 'participatory feature' and suggests that readers expect to be allowed to respond, when they see a website titled 'blog' (2008, p. 197). Indeed, comments enhance a blog's authenticity (Finin *et al.* 2008; Howard 2008; Scoble and Israel 2006; Sorapure 2003). Such views are endorsed by leading bloggers and social media professionals, such as Laurel Papworth (2009), who criticises marketing expert Seth Godin's refusal to allow comments on his blog. This has generated a lengthy debate in her blog's comments section, where a number of respondents insist that comments are a definitive feature of the blog that signal interactivity and engagement. The absence of comments limits self-presentation opportunities for the blogger through such interactivity.

In *Tony Wheeler's Travels* the absence of comments means that the text falls short of being 'standard' or 'participatory'. While a number of elements position the text as a personal blog, its exclusion of comments and its lack of engagement with readers undermine this impression. It can be argued that the narrative only goes through the motions of being a blog, adopting certain features while discarding others, particularly those that support interactivity with users or other bloggers. In view of Andreasen (2006) and Serfaty's (2004) arguments that readers' comments make blogs heteroglossic and polyphonic, it appears that some of these discursive qualities are lost as well. As there is no discussion of the views expressed in each entry, the narrative on the whole becomes authoritarian and impersonal, in the manner of a touristic text, in addressing its audience.

Notwithstanding the failings of *Tony Wheeler's Travels* with respect to comments and a blogroll, other elements still lend a blog-like structure to the text. These include the link to Tony Wheeler's profile in the top left-hand corner titled 'About Tony' (Wheeler 2009a), social media sharing buttons under each post, the aforementioned tag cloud along the right-hand margin and links across the top to pages that categorise blog entries according to subject – 'Places', 'Media', 'Living', 'Transport', 'Culture', and 'The Rest'. Categorised pages of posts are typical of many blogs but are not, in this instance, entirely unproblematic. The last two categories appear to be the least used, with the most recent entries at the start of 2016 dating back to the August of 2013 and 2015 respectively. In contrast, the most recent entries are under 'Places'. This is understandable given the blog's emphasis on Wheeler's 'travels', and it supports his self-presentation as a traveller who visits far-flung locations. However, viewed within Graham Dann's framework, a narrative largely driven and organised by destination may be perceived as a being guidebook-like by a discerning reader. Furthermore, the veracity of the narrative as a chronology of travel is destabilised by the constant switching of place in successive entries. Across a span of three days, Wheeler posts on India, Estonia, and then India again (see entries from 28 December 2015 to 1 January 2016), which could leave readers speculating about the currency of the posts and the actual location of their author (Wheeler 2015).

This emphasis on place is reiterated in the tag cloud, which opens onto a page with hundreds of alphabetically listed tags in the form of hyperlinked keywords mostly pertaining to destinations. Surprisingly, for a travel blog that dates its entries across a period of over twenty years, there was only one post tagged 'travel' as of 1 January 2016. In comparison, on the same day, *Traveling Savage*, an independently owned travel blog that dates back to 2009 listed approximately half a dozen posts each under the tags 'hikes', 'solo travel', and 'travel philosophy' in its much smaller and easily navigable tag cloud. The chapter on photography discusses tagging and folksonomies in greater depth, where such a discussion is more relevant. Here, it suffices to observe that tags contribute to the self-presentation of the blogger and the impression created on a reader about the nature of the narrative. The associations of authentic travel with solitary and adventurous experiences are stronger in Savage's blog than in Wheeler's. While the long tag listing of places complements Wheeler's presentation of a well-travelled self, it also has the effect of reading like the index page in a guidebook.

Outwardly, the narrative that is *Tony Wheeler's Travels* displays a blog-like structure; however, a closer perusal of its form and content give the lie to the narrative's claims to be a blog. This superficiality is to some extent determined by the conflicting discourses of travel and tourism in the text, both distinct, yet constantly collapsing into each other. *Tony Wheeler's Travels* wears two masks – one of a narrative of travel, as opposed to tourism, and the other of a blog – both of which are flawed. These weaknesses are perhaps best understood through a study of the travel and tourist discourses in the text.

Nothing personal

The 'silencing' of feedback, effectively a result of the absence of readers' comments, is a characteristic of tourist discourse, which is essentially monologic, unidirectional, and authoritarian (Dann 1996, pp. 62–67). The language of tourism, according to Dann, treats the addressee as being less experienced, asexual, ageless, and of indistinct socio-economic status. He argues that responses to tourist discourse are as rare as comments from a congregation listening to a sermon. These qualities are antithetical to those associated with blogs. In its omission of the comments section, *Tony Wheeler's Travels* appears to support the authoritarian voice of tourist discourse. Not only does the lack of feedback ensure that the discourse remains unidirectional, it also effectively prevents the audience from undermining the author's status as an expert.

A similarly authoritarian tone underpins some entries as well, reflecting the language of the guidebook. Take, for example, the first paragraph of an entry on the Meat Packing District in New York which advises readers, 'you can hardly get more hip' than this locale and 'you'll find Stella McCartney and Alexander McQueen', which declaration positions them as tourists and Wheeler as the knowledgeable and perhaps discerning tour guide (Wheeler 2009e). Another entry prosaically titled 'Ljubljana' begins in a chatty first-person voice, but suddenly breaks into guidebook-style direction: 'Leave the square, walk a short distance up Wolfova ulica and you'll find a terracotta figure of a woman....' The authoritarian voice of the tour guide is manifest in such imperative statements directed at an implied 'you' and these emphasise the unidirectional nature of tourist discourse.

Another distinguishing feature of tourist discourse is the ambiguity of the author's identity or an indistinct authorial voice (Dann 1996; Robinson 2004). This is a contrast to the discourse of blogs, which are often seen as personal narratives that have the distinctive stamp of their author's voice and personality (Kitzmann 2003; Serfaty 2004; Sorapure 2003; Walker Rettberg 2014). Although it is possible that this text could have multiple authors, it can be argued a text titled *Tony Wheeler's Travels* clearly presents Wheeler as the sole author. Despite the title's suggestion that this is Wheeler's personal narrative, however, individual entries themselves often tend towards an impersonal style. In the abovementioned entry describing New York, the word 'I' appears only once in the entire text, and twice in the captions accompanying the photographs.

It is interesting to note that Tony Wheeler's profile photograph, appearing at the top of every page (as it would in a blog) does introduce a personal touch to each entry. This was originally offset by the *Lonely Planet* logo, placed in the left-hand corner. As the brand name of a guidebook publisher, this association with the corporate face of tourism introduced discursive tensions, given the presentation of the individual as an independent traveller. Guidebooks are tourist paraphernalia and, as Butcher notes, *Lonely Planet* guidebooks have commercialised travel to the point of 'turning traveller heaven into tourist hell' (2003, p. 45). Thus, the banner over every web page was a visual representation of the tensions between the presentation of Tony Wheeler as a traveller and the blog as a personal narrative, and the presentation of Tony Wheeler as a tourism promoter and the text as an extension of the commercial discourse generally associated with *Lonely Planet* as a tourism organisation.

Following Wheeler's sale of the publishing house, the logo has been relegated to the bottom of the page. The banner now boasts a repetitive collage of travel photographs. Some of these display iconic tourist destinations, others show Wheeler posed against modes of transport, and still others are grip-and-grin photographs. It can be argued that a photograph of an individual posed against the backdrop of an iconic sight is touristic (Robinson and Picard 2009, p. 16). Certainly, photographs that show Wheeler biking on a dusty trail position him as a traveller going off the beaten path. In comparison, his posing against the Taj Mahal has a decidedly touristic flavour and is suggestive of the stereotypical camera-bearing tourist who looks for iconic monuments as a backdrop to his or her images. The collage itself appears to be an artless scattering of snapshots from across the years and many journeys, indicating a spontaneity associated with travel rather than tourism. However, a closer look reveals a considered arrangement of images that is repeated in three panels across the top of the web page that smacks of commercialism and a carefully crafted corporate image. On the whole, the discursive tensions may be less distinctive, but they are nevertheless present. More importantly, these are tensions that are constantly negotiated and re-negotiated as the narrative evolves.

Although this book devotes an entire chapter to travel photography in a later chapter, the photographs gracing the entries of *Tony Wheeler's Travels* merit further scrutiny here, also for their impersonal nature. The 'sender identification' that Dann finds typically lacking in most tourist discourse is also missing in most of the accompanying photographs in each post. These tend to resemble postcards rather than personal travel photographs since they rarely show Wheeler or his wife, who is often his travel companion. Of the eight entries for October 2009, only one has a photograph of the author, taken from a distance. Wheeler's presence in a photograph does not necessarily associate the image with travel discourse. Conversely, if the author's absence makes the photographs impersonal, this alone does not make them touristic. However, the images in this text are usually of sights that are unique to a travel destination – taxi cabs and the London Eye in posts on London, for example. This is a capturing of signs, itself a touristic practice (Urry 2002, p. 129). Also, the studied composition of many of the photographs suggests a professional touch, more in keeping with promotional tourist photography than an amateur effort.

Commercial tourist photography has certain distinct qualities. Urry and Larsen, for example, note that such photographs are usually idealised, positive images (2011, p. 169). This view is echoed in Dann's conclusion that most touristic communication is characterised by 'euphoria' and generally excludes anything negative (1996, p. 65). This is often true of the images in *Tony Wheeler's Travels*. The photographs for October 2009 are mainly positive, even artistic, images of various tourist destinations and icons such as the London Eye (Wheeler 2009c). The November entries are filled with photographs of statues in various Slovenian cities. On the whole, such images celebrate the popular and positive sights of a destination.

Equally euphoric is the language of some of the entries. 'Trieste', for example, describes 'the finest town square', 'impressive buildings', and 'elegant statuary' (Wheeler 2009g). Such positive descriptions tend to be impersonal. In conjunction with photographs that depict iconic sights at tourist destinations, they make for a text that reads very much like a guidebook in terms of narrative technique. Again, as readers are not allowed to comment on these photographs, there is no discussion of the experience each of these images represents. The photographs are closed to interpretation and, as a consequence, the depiction of the destination is, in this sense, both imperative and authoritarian. There is a touristic focus on place rather than personal experience. So, neither the former title of *Tony Wheeler's Blog* nor the current *Tony Wheeler's Travels* necessarily meets the expectation of this being a personal text or a personal narrative about Tony Wheeler.

In comparison, euphoria is absent in the entry on Ryanair that notes the flaws of its services (Wheeler 2009f). The entry is almost completely in a first-person voice. Its focus on the self and the apparent hardships endured while travelling with Ryanair presents this as a travel experience as opposed to a touristic one. The entry was first posted when the blog was still a part of the *Lonely Planet* website. As such, entries written in this vein authenticate the author's, and by extension *Lonely Planet*'s, association with travel. The personal tone of this entry is a contrast to the idealised descriptions of destinations in other entries. There is a resulting discursive tension between different posts in this text.

A turn of phrase

It is the author's voice, writes Mike Robinson, that distinguishes tourist discourse from travel discourse (2004, p. 309). In its avatar as *Tony Wheeler's Blog*, the website bore the slogan 'therefore I travel', on the bottom right-hand corner of every page. At the time, this association with travel was necessary to differentiate the blog from the promotional touristic discourse of *Lonely Planet* and conversely to validate the publisher's promotion of ostensibly authentic travel. It was also a clear statement of the author's position as a traveller and the presence of voice of the traveller in the text. It is this voice that one hears in entries such as 'Ljubljana'. The guidebook-style extract quoted earlier is preceded by a paragraph where Wheeler describes how he did 'tourist things' including climbing up to the local castle. He qualifies this, however, by adding in parentheses 'well I took the funicular up, I climbed down' (Wheeler 2009d).

Here then, is the language of travel. Although the author admits to doing 'tourist things', the phrase is dismissive of tourist activities, and it is the traveller identity that is emphasised in the solitary, first-person 'I'. Fellow travellers or tourists are conspicuously absent in the bus, the funicular, and at the castle. The impression created is one of independence and solitude. This is a traveller self that personalises the experience in doing the 'tourist things' a little differently, by climbing down, thus forsaking the beaten path. This focus on the self and the conversational tone of this paragraph directly contrasts with the impersonal and imperative voice of tourist discourse employed in subsequent paragraphs of the entry.

Sometimes the change from a travel style to a touristic one or vice versa occurs within a paragraph. For example, 'Trieste', which reads almost entirely like a guidebook entry, has a final paragraph that begins in tourist discourse but ends in the language of the solitary traveller: 'There are plenty of churches, museums, bits of Roman ruins and a solid old castle to distract you. The imposing Serbian Orthodox Chiesa di Santo Spiridione has colourful mosaics. I was passing through Trieste on my way to a literary festival in the town of Udine' (Wheeler 2009g).

The author occupies several positions within these few sentences. He is both tour guide and traveller. The entry, appropriately categorised under 'Places', lists the notable features of a church in Trieste in much the same way as a guidebook would. While the indication that the author was only 'passing through' suggests a superficial engagement with all that the destination offers, the fact that he is on the way to a literary festival nevertheless presents him as a person of some discernment. It also strengthens his self-presentation as a blogger and a writer. In other instances, an entire entry may read like travel discourse. The 'Ryanair' entry is written entirely in the first-person, describing an apparently solitary flight with no mention of fellow travellers. This is Wheeler at his most personal, and for once the guidebook-style advice directed at an anonymous, implied 'you' is absent. These variations make for a sort of ebb and flow between the discourses of travel and tourism.

Plotting the picaresque

Previous studies of travel discourse have analysed works generally classified as travel writing in order to identify the specific features of travel discourse (Dann 1999; Galani-Moutafi 2000). A definitive trait of this genre is its picaresque style (Fussell 1980, p. 207; Holland and Huggan 1998, p. 8; Mewshaw 2005, p. 5; Zilcosky 2008, p. 7). A picaresque narrative usually has travel as a central theme and is described as having a panoramic and episodic structure, a first-person point of view, a solitary protagonist in an 'inconstant world', many characters and themes such as an independent traveller who is free of 'the confines of ordinary social life' (Blaber and Gilman 1990, pp. 9–26; Wicks 1974, pp. 240–249). Some of these traits, such as the solitary traveller persona and first-person narration, are regarded as markers of travel discourse (Dann 1996).

Picaresque episodes are present both in fictional narratives featuring itinerant heroes – *Don Quixote* and *The adventures of Huckleberry Finn* are well-known examples – as well as many notable nonfictional travel narratives that are written in a fragmented style (Burton 2001; Cohen 1992; Holland and Huggan 1998, p. 7). Structurally and stylistically therefore, this has some parallels with the sequential entries of the blog. Although blog entries are in reverse-chronological order, each of these is usually a closed episode. The panoramic nature of the picaresque narrative also resonates with the blog form. The text of a blog is a work in progress, containing numerous entries, and is in this sense panoramic. In addition to this, the first-person point of view central to picaresque travel writing fits in well with the personal nature of the blog narrative and reinforces the notion that the text is a blog. As a narrative, *Tony Wheeler's Travels* is far from complete. With entries spanning over ten years and many destinations, it can easily be described as panoramic. In addition to this, each entry reads like a complete episode of the journey. The first-person point of view, as already noted earlier, finds expression either partially or fully in various entries. Thus, the picaresque elements of travel discourse accentuate the blog-like nature of the text and add credibility to its claim to be a blog.

Descriptions of the resilience of the picaresque traveller are also markers of travel discourse. The picaresque hero often describes a struggle to survive a 'chaotic landscape' (Wicks 1974, p. 245). Similarly, the real traveller, writes Galani-Moutafi, is depicted as someone who 'stoically endures uncomfortable and unpleasant experiences' (2000, p. 220). These travel experiences are generally associated with adventure, independence, exploration, and going off the beaten path (McCabe 2005, p. 97; O'Reilly 2006, p. 156). Therefore, it is the discourse of travel that is most emphasised in *Tony Wheeler's Travels* when the author adopts the persona of the traveller who forsakes the mundane. This was originally phrased in *Tony Wheeler's Blog* as a desire to 'investigate new travel possibilities or simply to experience something new' (Wheeler 2008a). Significantly, that description has since been replaced by the 'About Tony' profile that highlights Wheeler's interests in writing and book publishing and his promotion of his own travel books, both of which lend an undercurrent of commercialism to the narrative. This subtle turn in the self-presentation that now positions the self as a writer of travel texts rather than a publisher of guidebooks is significant for its dissociation with commercial tourist discourse and identification with travel. Nevertheless, the writer of travel potentially paves the way for the tourist who wishes to visit the places the former describes.

The presentation of self as a resilient traveller is played out variously in different parts of the narrative. At times, it is the choice of destination that marks an experience as travel. One such example is a trip to Afghanistan in 2006, filled with long journeys to various locations within a country that the author describes as 'definitely unsafe, although nothing like Iraq' (Wheeler 2006). For a reader aware of the ongoing conflict in the Middle East both at the time of the entry being written and in the following years, the display of the destination in its title may be perceived as a declaration of daring by the intrepid traveller rather than a touristic labelling of place.

Sometimes, the experience of travel manifests itself in a tale of survival limited to a single paragraph, as in an entry on Haiti, which is singular for its description of the dangers of being out after dark. Despite referring to the new *Lonely Planet* guidebook's warning that travellers should be careful, Wheeler nevertheless decides to brave the streets in the early hours to provide a firsthand account of what may happen to the unwary traveller. He finds 'nobody out on the streets and no transport to be found' and resolves this precarious solitude by finally begging a ride to the city's main square from where he navigates his way back to Pétionville (Wheeler 2008b).

Here, travel discourse is set against the warning of authoritarian tourist discourse. There is an element of promotion as well in the mention of the 'new Haiti edition' guidebook, an indicator of the narrative's original connection with the *Lonely Planet* website and its commercial activities. Yet, it is in disregarding the advice of the guidebook and being out after dark that the adventurous and resilient solitary traveller comes to the fore. Zilcosky observes that the getting lost in order to discover the self and so be 'found' is a long-used trope in travel writing (Zilcosky 2004). There is something of this need to find the undiscovered corners of cities that have been already mapped and explored in full in Wheeler's wanderings. In doing this, he assumes some of the qualities of a picaresque hero, wandering in search of new adventures, each of which forms an episode of his narrative. Like many picaresque encounters, there is the suggestion that there is something new to be learnt in each travel experience. Yet, in the very process of getting lost, the narrator documents the path of his journey, ensuring that he can be found not only by the reader but also by future travellers. In other words, by performing the traveller he sets the stage for future tourism. In this sense, the travel blog that presents itself as a narrative of authentic travel is simultaneously a guidebook for potential travellers or tourists and consequently collapses into tourist discourse.

The independent traveller plans his own journeys, and this too requires resilience. In entries such as 'Ryanair' and 'Ugly cars – I rented one', air travel and car hire become experiences that are not without their own difficulties. Criticising the 'weird extra charges', imposed by car rental companies, Wheeler is both caustic and humorous in his comparison of the evils of the Dodge Charger and the Cadillac Escalade. The latter, he observes, was driven by golfer Tiger Woods and notorious photographer Helmut Newton and is the sort of vehicle from which 'rap stars shoot at each other...the classic bling-mobile, the axle-of-evil' (Wheeler 2009h).

It is a voice that, by being dismissive of a comparatively touristic mode of transport (as opposed to a bicycle), positions the author as a knowledgeable individual. Likewise, if Wheeler must perforce rent a popular model, he is nevertheless a long-suffering traveller for having to use a vehicle that is 'horribly ugly'. There is also some glamour as well as danger in driving a vehicle that is positioned as having a somewhat criminal element associated with it. Both entries are written in a singular first-person voice, further emphasising the solitary and independent nature of travel. Where the voice of the traveller finds expression in an entry, it counters instances of touristic language in the narrative. The personal voice associated with travel discourse has a twofold function here. The first-person voice description of travel experiences provides a perfect foil for tourist discourse. Moreover, by bringing in the personal anecdote that is often characteristic of blogs, it validates the positioning of this narrative within the genre. Once again, these examples show that the degree of travel or tourist discourse varies across the entries.

The picture of travel

Although it is possible to trace the discourse of travel in the entries, it is far more difficult to locate it in the accompanying photographs. Much contemporary research on tourist photography is based on John Urry's theory that tourists reproduce symbols of tourism seen in brochures and other travel media, thus creating a 'circle of representation' (Caton and Santos 2008; Garrod 2009; Jenkins 2003; Urry 2002; Stepchenkova and Zhan 2013). Jenkins' study of backpackers, who often identify themselves as travellers, concludes that their personal travel photographs are no different from those present in commercial tourist discourse (Jenkins 2003; O'Reilly 2006). This not only confirms Urry's theory, but also suggests that there is little to distinguish between travel and tourist discourses in photography. On the whole, though, there is some ambivalence in the existing research. While Caton and Santos find in their study of tourist photography that the circle of representation is completed, Stepchenkova and Zhan's analysis concludes that there is only a partial completion of the same.

Images in *Tony Wheeler's Travels* generally lend credence to Urry's theory. The entries on Slovenia contain photographs of statues and heritage monuments. Dilley points out that such images are characteristic of tourist brochures for European destinations (qtd. in Jenkins 2003, p. 313). Similar is the case with photographs of a trip to London in October 2009. One of the images in the post on ferris wheels titled 'Big Wheels – London, Singapore, Melbourne' displays an aerial view of London shot from inside the iconic London Eye. It is rather telling that the photograph includes Big Ben and the Houses of Parliament – a popular tourist attraction associated with the destination. It could perhaps be argued that the angle from which this is shot (with a section of the wheel obscuring the view) is unusual, and that it signals the need to break away from the vicious circle of reproducing tourist images to add the personal touch of blog discourse or travel discourse. In fact, Garrod's comparative study of postcards and tourist photographs reveals subtle differences between the two, suggesting this is possible. Nevertheless, there needs to be more research on the photographic techniques employed by travellers to substantiate this view.

For the most part, however, the photographs in *Tony Wheeler's Travels* are touristic. A subsequent entry on his visit to the United Kingdom carries a photograph of the iconic London cab. Here, visual forms of touristic discourse are offset by a first-person entry placed directly below the photograph, where Wheeler relates what he has spent on the taxi fares in New York, Melbourne, and London, and asks of his readers, 'What did I get for my money?' (Wheeler 2009b). Thus, visual tourist discourse is set against the personal tone of travel discourse, particularly the voice of a traveller enduring the chaos of differing taxi fares.

The choice of image is equally interesting. This photograph of the taxis also appears on the bottom half of the cover of the 2008 edition of the *Lonely Planet London: city guide* (the top half of the guide carries a picture of Big Ben). The guidebook image has been sourced from Getty Images, but no credits appear under the online photograph, which is a cropped version of the same image simply captioned 'London taxis'. The book was published before the entry, suggesting that the photograph may have been deliberately included here for promotional purposes. For a reader who is aware of the previous contexts of this image, the inclusion of such a photograph in the post makes it touristic. It also destroys the impression that author is trying to create of the self as a genuine traveller and blogger. As the title *Tony Wheeler's Travels* conveys the impression that the text is a personal, original narrative by Tony Wheeler, such content weakens the credibility of the narrative and its author. Tourist discourse here is repurposed and presented as travel discourse and promotional material is presented as a personal text. Across the narrative, therefore, discourses of tourism either collapse into or feed those of travel and vice versa.

A blog in the narrative

In some respects, the narrative's claim to being a 'blog' is justified in *Tony Wheeler's Travels*. It has the heteroglossia and polyphony that is characteristic of most blogs. A number of different speech styles constitute the narrative – the personal tone of the blogger/traveller, the impersonal voice of the tour guide, and the picaresque style of travel writing – suggesting that at least some of the discursive qualities central to blogs are present in this text. To some extent, the multivocality of this text corresponds with Hevern's interpretation of the blog as an expression of a polyphonic self (2004, p. 332). According to Hevern, self-identity is constructed through the use of multiple voices that occupy various, sometimes oppositional positions (2004, p. 330). It is possible to identify such conflicting aspects to the self-presentation in *Tony Wheeler's Travels* in the authoritarian voice of the tour guide and the more personal voice of the traveller. As these tend to imbue the text with what may be described in Bakhtin's words as the simultaneous co-existence of a 'plurality of unmerged consciousnesses', it is easy to identify some degree of polyphony in the narrative (1984, p. 9).

Certainly, the text fulfils the condition that there should be an 'interaction and interdependence' of opposing voices in a polyphonic text (Bakhtin 1984, p. 36). The personal descriptions of the solitary traveller and the picaresque style of travel discourse are a distinct contrast to the impersonal voice of the tour guide and the authoritarianism of guidebook-style entries in the narrative. Nevertheless, the discourses of travel and tourism indicated by these voices are interdependent. Wheeler's presentation of the self as a traveller validates his position as a blogger but it also served to authenticate *Lonely Planet*'s promotion of tourism, particularly in the earlier entries written when the blog was a part of the publisher's website.

The second condition of polyphony is that the 'consciousnesses' present in a text must be equally authoritative. For Bakhtin, this does not result in a cancelling out of opposite views, but ensures that there is no monologic resolution in which voice emerges dominant (1984, pp. 18–26). It can be argued that such polyphony cannot exist in *Tony Wheeler's Travels,* as its frequently authoritarian tone, some of which is due to its lack of a social nature, does not allow for a real interaction of different voices. This means the personal voice of the blogger cannot be fully realised as valid or authoritative until the text incorporates more of the formal elements of a blog or participates more fully in the travel blogosphere through linking via blogrolls and responding to readers' comments. It should be noted, however, that Bakhtin's concept of polyphony was based on completed novels, whereas *Tony Wheeler's Travels* is at present a living text. It is possible that the text will continue to evolve, giving greater independence and validity to the personal voice of the blogger and inviting greater participation from its audience. It is equally possible that subsequent entries may give precedence to tourist discourse or focus on Wheeler's newer commercial interests and his self-presentation as a writer. Therefore, the narrative has the potential to incorporate other discourses and, as a consequence, a greater degree of heteroglossia and polyphony.

It should be noted that while heteroglossia and polyphony are concepts that offer a means of understanding the discursive tensions in *Tony Wheeler's Travels*, their presence is not enough to authenticate the narrative's positioning as a blog. Certainly, some features of the text give it the appearance of a blog. However, a closer look at the content suggests that the text would be better described as a website, and the new title is in this sense better suited to the narrative than the previous one. The presence of discourses of both travel and tourism in *Tony Wheeler's Travels* makes this a heteroglossic text. The authoritarian voice of tourism however does not allow a full realisation of the text's potential to be a personal narrative and a space for social interaction, both of which are intrinsic qualities of a blog. It also restricts presentation of the self as a traveller.

As a self-presentational narrative, *Tony Wheeler's Travels* is straightforward in its intent to position the author as a credible blogger and a genuine traveller. Various elements in the text act as cues to signal to the reader that the author is recounting a travel experience rather than a touristic one, that he is something of an adventurer and an explorer, and a serious writer. However, the success of this self-presentation is doubtful when a discerning reader or other bloggers can see through the superficial structure of a text that styles itself as a blog. As this textual analysis does not survey reader response, it is difficult to assess how audiences react to this text.

It should also be acknowledged that no single definition of the blog format is truly applicable to *Tony Wheeler's Travels*. That is to say, going by generic definitions it can be argued that the text is not a blog, despite its appearing to be one. However, as discussed earlier, definitions need to be flexible to take into account the ever-evolving nature of such narratives. Furthermore, there needs to be a more expansive definition for what constitutes a guidebook publisher's blog. Such a definition may allow for an inclusion of texts such as *Arthur Frommer*

Online, with its decidedly commercial content, and the multi-authored *Lonely Planet Blog* under this category. Conversely, it can be argued that guidebook publishers need to be more attentive to what audiences expect of a travel blog. Bearing this in mind, they need to both refrain from using the term loosely and show more than a cursory engagement with the blogosphere. *Tony Wheeler's Travels* may in time incorporate more elements of the blog and become a more credible execution of the format. Equally, it may shed the blog-like features it has and develop into a website in its own right. For now, despite its somewhat tepid engagement with other blogs, it deserves recognition as a ground-breaking narrative that has carved a place for itself in the blogosphere more resolutely and to a greater extent than any other guidebook publisher's travel blog.

References

Akehurst, G. 2009. User-generated content: the use of blogs for tourism organisations and tourism consumers. *Service Business* [Online], 3, 51–61. Available: http://link.springer.com/article/10.1007/s11628-008-0054-2 [Accessed 17 Apr. 2012].

Andreasen, L. B. 2006. Weblogs as forums for discussion – an alternative to the computer conference as a Standard in Online Learning. *In:* Buhl, M., Sørensen, B. H. and Meyer, B. (eds.) *Media and ICT – learning potentials.* Copenhagen: Danish University of Education Press.

Bakhtin, M. 1981. *The dialogic imagination: four essays,* Austin, TX, US: University of Texas Press.

Bakhtin, M. 1984. *Problems of Dostoevsky's poetics*, Minneapolis, MN, US:University of Minnesota Press.

Blaber, R. L. and Gilman, M. 1990. *Roguery: The picaresque tradition in Australian, Canadian, and Indian fiction,* Springwood, NSW, Australia: Butterfly Books.

Bosangit, C., McCabe, S. and Hibbert, S. 2009. What is told in travel blogs? Exploring travel blogs for consumer narrative analysis. *In:* Höpken, W., Gretzel, U. and Law, R. (eds.) *Proceedings of the International Conference on Information and Communication Technologies in Tourism.* Amsterdam: Springer.

Bruns, A. and Jacobs, J. 2006. *Uses of blogs,* New York: Peter Lang.

Burton, S. 2001. Difference and convention: Bakhtin and the practice of travel literature. *In:* Barta, P. I. (ed.) *Carnivalizing difference.* London: Routledge.

Butcher, J. 2003. *The moralisation of tourism: sun, sand ... and saving the world?*, London: Routledge.

Carson, D. 2008. The 'blogosphere' as a market research tool for tourism destinations: a case study of Australia's Northern Territory. *Journal of Vacation Marketing* [Online], 14. Available: http://jvm.sagepub.com/cgi/content/abstract/14/2/111 [Accessed 1 Apr. 2009].

Caton, K. and Santos, C. A. 2008. Closing the hermeneutic circle photographic encounters with the other. *Annals of Tourism Research* [Online], 35. Available: http://www.sciencedirect.com/science/article/B6V7Y-4RR8V8X-2/2/5ced5cd41d1abfd6aab42d694abc580b [Accessed 1 Dec. 2009].

Cohen, B. 1992. *Tourism,* Chippendale, NSW, Australia: Pan Macmillan.

Crotts, J. C., Mason, P. R. and Davis, B. 2009. Measuring guest satisfaction and competitive position in the hospitality and tourism industry: an application of stance-shift analysis to travel blog narratives. *Journal of Travel Research* [Online], 48. Available: http://jtr.sagepub.com/cgi/content/abstract/48/2/139 [Accessed 1 Nov. 2009].

Dann, G. 1996. *The language of tourism: a sociolinguistic perspective,* Wallingford, UK: CAB International.

Dann, G. 1999. Writing out the tourist in space and time. *Annals of Tourism Research* [Online], 26. Available: http://www.sciencedirect.com/science/article/B6V7Y-3VS7VK0-8/2/644ebe6402ad134ca201678b33b3afc4 [Accessed 30 Mar. 2009].

Finin, T., Joshi, A., Kolari, P., Java, A., Kale, A. and Karandikar, A. 2008. The information ecology of social media and online communities. *AI Magazine* [Online], 29(3), 77–92 [Accessed 22 Nov. 2009].

Frommer Media. 2016. *Arthur Frommer Online* [Online]. Available: http://www.frommers.com/community/blogs/arthur-frommer-online/ [Accessed 14 Jan. 2016].

Fussell, P. 1980. *Abroad: British literary traveling between the wars,* New York: Oxford University Press.

G.M. 2013. Bookend: the guidebook industry. *Gulliver* [Online]. Available: http://www.economist.com/blogs/gulliver/2013/04/guidebook-industry [Accessed 14 Jan. 2016].

Galani-Moutafi. 2000. The self and the other: traveler, ethnographer, tourist. *Annals of Tourism Research* [Online], 27(1), 203–224. [Accessed 30 Mar. 2009].

Garrod, B. 2009. Understanding the relationship between tourism destination imagery and tourist photography. *Journal of Travel Research* [Online], 47. Available: http://www.scopus.com/inward/record.url?eid=2-s2.0-58149508293&partnerID=40 [Accessed 1 Dec. 2009].

Hanlan, J. and Kelly, S. 2005. Image formation, information sources and an iconic Australian tourist destination. *Journal of Vacation Marketing* [Online], 11. Available: http://jvm.sagepub.com/content/11/2/163.abstract [Accessed 18 Apr. 2012].

Helmond, A. 2010. Identity 2.0: constructing identity with cultural software. Digital Methods Initiative. *Anne Helmond* [Online]. Available: http://www.annehelmond.nl/wordpress/wp-content/uploads//2010/01/helmond_identity20_dmiconference.pdf [Accessed 22 June 2010].

Hevern, V. W. 2004. Threaded identity in cyberspace: weblogs and positioning in the dialogical self. *Identity* [Online], 4(4). Available: http://www.tandfonline.com/doi/pdf/10.1207/s1532706xid0404_2. [Accessed 17 Mar. 2009].

Holland, P. and Huggan, G. 1998. *Tourists with typewriters: critical reflections on contemporary travel writing,* Ann Arbor, MI, US: University of Michigan Press.

Howard, R. G. 2008. Electronic hybridity and the vernacular Web. *Journal of American Folklore* [Online], 121(480), 192–218 [Accessed 16 Oct. 2009].

Jenkins, O. 2003. Photography and travel brochures: the circle of representation. *Tourism Geographies: An International Journal of Tourism Space, Place, and Environment* [Online], 5. Available: http://www.informaworld.com/10.1080/14616680309715 [Accessed 1 Dec. 2009].

Jones, S. 2003. *The encyclopedia of new media,* Thousand Oaks, CA, US: Sage.

Kitzmann, A. 2003. That different place: documenting the self within online environments. *Biography* [Online], 26(1), 48–65. [Accessed 26 November 2009].

Lonely Planet. 2016a. *About us and our authors*. [Online] Available: http://www.lonelyplanet.com/about/our-authors [Accessed 14 Jan. 2016].

Lonely Planet. 2016b. *Lonely Planet Blog* [Online].. Available: http://www.lonelyplanet.com/blog/ [Accessed 14 Jan. 2016].

Lonely Planet. 2016c. *Pathfinders* [Online]. Available: http://www.lonelyplanet.com/pathfinders [Accessed 14 Jan. 2016].

Lovink, G. 2008. *Zero comments: blogging and critical Internet culture,* New York: Routledge.

McCabe, S. 2005. 'Who is a tourist?': a critical review. *Tourist Studies* [Online], 5(1), 85–106. Available: http://tou.sagepub.com/content/5/1/85 [Accessed 13 Nov. 2009].

Mewshaw, M. 2005. Travel, travel writing, and the literature of travel. *South Central Review* [Online], 22. Available: http://muse.jhu.edu/journals/south_central_review/v022/22.2mewshaw.html [Accessed 21 May 2009].

O'Reilly, C. C. 2006. From drifter to gap year tourist: mainstreaming backpacker travel. *Annals of Tourism Research,* 33, 998–1017.

Papworth, L. 2009. *No comments, no engagement* [Online]. Available: http://laurelpapworth.com/non-engagement-seth-godin/ [Accessed 13 Nov. 2009].

Pühringer, S. and Taylor, A. 2008. A practitioner's report on blogs as a potential source of destination marketing intelligence. *Journal of Vacation Marketing* [Online], 14(2), 177–187 [Accessed 7 Oct. 2009].

Robinson, M. 2004. Narratives of being elsewhere: tourism and travel writing. *In:* Lew, A. A., Williams, A. M. and Hall, C. M. (eds.) *A companion to tourism.* Malden, MA, US: Blackwell.

Robinson, M. and Picard, D. 2009. Moments, magic, and memories: photographing tourists, tourist photographs, and making worlds. *In:* Robinson, M. and Picard, D. (eds.) *The framed world: tourism, tourists, and photography.* Farnham, UK: Ashgate.

Rosenberg, S. 2009. *Say everything : how blogging began, what it's becoming, and why it matters*. New York: Crown.

Rough Guides. 2016a. *Rough Guides*. Available: http://www.roughguides.com/ [Accessed 14 Jan. 2016].

Rough Guides. 2016b. Rough Guides [Online]. *Twitter*. Available: https://twitter.com/RoughGuides [Accessed 14 Jan 2016].

Schmallegger, D. and Carson, D. 2008. Blogs in tourismchanging approaches to information exchange. *Journal of Vacation Marketing* [Online], 14. Available: http://jvm.sagepub.com/cgi/content/abstract/14/2/99 [Accessed 15 May 2009].

Schmidt, J. 2007. Blogging Practices: An analytical framework. *Journal of Computer-Mediated Communication* [Online], 12. Available: http://dx.doi.org/10.1111/j.1083-6101.2007.00379.x [Accessed 24 Feb. 2011].

Scoble, R. and Israel, S. 2006. *Naked conversations: how blogs are changing the way businesses talk with customers.* Indianapolis, IN, US: Wiley Technology.

Serfaty, V. 2004. *The mirror and the veil: an overview of American online diaries and blogs,* Amsterdam: Rodopi.

Sorapure, M. 2003. Screening moments, scrolling lives: diary writing on the Web. *Biography* [Online], 26(1) 1–23. Available: https://muse.jhu.edu/article/42425. [Accessed 14 Sept. 2009].

Stepchenkova, S. and Zhan, F. 2013. Visual destination images of Peru: comparative content analysis of DMO and user-generated photography. *Tourism Management,* 36, 590–601.

Time Out. 2016. *Time Out*. Available: http://www.timeout.com/ [Accessed 14 Jan. 2016].

Urry, J. 2002. *The Tourist Gaze*, London: Sage.

Urry, J. and Larsen, J. 2011. *The tourist gaze 3.0,* Los Angeles, CA, US: Sage.

Van Nuenen, T. 2015. Here I am: authenticity and self-branding on travel blogs. *Tourist Studies,* 1–21[Online]. Available: http://tou.sagepub.com/content/16/2/192 [Accessed 24 Sept. 2015].

Walker Rettberg, J. 2014. *Blogging,* Cambridge, UK: Polity.

Wenger, A. 2008. Analysis of travel bloggers' characteristics and their communication about Austria as a tourism destination. *Journal of Vacation Marketing* [Online], 14.

Available: http://jvm.sagepub.com/cgi/content/abstract/14/2/169 [Accessed 27 Oct. 2010].

Wheeler, T. 1994. Coast to coast by Cadillac. *Tony Wheeler's travels* [Online]. Available from: http://www.lonelyplanet.com/tonywheeler/ [Accessed 13 Jan. 2016].

Wheeler, T. 2005. Travel blogs. *Tony Wheeler's blog* [Online]. Available from: http://www.lonelyplanet.com/tonywheeler/travel_blogs/ [Accessed 23 Nov. 2009].

Wheeler, T. 2006. Afghanistan practicalities. *Tony Wheeler's travels* [Online]. Available from: http://www.lonelyplanet.com/tonywheeler/my_lists/afghanistan_practicalities/ [Accessed 13 Jan. 2016].

Wheeler, T. 2008a. *My profile* [Online]. *Lonely Planet*. Available: http://www.lonelyplanet.com/tonywheeler//profile/my_profile/ [Accessed 3 Dec. 2009].

Wheeler, T. 2008b. Port-au-Prince – Naïve art, voodoo music and a slave-hero. *Tony Wheeler's travels* [Online]. Available from: http://www.lonelyplanet.com/tonywheeler/travel_blogs/haiti/portauprince_naieve_art_voodoo/ [Accessed 13 Jan. 2016].

Wheeler, T. 2009a. About Tony. *Tony Wheeler's travels* [Online]. Available from: http://www.lonelyplanet.com/tonywheeler/ [Accessed 14 Jan. 2016].

Wheeler, T. 2009b. Airport transport – London, Melbourne, New York. *Tony Wheeler's travels* [Online]. Available from: http://www.lonelyplanet.com/tonywheeler/my_lists/airport_transport_london_melbo/ [Accessed 14 Jan. 2016].

Wheeler, T. 2009c. Big wheels – London, Singapore, Melbourne. *Tony Wheeler's travels* [Online]. Available from: http://www.lonelyplanet.com/tonywheeler/travel_blogs/big_wheels_london_singapore_me/ [Accessed 13 Jan. 2016].

Wheeler, T. 2009d. Ljubljana. *Tony Wheeler's travels* [Online]. Available: http://www.lonelyplanet.com/tonywheeler/2009/11/19/ [Accessed 13 Jan. 2016].

Wheeler, T. 2009e. New York – the meat packing district. *Tony Wheeler's travels* [Online]. [Accessed 13 Jan. 2016].

Wheeler, T. 2009f. Ryanair – and the romance of air travel. *Tony Wheeler's travels* [Online]. Available from: http://www.lonelyplanet.com/tonywheeler/2009/11/13/ [Accessed 13 Jan. 2016].

Wheeler, T. 2009g. Trieste. *Tony Wheeler's travels* [Online]. Available: http://www.lonelyplanet.com/tonywheeler/2009/11/14/ [Accessed 13 Jan. 2016].

Wheeler, T. 2009h. Ugly Cars – I rented one. *Tony Wheeler's travels* [Online]. *Lonely Planet*. Available: http://www.lonelyplanet.com/tonywheeler/my_lists/ugly_cars_i_rented_one/ [Accessed 3 Dec. 2009].

Wheeler, T. 2015 Archive. *Tony Wheeler's travels* [Online]. Available: http://tonywheeler.com.au/2015/ [Accessed 18 July 2016].

Wheeler, T. and Wheeler, M. 2006. *Once while travelling: the Lonely Planet story,* Camberwell, VIC, Australia: Penguin.

Wicks, U. 1974. The nature of picaresque narrative: a modal approach. *PMLA* [Online], 89. Available: http://www.jstor.org/stable/461446 [Accessed 10 June 2009].

Zilcosky, J. 2004. The writer as nomad?: The art of getting lost. *Interventions,* 6, 229–241.

Zilcosky, J. 2008. Writing travel. *In:* Zilcosky, J. (ed.) *Writing travel: the poetics and politics of the modern journey.* Toronto, Canada: University of Toronto Press.

3 The voice(s) in the paratext

Presenting the author(s) of sponsored travel blogs

A large number of travel blogs are hosted on travel-specific websites sponsored by third-party advertising. For the most part, analyses of these blogs focus on the significance of a travel blogger's identity as a consumer of tourism for the perceived credibility of a blog's content and its promotion of various destinations (Banyai and Havitz 2013; Pühringer and Taylor 2008; Schmallegger and Carson 2008, p. 74; Wenger 2008). Little has been written about how the formal elements of blogs contribute to this online identity, how web hosts influence the different positions that an author occupies in the text – traveller or tourist, travel expert or tour guide – or the part played by discourses of travel and tourism. This chapter seeks to address this gap by exploring the concept that blogs are personal narratives whose formal features give some idea of an author's online self, with respect to blogs hosted on travel-specific web hosts. Gérard Genette's theory of paratexts (1997) provides a useful starting point for arriving at an understanding of how the content and other formal features provided by travel-specific web hosts and their sponsors complicates the identification of authorial voice and introduces discursive tensions in these narratives. It is employed here in the interrogation of a number of travel blogs on *TravelBlog*, *TravelPod*, and *BootsnAll*. Certainly, travel blogs may also be hosted, free of advertising, on blog hosting sites such as *Blogger* or *Wordpress*. However, the focus here is limited to those found on travel-specific web hosting services driven by advertising sponsorship, mainly to ascertain how web-host-provided paratextual elements combined with third-party advertising and user-generated text contributes to or detracts from the self-presentation of these travel bloggers.

There have been arguments both for and against the centrality of the author in online narratives. For some, texts such as blogs signal the 'death of the author', since these platforms allow readers to engage with the author, hence undermining authorial control over the text (Barthes 1977; Landow 2006). For others, blogs celebrate authorship. Chris Chesher, for example, proposes that the features of a blog should facilitate author identification (2005). This view is reiterated in Warschauer and Grimes's assertion that the consistent voice and visual elements of a blog's posts testify to its 'personal ownership and authorship' (2008, p.8). Likewise, Viviane Serfaty observes that while the features of a blog may make it a polyphonic text where conflicting discourses interact, the author still remains in control (2004, p. 61). Certainly, in the case of personal blogs, it is usually the blogger who selects and provides such elements as links to other blogs in the form of a list known as a blogroll, which becomes an expression of his or her interests (Lomborg 2009). Not only does such linking manifest the blogger's interests, affiliations, and authorial intent, it also leads to a 'cementing of certain chosen connections' that situates the narrative in a network of associated texts (Lovink 2008; Syverson 2007, p. 433). As mentioned in the introductory chapter, and as corroborated by several other similar studies, formal features are self-presentational elements that offer some sense of who the author is and locate the text in its genre (Nardi *et al.* 2004, p. 42; Schmidt 2007, p. 1415).

Admittedly, an author's personality is usually writ large in personal travel blogs that are hosted independently. In comparison, it is less prominent in the amateur travel blogs found on commercially sponsored travel-specific web hosts such as *TravelPod*, *TravelBlog*, and *BootsnAll* where many other voices also claim a reader's attention – that of the web host or advertisers. These voices generally find expression in paratextual elements[1] such as logos, titles, maps, hyperlinks, blogrolls, and other formal elements provided by the web hosts and their commercial sponsors. Such paratextual 'on-site elements' also help position online narratives in terms of genre and reader expectations (Stewart 2010, p. 64). Most blogs are also usually, but not always necessarily, open to comments, making them spaces where the many voices of readers and authors interact (Serfaty 2004, p. 61; Walker Rettberg 2014, p.34). When travel bloggers adopt different voices and write as travellers, tourists, or travel experts, this only adds to the polyphony of the conversation. While it can be agreed, with George Landow (2006, p. 56) and Viviane Serfaty (2004, p. 61), that such multivocality is a defining characteristic of such online narratives, the degree to which authorial voice remains distinct differs from travel blog to travel blog and this can be problematic under certain circumstances.

Despite suggestions to the contrary, such blogs on travel-specific web hosts are still largely personal in that they generally comprise first-person-voice posts describing the bloggers' travel experiences. Their web hosts use these posts as a foundation for producing commercial content, in the form of advertisements and links to other travel-related information, which accompanies each post. Bloggers, in their turn, rely on web hosts to provide space for their personal travel narratives. There is, therefore, an interdependence of travel-themed content provided by bloggers and the generally touristic commercial content from both the web host and third-party advertisers. The notion of authorial control is far more complicated when the web host and commercial sponsors contribute to the form and content of travel blogs. Their creating and adding content makes it difficult to ascertain the extent to which the bloggers themselves control various elements of their narratives. In addition to this, features such as advertisements contribute to the heteroglossia and polyphony of the text, which mixing of discourses can potentially blur personal and commercial interests (Howard 2008, p. 194). As a consequence, some elements of travel blogs found on such hosting sites may, in fact, obscure rather than define authorial identity. They may also confound the positioning of the blog as either a commercial text promoting a destination or as a personal narrative describing a travel experience.

Genette's theoretical framework of paratexts offers a means of understanding how web hosts such as *TravelBlog*, *TravelPod*, and *BootsnAll* and their commercial sponsors contribute towards the discursive tensions between travel and tourism in their travel blogs and how this complicates issues of authorship in these narratives. Paratexts are rarely the focus of academic debates on blogging. Nevertheless, their contribution to the self-presentation of a travel blogger, their role in the positioning of the text, and their implications for centrality of authorial voice need to be investigated further, particularly given the multivocality that arises when content produced by web hosts or commercial sponsors frames posts and photographs created by travel bloggers. This also requires an examination of the various narrative techniques incorporated in these blogs.

A twist in the title

The idea of paratext was originally used by Gérard Genette with regard to printed books (1997). According to Genette, the paratexts of a narrative include both 'external presentation' elements (peritext), such as the title and the name of the author that are located around the text, as well as 'distanced elements', or other related texts (epitext). This concept has been adapted, in film and television studies, in order to analyse trailers, spin-offs, and fan-created texts. Some paratexts are seen to guide viewers' selection, expectation, and interpretation of texts, while others change an audience's initial understanding of a text over time (Gray 2010). Consequently, paratexts play a significant role in positioning a text and so guide a reader's or viewer's response to the same. The concept has also been useful in the study of online texts. Applying Genette's theories to his analysis of the *Inanimate Alice* website, Gavin Stewart (2010, pp. 64–65) interprets banners, images, links, and page layout as paratextual elements that contribute to a reader's understanding of the content and positioning of the narrative. All of these are characteristic features of web pages and blogs, including those created on travel-specific hosting sites. Here, the web hosts produce banners, browser tab text, and URLs (Uniform Resource Locators). Indeed, the principal contribution of the web host is the template of the blog itself – the general layout of formal elements and their overall appearance. These are part of the peritext that frames the blog entries. Although it is usually the author who chooses a user name and a title for the blog, the design and manner of presentation of this information, by means of a browser tab title, URL, and user name placed prominently over each blog post, is decided by the web host. Ultimately, the web host positions the blog and its entries, manipulates the self-presentation of the blogger, and so influences a visitor's evaluation of the narrative.

It is reasonable to assume that a text owes its positioning as a narrative of travel largely to the title chosen by its author and the URL displayed in a browser's navigation bar. It is also fair to assume that the user name employed by the author indicates a prevalence of authorial voice and identity over other voices in the text.

Even so, in these travel blogs, the content provided by the web host often competes for attention alongside titles and posts created by the bloggers in a manner that can influence readers' impressions of the narrative and the online self that a blogger presents. Also, at times, the corporate identity of the web host looms large in the form of logos and banners and jostles for space with the online self-presentation of the blogger. In order to be heard, the authorial voice – and often this is the voice of a traveller – must compete with the voices of commercial tourism. This complicates both authorial identification and authorial control. Therefore, an examination of the extent to which titles and banners contribute towards a blogger's online self-presentation and the discourses of travel and tourism present in the narrative is particularly pertinent to a discussion of textual positioning and authorial identity within these travel blogs.

At the time of initial access in February 2010, *Darryl and Sarah – Wallaby Wanderers* was listed as a 'featured' travel blog on the *TravelBlog* home page, suggesting that the text enjoys some popularity (Howell and Howell 2010a). With over 300 entries and more than 4000 photographs the contribution of the British bloggers, Darryl and Sarah Howell, is substantial. Yet, the banners and URL, part of the template provided by the web host, detract from the presentation of this text as a unique personal narrative written by the blogger. All pages hosted on *TravelBlog* carry the website's signature horizontally scrolling banner. This displays a series of silhouettes of iconic sights from across the world – the Parthenon, the Eiffel Tower, the Sydney Opera House, the Petronas towers, Rio's Statue of Christ the Redeemer, and animals in the African savannah among others. The authors' title for each entry appears immediately under this logo, but the URL correlates with the geographical location of the place described in the post. For example, 'A Peak too Far' may be found by typing the URL: http://www.Travelblog.org/Oceania/Australia/Tasmania/Cradle-Mountain/blog-479978.html (Howell and Howell 2010g). *TravelBlog* differs in this respect from other blog hosts like *Blogger* and *Wordpress* that allow bloggers to use their blog title as a part of the URL. In this instance, the web host uses the URL to position the post as a text on Tasmania, rather than a personal travel narrative. In addition to this, although the words in the tab title display the bloggers' names, it is the corporate identity of *TravelBlog* that looms large in the banner and logo immediately below this.

Although there has been research to support the notion of banner blindness of readers, animated banners have been found to be more noticeable than static ones (Benway 1998; Hamborg *et al.* 2012). Indeed, owing to the prominently placed scrolling banner, the voice of commercial tourism clamours for attention alongside the voice of the traveller in the narrative. The silhouettes periodically shift from right to left, in a manner that resonates with tourism's imperative to consume sights continuously but superficially, without stopping to truly absorb the experience or enjoy the view. The graphic capturing of iconic sights and touristic signs in a series and the carefully timed display are at odds with the timelessness of travel. In contrast, the title below this banner associates the experience described in the entry itself with travel. The traveller must climb a 'peak' which is 'too far', suggesting an arduous journey. This is validated by the post, which describes a difficult trek via tracks that are alternatively 'hard', 'rough', and 'steep' (Howell and Howell 2010g). The peak itself, Tasmania's Cradle Mountain, is presented as an unattainable goal, unlike the touristic destinations displayed above the entry that are so easily reached. Yet, the accomplishment of having tried to reach the peak, and the description of the climb up a rugged path, unintentionally taking the wrong route despite having a map, imbues the experience with a sense of spontaneity and remoteness associated with off-the-beaten-path travel. Framed as it is within advertising for tourism services and headed by a URL that categorically traces the route from Oceania to Australia to Tasmania all the way to Cradle Mountain, the entry effectively turns the unreachable destination into something that can be reached by future visitors. In this sense, travel and its attendant discourses paves the way for potential tourism. Moreover, the bloggers' entries about travel underwrite the promotional discourses of tourism present in the accompanying advertisements.

There is a similar collapse of travel into tourism in *TravelPod* whose blogs resemble those of *TravelBlog* with respect to tab titles and banners. A case in point is *Global Roaming: Overland from Sydney to Scotland via a wintry Siberia* written under the user name Technotrekker. The blog enjoys some little fame – both the narrative and its author, Ross Pringle, have been featured in the media (Timson 2006). Although this blog is now complete, Pringle continues to write an independent travel blog titled *The Longest Way Home* that is widely networked across other social media platforms such as *Facebook* and *Twitter* (Pringle 2016). When first accessed in April 2010, *Global Roaming* was listed as *TravelPod*'s best travel journal (Pringle 2005b). At the time of writing, it was still rated as a 'top pick' by the web host. As in other *TravelPod* blogs, the blogger's user name followed by the phrase 'travel blog' appears in the browser tab. The web host modifies this by adding a qualifying phrase that locates each post in terms of the destination it talks about. So a post ambiguously titled 'Life on the Fringe' bears the tab title 'Technotrekker's Travel Blog – Edinburgh, United Kingdom, August 18, 2007' (Pringle 2007b). In addition to this, the web host provides an interactive map, immediately under the title, which plots the destination as well as the route taken to reach it. Destinations mentioned in each entry are also plotted on an interactive timeline that runs across the top of the map, in a series of pinpoints accompanied by the name of the place and an icon of the country's flag. The timeline numbers each entry and positions it in relation to other posts on the journey. This indicates where and when a particular destination was reached not just on the journey, but in the travel narrative of the blog as a whole. This feature effectively structures the narrative and gives what is presented as a spontaneous 'roaming' of the world the planned appearance of an itinerary. These paratexts make the narrative more place-specific and locate it as a travel text on Edinburgh.

Here again, the title of the post associates the experiences described therein with travel as opposed to tourism. 'Life on the Fringe', an oblique reference to the Edinburgh Fringe festival, could also allude to living life on the edge. The festival itself is known for its inclusion of experimental art, and is in this regard unconventional. Pringle's participation in cultural activities enhances his presentation of the self as an individual of refined tastes, a quality that is characteristic of travellers rather than tourists. Yet, the Fringe Festival is also a well-established event and has developed over the years into a recognisable mainstream tourist attraction. For this reason, the festival itself may not be regarded as an experience that goes off the beaten path, despite the blog entry's association of this with travel. The connection, made by the web host, between 'Fringe' and 'Edinburgh' authenticates the entry and contextualises an otherwise ambiguous title by designating a location. For web hosts and their sponsors, such titles situate the destinations described as places that offer travel experiences, which in turn validates the accompanying advertisements for various travel services. While supporting Pringle's narrative of travel, these promotional discourses make the destination more accessible and attractive for potential tourists.

Inasmuch as these are personal narratives of travel, the discourses of corporate tourism are conspicuous in the logos and URLs of *TravelPod* blogs, almost displacing authorial voice. As with *TravelBlog*, the corporate logo enjoys a prominent position at the top left-hand corner of the page. The location of the logo is significant. Although readers may ignore banners, nevertheless they scan web pages beginning at the top-left quarter (Benway 1998; Francisco-Revilla and Crow 2009). Granted, there is sufficient space for authorial expression – a thumbnail picture and a link to an 'About the Author' page along the right-hand margin. Also, unlike *TravelBlog*, the URL includes the user name 'Technotrekker', lending a clue to the blogger's online self. This user name appears again, almost as an afterthought, placed as it is in a much smaller font under the post's title. Discourses of tourism are strategically placed and enjoy greater visibility than the self-presentational elements that lend some clue to the author's online self and the various roles they occupy in their narratives. Yet, user names, including such terms as 'trekker', validate the blog as a whole and the promotional discourses that subsist on this narrative.

In comparison, the same paratextual elements in *BootsnAll* blogs present a clearer sense of the authors' online self. *For Mom, Love Steve* (Nakano 2010a) was once listed as a top blog on this website, in terms of number of posts. As with other *BootsnAll* blogs, the entry's title, which chosen by the blogger, appears unmodified in the browser tab. The blog itself can be located using the URL http://blogs.bootsnall.com/nakano/. This particular *BootsnAll* travel blog also has an alternative URL, www.steveislost.com, indicating that the web page is now an independent website, although it continues to use the *BootsnAll* template and is accessible through the web host's home page (Nakano 2010a). The logo for this web host is fairly unobtrusive, occupying only a small corner in the top right of the web page. When it comes to choosing a banner for their web pages, users may choose between images of a pair of boots, as is the case with *For Mom, Love Steve* (Nakano 2010a), or the Sydney Opera House, as seen in *Holly's Travels* (Holly 2010) or a pier at sunset, as displayed in *The Wanderings of busman7* (Hawke 2016) among others. In general, the template offered by this web host places greater emphasis on the concept of travel or tourism than on the corporate identity of the hosting service. Rather than highlighting the destination being described in the post, paratextual elements in these blogs allow a better expression of the authors' position and the themes of their narratives. The individualism is limited, though – the hiking boots in Nakano's blog could well feature in a number of other travel blogs on *BootsnAll*. However, users may choose a template that correlates best with the online self they wish to present. In this case, the banner enhances Nakano's self-presentation as someone who is 'lost' while travelling. The image creates an association with forms of independent travel such as backpacking while also reiterating the name of the web host. This supports the web host's corporate image as a resource on independent travel as opposed to organised tourism.

This is hardly an exhaustive study of the various advertising-sponsored, travel-specific platforms that host blogs. Nonetheless, these findings indicate that discussions of the role of blog features in author identification must recognise the possibility of the text having multiple authors in the form of a web host and a blogger. Furthermore, it is likely that these bloggers have little control over the creation of tab titles or URLs, which are probably generated by the software used by the hosting website. On the whole, these blogs consist of some elements created by the blogger-authors and others, which are really paratexts, appearing courtesy of the web-host publisher. Such travel blogs support Genette's belief that both author and publisher share the responsibility for authorship of elements such as titles (1997, p. 74). Regardless of whether the web host is seen as a co-author or publisher, arguments that a blog's features emphasise the author's ownership and identity need to acknowledge the possibility that formal elements need not necessarily identify the blogger.

The multiple voices of the bloggers, the web host, and the sponsors manifest the heteroglossia in these blogs. However, there is not necessarily any parity between these voices or the discourses they represent. Corporate discourses of the web host and sponsors can take precedence over the personal discourse of bloggers. To a certain extent, a blogger's presentation of the self as traveller or of a travel experience is either superseded by the corporate identity of the web host or sidelined by the need to give prominence to the destination of the journey described. Any discussion of authorial identity or control in such blogs found on hosting sites must, as a consequence, recognise that not all elements in the text reflect aspects of the online self that bloggers wish to present to their readers.

The language of links

Conversations about links usually pertain to the links list known as a blogroll, which often appears alongside the text entry. This may be regarded as a paratext for several reasons. First, it contextualises the blog by situating it in a network of other blogs that share the same culture (Lovink 2008, p. 252; Serfaty 2004, p. 26). Second, in personal blogs, such as those found on *Blogger* or *Wordpress*, bloggers determine the content of their blogrolls and, through their choices, present aspects of their online self. The blogroll, therefore, is a feature that contributes to a reader's impression and interpretation of the author and the narrative it accompanies. Yet, with travel blogs where web hosts generate the links instead of the blogger, both authorial self-presentation and textual positioning become problematic. Although posts on these travel blogs are usually accompanied by links to other blogs, these link lists are not always blogrolls in the traditional sense of a static list of links that appears alongside all posts. Instead, the list generally comprises links to advertisements and other, often annotated, external and internal links also generated by the web host.

The breadcrumb trail in *Wallaby Wanderers* is a good example of how web hosts provide internal links to promotional content and position the narrative as a text on a specific destination. This is a series of links that appears horizontally across the top of each page, just below the banner, that indicates the hierarchy of web pages in the website. In *Travelblog* blogs, this breadcrumb trail contains links to other blog posts on the same country, region, or destination. So, a post on Narooma in Australia carries the breadcrumb trail 'Oceania >> Australia >> New South Wales >> Narooma' (Howell and Howell 2010e). Each of these terms links to a series of other blog posts and photographs on the same destination as well as a description of the place provided by the web host. A reader who chooses to click on 'Narooma' will be able to view other blog posts on the same destination. This 'blogroll' then, changes for each entry, as do the accompanying links. The breadcrumb trail maps a route to destinations that may be otherwise presented as being off-road, remote, or unexplored and, therefore, as experiences associated with travel. In the very moment that the blogger posts the entry, the web host authenticates it by locating it on a map, assigning a path, and providing guidebook-style descriptions of the same. A narrative of travel thus serves to further interests that are commercial and collapses into the discourse of tourism.

TravelPod entries similarly display a series of links pertaining to the destination visited, the only difference being that these are located just over the date of the entry. In 'Life on the Fringe', clicking on the link to 'Edinburgh' opens a page with links to other blog posts, photographs, and videos on the same destination. The links effectively fragment the blog, treating each entry as a separate text on a specific destination, rather than preserving the integrity of the narrative as a whole. Moreover, this place-associated linking is technology-driven and does not necessarily indicate any real affiliation between the authors of these posts, who are probably unaware of their fellow travellers and bloggers. Both *TravelPod* and *TravelBlog* do allow bloggers to nominate 'favourite bloggers' or 'follow' other blogs, respectively, by providing links to these from their 'About' page. However, these are exclusively internal links to other blogs on the same website. Among the three web hosts selected for this study, *BootsnAll* is the lone exception in allowing its bloggers to display a conventional blogroll as a list alongside the posts that includes links to both blogs and other online texts selected by the blogger.

TravelBlog, *TravelPod*, and *BootsnAll* also provide links to other web pages and advertisements. Directly below the corporate banner in each *TravelBlog* blog post is a menu with navigational links to web pages with information on every continent. Each of these contains maps, factual descriptions of the region, travel advice, advertisements, and links to other relevant resources. *TravelPod* is far more simplistic in its display of a single link to 'Destinations' over each entry, which in turn opens a page with links to hotel reviews alphabetically listed by destination. In both *TravelBlog* and *TravelPod*, such links are internal, leading to pages within the same web site. A similar style is seen in *BootsnAll* blogs, with the only difference being that there are usually a few external links as well. While bloggers may describe an experience or destination as being off the beaten path in a post, web hosts locate the same experience by giving the ostensibly remote destination a name, mapping a path to it, and even providing information on accommodation and sightseeing. When web hosts repurpose content to promote destinations, travel inscribes a path for tourism.

Both *TravelBlog* and *TravelPod* control and limit the networking capabilities of their blogs and authors. Far from facilitating an engagement with the 'enclave culture' of blogs (Lovink 2008, p. 252), these web hosts' restrictions effectively frustrate a blogger's positioning of the narrative among other similar texts. The narratives behave as personal blogs and participate in the blogosphere only as far as their web hosts permit. Indeed, if an entry is listed with other similar blog posts on the same place, this association is subject to the software used by the web host and serves mainly to generate or supplement its own (often promotional) content on the same destinations. The narratives cannot 'travel' by extending their content and connections to platforms external to their chosen web host. For a reader, navigating these blogs is an experience not unlike that of a guided tour, whose guide marks out a fixed route or itinerary.

As a result, there is little presentation of a blogger's self in *TravelPod* and *TravelBlog* 'blogrolls'. These mainly expand the post's potential to be a resource on a specific destination. Also, this network is largely contained within the same website. In addition to this, the 'blogroll' and links break rather than bind the blog narrative, making use of the episodic structure to turn it into a number of texts on various places, and indeed try to position each entry as a stand-alone text on a particular destination. Instead of preserving and promoting the interpretation of these blogs as personal narratives, they manipulate the text to serve the web hosts' commercial ends by firmly situating each post among online texts dedicated to tourism marketing. The host-provided links in such blogs fail as paratexts in that they do not, to quote Syverson (2007, p. 433), 'cement connections' that are personal, so giving a sense of the author, but instead position these blogs among other corporate and commercial texts. This strategy serves mainly to guide readers to a point of purchase and encourage them to avail themselves of various travel-related services. As for the question of authorial control, in the case of links in these travel blogs, the web host wields the baton.

Making sense of advertising

Blogs in *TravelBlog* and *BootsnAll* often contain advertisements that appear over, below, or alongside entries. These advertisements are generated by third parties.

The web hosts use Google AdSense, a software program that analyses the words in each blog post and places small advertisements relevant to the content (Auletta 2009, p. 91). For example, 'Needle in a Haystack', the *Wallaby Wanderers* post on Orange (Howell and Howell 2010f), is accompanied by advertisements placed beside the title and alongside the entry for airfare discounts from Flight Centre, hotel accommodation, and a spa service. Similarly, advertisements for travel and tourism services appear in a little box alongside posts in *For Mom, Love Steve*. Advertisements that focus on the place and commercialise the text often do little for the positioning of the blog as a personal narrative. It should be noted here that these web hosts do not have complete control over such third-party advertising. Programs such as AdSense may also take a reader's interests and geographical location into account while generating advertisements. In the case of posts on obscure destinations, banner advertisements may not supplement the text at all, and may only be generated for the region, or a user's geographical location. Thus an Australian visitor to a *TravelBlog* post is likely to see advertising for services in that country whereas a visitor from the United Kingdom will see different advertisements framing the same content. While this advertising can supplement the presentation of a destination, it does little for the presentation of the blogger. In fact, advertisements form a symbiotic relationship with blog posts, feeding off them in order to exist. Conversely, their very presence on the page also pays for the existence of the travel narrative itself and the online self it presents.

There are no sponsored advertisements visible in *Global Roaming*, owing to the different structure of the *TravelPod* platform. The destination name appearing over each entry in *TravelPod* blogs links to a page that promotes travel services pertaining to the destination described in the post. This page contains place-specific advertising from *TravelPod* sponsors such as Expedia. These advertisements are dependent on the text generated by the blogger, suggesting that the blogger has some degree of authorial control over content generated by the web host, however indirect or involuntary this may be. However, the page itself serves a commercial purpose that has nothing to do with promoting or interpreting the blog narrative to which it is linked, and a lot to do with selling travel-related services for the destination mentioned in the post.

The content provided by these travel blog hosting sites and their sponsors generally uses narrative techniques such as an authoritarian and impersonal tone, a lack of sender identification, euphoric description, and repetition. In *Global Roaming*, short but imperative hyperlinked phrases encourage readers to share the blog via social media, 'map your own trip', 'post your own travel photos', and 'turn blog into book' (Pringle 2005b). *TravelPod* has a commercial purpose in soliciting these actions. Each entry is a promotional tool to draw potential contributors who will, by writing their own travel narratives, generate content that can be manipulated towards the promotion of various travel-related services. Each blog is also offered as a print book, either softcover or hardcover, at a price that varies according to its length.

This authoritarian voice is more pronounced in the text of advertisements. An advertisement for Kokoda Spirit in *Wallaby Wanderers* is both imperative and euphoric: 'Walk in the footsteps of heroes. One of the world's great adventures' (Howell and Howell 2010f). Advertisements in a *BootsnAll* blog entry on Guatemala echo this tone: 'Great hotels in Guatemala Official site. Book online today' (Nakano 2010c). The language of such advertisements is largely impersonal, although the sender may be identified in the advertiser's website URL that appears in fine print. This style, usually typical of guidebooks, brochures, or advertisements that promote tourism, is characteristic of tourist discourse (Dann 1996). This association with forms such as guidebooks and brochures positions the blog as an informational travel text, and this may strengthen the author's reputation as an expert on travel. However, it is the voice of the web host and the sponsor and not that of the blogger that is clearly heard and identifiable here. It weakens the positioning of these travel blogs as purely personal narratives comparable to forms such as the diary by adding touristic overtones. Certainly, it is not authorial voice that is foremost, although the other voices in the text may add to the perceived credibility of the author's narrative and vice versa.

On the one hand, the touristic discourse represented by these advertisements sets up a tension with entries that associate a destination with a travel experience. The promotion of hotels in Guatemala makes this a destination that is easier to access and experience for potential tourists while the same country is presented as being off the beaten path in Nakano's blog. In addition to this, there is sometimes a tension within the advertisements themselves. The Kokoda trail in New Guinea referred to in advertisements appearing in the *Wallaby Wanderers* blog is generally held to be a harsh and difficult route where many lives were lost during the Second World War. It has since been commercialised as a tourist attraction. Although the advertisers draw on this association with travel, some of the gravity of the experience is lost when it is described as a 'great adventure'.

When considering banner advertising, it should be noted that the discursive tensions set up by the presence of such advertising and web-host-generated content may not be recognised by a visitor to the blog, not merely due to banner blindness. To begin with, discussions of advertisements become immaterial when a reader uses filters or ad-blockers that prevent their appearance in the browser. Furthermore, readers may ignore a significant proportion of the banner advertisements on a page, even if they do not physically remove these (Drèze and Hussherr 2003). Such avoidance of advertising is not exclusive to online texts. Studies of television advertising indicate that viewers either deliberately ignore commercials or fail to absorb the message therein after repeated viewing (Calder and Sternthal 1980; Elpers *et al.* 2003). However, Drèze and Hussherr suggest that at least some readers recall the advertisements they do look at online. This is corroborated by Hamborg *et al.*'s findings on the greater visibility of animated banners (2012). Therefore, it is possible that in such cases the banner advertisements do complicate the positioning of the text as a narrative of travel and introduce a tension between the discourses of travel and tourism.

Advertisements contribute to the heteroglossia and polyphony of the text. This in turn raises several questions about authorial control. A blog visitor's ability to either physically block advertisements or read the entry while ignoring the accompanying advertisements has several implications. First, there may not always be a perceptible discursive tension between blogger- and web-host-provided content, particularly if the web host's contribution is a banner advertisement. Second, although such travel-specific blog hosting sites often have the power to place advertisements, a reader's ability to block these suggests that ultimately the responsibility for the formal appearance of the blog is not the author's alone but is, in fact, shared between blogger, web host, and reader. Finally, such advertising introduces a number of third parties and their attendant voices to the narrative. This adds to the polyphony of the text, but does little to enhance the self-presentation of its author or add to the clarity of authorial voice.

In the blogger's boots

Bloggers often make use of an 'About' page in order to describe themselves and the purpose of their blog. This is perhaps the most obvious means of identifying the author of the posts. All blogs on *TravelBlog* and *TravelPod* have this feature. *Wallaby Wanderers* contains a picture of the authors and a description of the blog itself (Howell and Howell 2010a). The authors present themselves using only their first names, Darryl and Sarah, and it is only by consulting the bloggers directory in the website that visitors will know that the blog is written by Darryl and Sarah Howell. Similarly, clicking on the blogger's user name in *Global Roaming* takes a reader to Technotrekker's 'About the Author' page (Pringle 2005d). In all *TravelPod* blogs, this page provides details of the blogger's place of origin, profession, and interests. The amount of detail provided differs from blog to blog. For example, Technotrekker chooses not to provide his real name here although the page does contain a photograph of the author and some posts and replies to readers' comments are signed 'Ross'. In comparison, *TravelPod* blogger Woodsy79 is quite reticent and only provides a username, photograph, and the name of his hometown (Woodsy79 2010). The *BootsnAll* template does not provide an 'About' page, but Steve Nakano's post 'Now About Me' serves to describe both the blogger and his narrative. This is a technique also used by other bloggers such as Dave Hawke, who writes as 'busman7', to make up for the deficiencies of this platform (Hawke 2016).

Upon comparison, the profile page of *TravelPod* blogs is somewhat restrictive in its format and only permits the entry of certain details. It also contributes to the presentation of an online self only so far as a blogger utilises it for this function. In contrast, *TravelBlog* allows greater freedom of self-presentation, and its bloggers may write several paragraphs about themselves, choosing what information they wish to share or withhold. The fact that *BootsnAll* bloggers choose to create posts that function as 'About' pages suggests author identification is indispensable to the presentation of an online self. Also, creating an 'About' post to make up for the absence of a feature generally held to be essential to blogs is a strategy that highlights these authors' awareness of the requisite practices in a presentation of the self as a genuine blogger and this may strengthen the perceived credibility of the narrative.

The user name a blogger chooses to adopt reflects the roles he or she wishes to occupy online. Some bloggers use their own names, as is the case with *Wallaby Wanderers* where both travellers take turns at writing entries. On the other hand, 'Technotrekker' and 'Woodsy79' are aliases created specifically for the purpose of narrating these bloggers' travel experiences. Pseudonyms and their connotations create an image of the author for readers, thus influencing the latter's perception of the text (Genette 1997, p. 50). In general, the user names reflect the blogger's real identity – take the Howells or busman7, for example – or suggest a traveller self in their use of travel-related words such as 'nomad' or 'trekker'. The travel theme is woven into titles and URLs as well, as in the case of *Global Roaming* or *Wallaby Wanderers* and www.steveislost.com. A well-chosen user name or title can reinforce a blogger's connection with other bloggers as well, thus enhancing his or her credibility. The *Wallaby Wanderers* blog, for example, links to KangarooJack's blog (Howell and Howell 2010b). User names thus offer a clear sense of the self a blogger wishes to present in his or her travel blog.

The different positions bloggers occupy are usually more distinct in blog posts. Hevern's observation that there may be multiple aspects to the online self of a single blogger is validated by travel blogs such as *Wallaby Wanderers* or *For Mom, Love Steve* (Hevern 2004, p. 322). Here, the authors consciously refer to their positions as travellers and bloggers as well as the connection between the self as writer and as traveller. For the Howells, starting a diary is part of their trip preparation, and the first few entries reflect this awareness of the self as blogger. They write about acquiring the necessary skills – 'Back in the warm we settle down for a bit of *TravelBlog* and *Facebook* training' (Howell and Howell 2010d) – and contemplate the logistics involved – 'whether we'll manage daily uploads very much depends on the amount of McDonalds and Starbucks Coffee houses we can find!' (Howell and Howell 2010c).

Writing with some regularity clearly lends conviction to a presentation of the self as a travel blogger. Seeking out McDonalds and Starbucks, places offering free wi-fi services, reflects the thriftiness of backpacker travel. Yet, the two fast food chains also represent a convenience and familiarity, which are at odds with the concept of travel as an adventure or an escape. The narration of 'adventure' through regularly updated entries relies on the proximity of these established and recognisable icons of commercialism and consumerism.

A similar awareness of the self as a blogger, who is responsible to his readers, is evident in Steve Nakano's blog where he explains, 'I write a blog to let everybody know what I am doing...' (Nakano 2010e). In both these narratives blogging and travel are interlinked, each influencing the other in that blogging may provide the impetus for travel or be integral to the travel experience, while the journey itself inspires the content for the blogs.

Technotrekker does not make such connections between travel and blogging, but he does describe himself as an author of a 'travelogue' or 'diary' in his eighth post in *Global Roaming*:

> I also have delusions of grandeur and yearning to write. At least I want to try and give it a go. I have reasonably advanced plans for a novel and am interested in writing articles, reviews and things like this travel diary. I'll get an idea of how people react to and accept my writing and if worst comes to worst, I'll have a substantial body of work in this diary that will be interesting to both myself and [sic] variety of other people.
>
> (Pringle 2005g)

He also reflects on the writing process in the first entry of the blog, which has clearly been written after the blog was completed. This introductory post lists links to what he feels are his best entries. It describes the entire blog as a 'one serious overland odyssey' culminating in Sydney and concludes with more links to posts on the hardware and software used to create the blog, this last establishing the self as a tech-savvy traveller as suggested by his user name (Pringle 2005f). In such posts, Technotrekker plays the mentor, giving advice on the blogging process through both entries and answers to comments from readers. Not all blogs contain such reflections on the writing process, and not all bloggers identify themselves as bloggers or emphasise their position as authors. That said, such entries suggest that posts, titles, and user names offer the best means of expressing various aspects of the online self.

Blogging travel

The presentation of self in the role of a traveller has previously been employed by hosts of television travel programmes, authors of travel books, and writers of backpacker narratives (Dann 1999; Dunn 2005; O'Reilly 2005). Here, the traveller self is constructed by means of narrative techniques such as writing out the tourist, using a first-person voice, and focusing on the journey rather than the destination, to create the impression of detachment, solitude, and timelessness (Dann 1999). Descriptions of the discomforts, difficulties, and dangers of a journey are integral to narrating the self as a traveller (O'Reilly 2005). These narrative techniques are often discernible in blogs on *TravelBlog*, *TravelPod*, and *BootsnAll* whose authors present a traveller self via blog posts. These entries are usually written in the first-person voice, creating the impression of a solitary journey. There is a sense of detachment from home and routine when Technotrekker writes about setting off:

> After many months of planning, I finally left Sydney at 14.55 yesterday....As I passed the first sight of the trip, the disused Regent St station which is sometimes referred to as Mortuary station due to it's [sic] gothic composition, I began to hope that it might not be a [sic] omen of things to come.
>
> (Pringle 2005a)

The 'disused' station and the implicit image of death suggest a breaking of ties with the familiar and pave the way for the adoption of the traveller self who then describes the train journey as one not totally free of hardship:

> Trying to sleep was not so easy. It was a surprisingly bumpy ride all night, especially in later stages beyond Orange where I think some of the labour who built the railway were so pissed at being stationed way out here that they deliberately built the rails less than perfectly parallel. From the rampant shaking it felt like it anyway. Even if the rails were straight, the Kangaroo class seats aren't made for posturepedic feeling, but I managed to catch a few Zs in spite of them.
>
> (Pringle 2005a)

A later entry in his blog, inspired by a trip to Myanmar also paints this traveller self as something of a survivor:

> To get here, the bus ride from Yangon was a sixteen hour adventure sport over one of the world's worst major arterial highways. The bus was packed to the gills, with special fold out seats at regular intervals in the aisle completing the concept of sardine heaven. We continuously jolted over ruts and potholes large enough to swallow mopeds, stopped at roadside diners so seedy the moths went elsewhere to buzz the lights, and I doubt we changed driver the whole way through. Whatever your guidebook says – pay the extra money and GET A TRAIN OR PLANE!
>
> (Pringle 2005e)

Such descriptions of the physical discomforts of travel are a marked contrast to the more euphoric language of tourism in web-host-provided content and as such contribute to the discursive tensions in the blog. Writing about getting to a destination is as important as describing what is there to see. By wearing the badge of the weary and long-suffering traveller, Pringle positions himself as a more credible authority than a guidebook. At the same time he also employs the touristic discourse generally associated with guidebooks and implicitly promotes a more touristic mode of travel when he advises potential travellers to 'pay the money' and 'get a train' (Pringle 2005e).

This implied promotion of tourism is in all likelihood unintentional for, even when writing about places they visit, Technotrekker and *BootsnAll*'s Nakano distance themselves from tourists and experiences that may be seen as common touristic pursuits. Technotrekker merely avoids company to seek the solitude necessary for a 'travel' experience:

> As attractive as Pangandaran is, I wanted something more than your average Indonesian tourist town (litter and vendor huts crowding out the nice view), so I left the few local holidayers to their paddling in the surf and headed further round the bay.
>
> (Pringle 2005c)

Meanwhile, Nakano is dismissive of 'tourist crap', and feels the need to justify his visit to Mayasa in Nicaragua, which he describes as: 'the epicenter for the artisans who make all the touristy stuff...there was a pretty well-known crater lake just outside the city limits...a distraction from having to look at tourist crap' (Nakano 2010d).

Both bloggers write of going off the beaten path and being spontaneous. These discourses of travel position them as travellers. And yet, although the entries focus on presenting the authors as travellers, this is achieved by defining their activities against that which is touristic. On the whole, the blog posts mentioned here strengthen the position of the text as a personal narrative. If tourist attractions are mentioned, they are nevertheless dismissed completely or merit little description. By offering little information about the destination they refer to, these passages effectively write out the tourist.

The blogger as tourist

Although many prefer to dissociate themselves from tourism, not all bloggers write as travellers. A case in point is *TravelBlog* author Kylie Munaro who, writing as Bluekat, describes a 16-day European bus tour. Unlike the bloggers discussed earlier, her trip has been planned by a tour operator, and her adherence to an itinerary marks her as a tourist. There are frequent references to recommended activities such as, 'We headed off to get pancakes for lunch, as we were told they should be tried' or 'We didn't go to the dinner and was [sic] told we could easily walk along the back streets to a set of shops visible from the hotel', and 'We had been heavily warned against trying to go to Capri and look around by ourselves as we would apparently be totally ripped off ...' (Munaro 2010g; 2010c; 2010a). Tourists are often seen as 'unadventurous' (Galani-Moutafi 2000, p. 210), and Munaro's online tourist self exhibits touristic caution in following advice and heeding warnings. This tourist self is more passive than the travellers of *Global Roaming* and *For Mom, Love Steve*.

Yet, this is not the only voice in which Munaro's online self speaks. She also offers her own recommendations as an informed tourist, or perhaps a traveller within a tourist. Even though she positions herself as a tourist, she is also discerning and critical of the tourist discourse that places her in this position. She sets herself apart from the situation she finds herself in and offers her own recommendations, as an expert on not just a travel destination, but on being a tourist, thus personalising an experience that has been packaged for mass consumption. Her entry on Capri is written in a tone that is at once authoritative and imperative:

> If you are looking at going to Capri as part of a Cosmos tour, please feel free to email me, and I can show you exactly what we did on a map, and you could easily achieve this yourself and save bucket loads of money. Also they try to scare you in saying alot [sic] of things will be closed and all, we didn't notice that anywhere! Have found this website http://www.capritourism.com/en/timetable-and-prices for 6.90 euro, you can purchase a two way chairlift ride and have access to the bus system for the entire day!
>
> (Munaro 2010g)

At other times, she is critical of the tour itself, and here the blogger turns reviewer, commenting on the food and facilities offered by the tour operator:

> Tea was included that night. I guess in the hotel, the front lobby staff were really nice, the ones in the dinning [sic] room were a bit abrupt though. From all the places we went to, it just stood out that these were not the friendliest by a distance.
>
> (Munaro 2010d)

Descriptions of hotels and meals are accompanied by photographs. She also frequently mentions availability of Internet facilities at each hotel or destination, displaying an awareness of herself as a blogger who is obliged to update her narrative. Her post on Pompeii illustrates this:

> Our hotel…had free internet but if you sat in their lobby (oh the second night, I was up past 11pm in their lobby trying to update my photos for those back home, and apparently upset the owners that wanted to turn out the lights! …)
>
> (Munaro 2010f)

Munaro writes as both participant and observer, positioned inside as well as outside the touristic experience. She refers to herself as a tourist but it is a tourist self as expert and critic that finds expression in the narrative.

The positioning of the blog itself is, however, far more complicated. The narrative technique and content of the commentary shifts from entries that read like a review of the tour, enumerating things to see and do, to posts that describe personal experience, have no references to fellow tourists, and little description of the sights at destinations visited. One stop between Cologne and Heidelberg is described only as 'a cute little town' (Munaro 2010b), while the entry on the Colosseum, a popular attraction in Rome, is a single paragraph that says little about the monument but a lot about the tour guide:

> We arrived at the Colosseum. Ok, now this was impressive. We were all handed little earphones to be able to listen to our guide. It was kind of funny because she was getting a touch grumpy with our group as she was barking out commands in Italian, and obviously no one had any idea as to what she was talking about so we all just stood around. She also didn't like that an older couple were too "slow" for her liking. It was a case of jump in your chariot and go style! I had to admit she totally lost me inside and I had more fun just looking around at the structure imaging the history that took place within these walls
>
> (Munaro 2010e)

Here, Munaro writes as a detached observer as she assesses the tour guide, and although the Colosseum is 'impressive' (Munaro 2010e), more attention is paid to details of the experience rather than to the monument itself. Such distancing and lack of emphasis on the destination are narrative techniques often employed in travel writing or narratives employing a traveller persona (Dann 1999; Dunn 2005). This entry is supplemented by photographs of the Colosseum, but the post itself contributes little to the identity of the web page as a destination narrative. Instead, it is intensely personal in opinion and tone, and this adds to the tensions between commercial and personal or touristic and travel discourses within her own blog on the Cosmos tour.

Blogging with a lens

The study of tourism is inextricably bound up with theories of photography and visual culture. A good deal of this research stems from the works of Judith Adler, Susan Sontag, and John Urry. For the most part, it examines the ocularcentric nature of Western culture and discusses sightseeing and photography as integral to the tourist experience (Urry and Larsen 2011; Adler 1989; Sontag 1977). Sontag argues that tourists use photography both to participate in and to distance themselves from places they visit (Sontag 1977). Her view of tourist photography as something that is used to control and possess place is similar to Crawshaw and Urry's equating the tourist's camera to an instrument of surveillance (1997). Academic arguments that build on these findings often focus on tourists' engagement with and representation of a place and indicate that tourist photography can reveal much about destination image. In particular, Urry's suggestion that tourists try to replicate media depictions of destinations, thus creating a circle of representation, has engaged a number of critics who have since tried to either confirm or refute this theory (Caton and Santos 2008; Garrod 2009; Jenkins 2003).

More recently, there have been attempts to shift the focus from the place that lies before the lens to person who stands behind it and to consider the role of tourist photography in the creation of memories and self-identity. Caroline Scarles' observation that tourist photographs are filtered and selected before they are displayed suggests that photographs in travel blogs may also be similarly chosen by the blogger (2009). Similarly, Steve Garlick's argument that contemporary tourist photography can offer perspectives of a destination that differ from the dominant images of that place indicates that there is some degree of personalisation (2002). Although images in amateur travel blogs may be viewed, from Urry's theoretical perspective, as merely replicating visual tourist discourse, these later findings open up the possibility they may also be personalised and offer some sense of their authors. This chapter is concerned in particular with the extent to which photographs in these travel blogs present the author's online self. A more detailed discussion of the visual forms of travel and tourist discourse follows in Chapter 6.

Although frequently analyses of tourist photographs consider the image in isolation, studies of established media such as postcards as well as newer digital media are testament to the academic interest in the way tourists use both text and images for communicating their holiday experiences. Some analyses of postcards examine both the dominant photographic representations of places as well as the messages written by tourists, while similar research into the use of cell phones has demonstrated how digital technologies can be used to create travel narratives consisting of text messages and photographs (Bell and Lyall 2005; Kennedy 2005). Travel blogs are, in general, good sources of tourist photography accompanied by text pertaining to the images. Photographs may locate a post and clearly associate this with a specific destination. Particularly in blogs found on travel-specific hosting sites, photographs may even supplement the place-related content provided by the web host or its sponsors. However, there is little discussion of the relationship between photographs and text entries in blogs, or how they contribute to the online self of the bloggers.

Robinson and Picard propose that personal holiday photographs, as opposed to professional travel photography contained in tourist discourse, can be used for 'the communication and projection of self' (2009, p. 20). The framing and composition of photographs in travel blogs may therefore offer insights into the blogger's online self and indicate whether the blogger plays the tourist, replicating images seen in media representations, or consciously plays the traveller, capturing more personalised images. Although Robinson and Picard argue that the advent of digital photography and the ability to take many photographs and edit them has drained holiday photographs of their former 'honest' spontaneity (2009, p. 22), it is likely that such technological advances have nevertheless allowed a greater expression of authorial voice. It is possible that bloggers actively select and discard digital photographs, both at the time of framing and capturing the sight and when deciding which of these images they will make publicly available on their blog as a supplement to the post. Each photograph, then, as a clear expression of the blogger's viewpoint, is a device for presenting some aspect of his or her online self.

Bloggers on *TravelBlog*, *TravelPod*, and *BootsnAll* differ greatly when it comes to making decisions about posting photographs online. Apart from a thumbnail profile picture, there are no photographs in Woodsy79's blog on *TravelPod*. In contrast, Technotrekker's blog on the same website is rich in photographs. Although some entries are free of images, many have over ten images, with one entry on canal boating in the UK incorporating forty-six photographs and a short video clip among the paragraphs (Pringle 2007a). As with most other entries in this blog, most of the photographs that appear in this post display scenic landscapes, landmarks, or features that are, for Technotrekker, iconic of the places he visits. Some of these pictures are of river banks, valleys, and fields that could be anywhere in England. Their location is only occasionally indicated by captions, although the accompanying web-host-provided links to websites of hotels in Llangollen in Wales do give a general idea of where these photographs are taken (Pringle 2007a). Only three photographs show the blogger himself, although all of the photographs are captioned and are placed between paragraphs of the entry, alongside descriptions of the views. Some of the photographs showing Pringle are in fact contributed by his travelling companions. For the most part, then, Pringle chooses not to emphasise his presence, and presents himself as a solitary observer of the English countryside. While his travelling companions – his parents and their friends – do rate a mention in his post, there is only the one photograph of them, and much in the manner of travel writers who write out tourists, he leaves them out of the picture. There is no touristic foregrounding of the author and his companions against iconic sights. Also, Pringle's absence from a majority of the photographs and the lack of characteristic features that anchor these scenes to specific occasions or destinations create a sense of timelessness and solitude that is an effect often used by travel writers to emphasis the experience of travel.

Not all travel blog photographs show such an emphasis on isolation. Subjects vary across blogs. Tourists may photograph recognisable icons or focus on people (Robinson and Picard 2009, p. 16). The *Wallaby Wanderers* blog contains a large number of entries describing visits with family and friends, and it is photographs of people rather than places visited that occupy such entries. In 'Such is Life', a post on the bloggers' visit to an animated theatre and exhibits on Australian outlaw Ned Kelly, photographs of the displays appear alongside personal snapshots taken at a film premiere attended on the same day (Howell and Howell 2010h). In this blog, photographs reflect an atmosphere of companionship that is markedly different from the solitary views of *Global Roaming*. While such photographs present different aspects of these bloggers – that of a friend or a relative rather than solitary traveller – they give little emphasis to the destinations visited. More to the point, however, they facilitate the presentation of the online self.

Meanwhile, photographs feature more prominently than text in some entries of *For Mom, Love Steve*, as in his entry on Mexico City in which he explains how he was 'just strolling around taking snapshots' to capture the essence of the place (Nakano 2010b). For Nakano, photographs of Mexico City provide evidence of his visit, but uploading these images reminds him of his identity as a blog author, makes him conscious of the technical considerations of supplementing the online narrative with visuals, and leads him to warn his readers of the lack of organisation in his visual material. His images are personal in that he selects 'interesting things', not necessarily popular tourist attractions most of which, he writes in this post, were closed on that day (Nakano 2010b). Images of historical buildings are few, while those of protest marches and crowds predominate. Here, Nakano creates an online self that is consciously non-touristic by presenting the traveller's perspective of Mexico City (Nakano 2010b). His presentation of a 'walking tour', as stated in the title, is not the touristic activity involving a capturing of iconic sights that the phrase suggests. Instead, the disordered presentation of a series of photographs associates the entry with a travel experience (Nakano 2010b).

For both the Howells and Nakano, photographs are a feature that enables their authorial voice to be heard. In these instances, the photographs serve to supplement a personal narrative and the discourses of travel in their blogs. This is not to say, however, that bloggers may not seek to replicate images seen in media representations of a particular destination as described by Urry's hermeneutic circle of representation. Tourists often anticipate the quintessential shot of a sight that best symbolises a destination, expressing disappointment and frustration when this is difficult to achieve (Robinson and Picard 2009; Scarles

2009). They often use techniques such as excluding other tourists from the photographic frame in order to achieve the impression of solitude (Robinson and Picard 2009). This is evident in the *Cosmos* blog, particularly in Kylie Munaro's photographs of Rome and Pisa. The Rome entry has eleven photographs of the Colosseum, and she significantly omits or at least minimises the presence of other tourists through careful framing. Of particular interest is 'Colosseum 2', a photograph captioned 'the group photo was taken in this spot as a panoramic shot including both items' suggesting that capturing this view is a mandatory part of the tourist experience. However, the inclusion of this photograph, which is nearly empty of fellow tourists, instead of the admittedly touristic group photograph, indicates that Munaro seeks to personalise the scene. Munaro's description of her efforts to photograph her son striking a typical pose at the Leaning Tower at Pisa also indicates a touristic need to capture the view that exemplifies the destination. She writes:

> Everyone was there taking their token photos holding up the tower and I attempted to get my son to do it as well! Weak as effort child! When we got around the corner he played along a bit better. He didn't want to feel like a dork in the wide open I guess.
>
> (Munaro 2010i)

She posts the 'token photos' on her blog, but describes her second shot taken from around the corner (also in the post) as the better picture (Munaro 2010i). The caption assures readers that it 'was taken around the corner so it was Pisa' (Munaro 2010i). Once again, she is careful to leave fellow tourists out of the frame. This second shot presents a more extraordinary view of the tower. Furthermore, it is described as being more natural, and therefore perhaps more authentic, than the earlier image of the touristic 'dork'. The post also contains photographs of her hotel room and various dishes sampled at a restaurant. These last are similar to photographs of food and facilities in other entries. While being personal, these also position the blog entries alongside the kind of tourist discourse that promotes places on the basis of sights to see, things to do, and where to stay or eat.

So, while Munaro's blog is openly touristic in its capturing of scenes that stand for particular destinations, there are also photographs that are to some extent placeless, in that they cannot be identified with any particular destination, although they do signify the tourist experience in some way for the blogger. Shots of cats and flowers are interspersed with pictures of Capri, while the bus trip to Florence inspires a photograph of a cigarette stub in the snow captioned 'ok, I think it looks kinda like art' (Munaro 2010h). Such photographs are a self-presentational strategy inasmuch as they offer insight into the blogger's interests. Others, such as some of the Colosseum photographs, focus on place and validate the post as a destination narrative. Still others, such as the 'group shot' view of the Colosseum and the Pisa photographs, serve both purposes, offering a personal slant on the commercialised view of the monument. Munaro's blog thus includes images that complete Urry's circle of representation, but also personal photographs that frame a travel experience that is uniquely hers alone. Photographs then become a feature through which authorial control may be exercised, consequently influencing the positioning of the entry and the narrative as a whole. They may also heighten the tensions between commercial discourses that enter the blog, via the web host and third-party sponsors, and personal discourse contributed by the blogger in the form of entries, depending on how personal or place-oriented these pictures are. Finally, they complement the presentation of an author's online self and so clarify the various roles he or she occupies, be it that of traveller or tourist.

Whose blog is it anyway?

Those who analyse blogs hosted on travel-specific web hosts must recognise that the web hosts play a significant role in the positioning of these narratives. While bloggers write each entry as an episode of a longer travel narrative, web hosts tend to fragment this larger blog narrative, treating each post as a unique text on a single destination. Often the web host provides paratexts, in the form of maps or title bars that emphasise the destination being written about, while downplaying the personal experience of a journey. Even if the photographs and accompanying descriptions remain neutral, focusing on time spent with family and friends, with no reference to place, the content generated by the web host may still position the entry as a text on a particular destination.

In varying degrees, these web hosts manipulate blog features commercialising personal discourse, changing the positioning of the text, and emphasising their corporate identity over that of the bloggers. While bloggers create user names and titles that reflect their individuality, the corporate identity of the web hosting service looms large in the form of logos, banners, and title bars. Also, templates, URLs, title bar texts, and maps that foreground the reference to place rather than person in a post can detract from a blogger's presentation of an online self. However, the extent to which formal elements contribute to blogger identification varies across features within the blogs and across web hosting services as well. Furthermore, the kind of linking and networking present in blogs on some other web hosting services that assists in the presentation of various aspects of self is often not possible on these travel-specific web hosting services. Web hosts such as *TravelPod* and *TravelBlog* restrict linking, generally regarded as the bloggers' preserve, in a manner that makes it difficult to get a sense of the author through the links. Bloggers using these services cannot express authorial identity by linking to other external blogs or other websites.

The amount of third-party advertising and destination-specific links to sponsors web pages in these blogs also varies across individuals and web hosting services. Such content contributes to the heteroglossia in these blogs by incorporating commercial and tourist discourses. However, much of this content can hardly be said to play a significant role in identifying the authors. The nature of programs such as AdSense suggests that advertising content may offer a tenuous link to the blogger through the post that is responsible for generating the advertisement, but then this content may equally be determined by the geographical location or interests of the readers. Furthermore, these third parties ensure that these travel blogs are polyphonic and heteroglossic. The blogs provide a space for multiple voices to interact – that of the web host, the sponsor, bloggers, and readers. Depending on the nature of the web host, each element in a blog may reflect the voice of a different individual or entity, not necessarily that of the blogger. Moreover, each of these voices can contain multiple discourses. Thus, sponsored content influences the discursive tensions in the blog, and also restricts the self-presentation of bloggers.

How then, does one get a sense of who the author is? The principal means of presenting the author online is via the photographs and entries in these blogs. In their entries, bloggers can occupy a variety of positions such as that of the traveller or the tourist. Similarly, the photographs they choose to display offer insights into the blogger's online self, while also authenticating the travel experience and supplementing commercial discourse by offering a sense of place. Certainly, the titles and user names selected by the bloggers are also self-presentational. Even so, those who view such blogs as a source of information about consumer behaviour must be aware that features that allow authorial expression on one platform may not necessarily serve the same purpose on another similar service. It is also worth keeping in mind, as Genette did, that both publisher and author are responsible for paratextual elements such as titles, and as such not all formal features in these travel blogs contribute to a sense of who the author is. Furthermore, the paratexts in such narratives can confuse and complicate rather than clarify the positioning of these travel blogs. Ultimately, in such texts, there are limitations to a travel blogger's presentation of self.

Note

1 Gerard Genette includes titles and pseudonyms in his description of what constitutes the paratexts of a book. This concept has been adapted for the study of film and web pages, notably in Jonathan Gray's *Show Sold Separately: Promos, Spoilers, and Other Media Paratexts.*

References

Adler, J. 1989. Origins of Sightseeing. *Annals of Tourism Research* [Online], 16. Available: http://www.sciencedirect.com/science/article/B6V7Y-460P4F2-33/2/b59a98b7bd314caae047d2c5b4e28852 [Accessed 10 Mar. 2009].

Auletta, K. 2009. *Googled: The end of the world as we know it,* New York: Penguin.

Banyai, M. and Havitz, M. E. 2013. Analyzing travel blogs using a realist evaluation approach. *Journal of Hospitality Marketing and Management,* 22, 229–241.

Barthes, R. 1977. *Image, music, text,* New York: Noonday.

Bell, C. and Lyall, J. 2005. 'I was here': pixilated evidence. *In:* Crouch, D., Jackson, R. and Thompson, F. (eds.) *The media and the tourist imagination: converging cultures.* 1st ed. London: Routledge.

Benway, J. P. 1998. Banner blindness: the irony of attention grabbing on the World Wide Web. *Proceedings of the Human Factors and Ergonomics Society Annual Meeting,* 42, 463–467.

Calder, B. J. and Sternthal, B. 1980. Television commercial wearout: an information processing view. *Journal of Marketing Research* [Online], 17. Available: http://www.jstor.org/stable/3150928 [Accessed 19 Apr. 2010].

Caton, K. and Santos, C. A. 2008. Closing the hermeneutic circle photographic encounters with the other. *Annals of Tourism Research* [Online], 35. Available: http://www.sciencedirect.com/science/article/B6V7Y-4RR8V8X-2/2/5ced5cd41d1abfd6aab42d694abc580b [Accessed 1 Dec. 2009].

Chesher, C. 2005. *Blogs and the crisis of authorship* [Online]. Sydney. Available: http://incsub.org/blogtalk/?page_id=40 [Accessed 14 Mar. 2010].

Crawshaw, C. and Urry, J. 1997. Tourism and the photographic eye. *In:* Rojek, C. and Urry, J. (eds.) *Touring cultures: transformations of travel and theory.* London: Routledge.

Dann, G. 1996. *The language of tourism: a sociolinguistic perspective,* Wallingford, UK: CAB International.

Dann, G. 1999. Writing out the tourist in space and time. *Annals of Tourism Research* [Online], 26. Available: http://www.sciencedirect.com/science/article/B6V7Y-3VS7VK0-8/2/644ebe6402ad134ca201678b33b3afc4 [Accessed 30 Mar. 2009].

Drèze, X. and Hussherr, F.-X. 2003. Internet advertising: Is anybody watching? *Journal of Interactive Marketing* [Online], 17. Available: http://dx.doi.org/10.1002/dir.10063 [Accessed 19 Apr. 2010].

Dunn, D. 2005. Venice observed: the traveller, the tourist, the post-tourist and British television. *In:* Jaworski, A. and Pritchard, A. (eds.) *Discourse, communication, and tourism.* Clevedon, UK: Channel View.

Elpers, J. L. C. M. W., Wedel, M. and Pieters, R. G. M. 2003. Why do consumers stop viewing television commercials? Two experiments on the influence of moment-to-moment entertainment and information value. *Journal of Marketing Research* [Online], 40. Available: http://www.jstor.org/stable/30038877 [Accessed 19 Apr. 2010].

Francisco-Revilla, L. and Crow, J. 2009. Interpreting the layout of web pages. *Proceedings of the 20th ACM conference on hypertext and hypermedia.* Torino, Italy: ACM.

Galani-Moutafi. 2000. The self and the other: traveler, ethnographer, tourist. *Annals of Tourism Research* [Online], 27(1), 203–224 [Accessed 30 Mar. 2009].

Garlick, S. 2002. Revealing the unseen: Tourism, art and photography. *Cultural Studies* [Online], 16(2), 289–305 [Accessed 19 May 2010].

Garrod, B. 2009. Understanding the relationship between tourism destination imagery and tourist photography. *Journal of Travel Research* [Online], 47. Available: http://www.scopus.com/inward/record.url?eid=2-s2.0-58149508293andpartnerID=40 [Accessed 1 Dec. 2009].

Genette, G. 1997. *Paratexts: thresholds of interpretation,* Cambridge, UK: Cambridge University Press.

Gray, J. 2010. *Show sold separately: promos, spoilers, and other media paratexts,* New York: New York University Press.

Hamborg, K. C., Bruns, M., Ollermann, F. and Kaspar, K. 2012. The effect of banner animation on fixation behavior and recall performance in search tasks. *Computers in Human Behavior,* 28, 576–582.

Hawke, D. 2016. Who is busman7. *The wanderings of busman7* [Online]. BootsnAll. Available: http://blogs.bootsnall.com/busman7/ [Accessed 1 Feb. 2016].

Hevern, V. W. 2004. Threaded identity in cyberspace: weblogs and positioning in the dialogical self. *Identity* [Online], 4(4). Available: http://www.tandfonline.com/doi/pdf/10.1207/s1532706xid0404_2 [Accessed 17 Mar. 2009].

Holly. 2010. *Holly's Travels*. BootsnAll. [Online] Available: http://blogs.bootsnall.com/hollyms/2010/01 [Accessed 2 Apr. 2010].

Howard, R. G. 2008. Electronic hybridity and the vernacular web. *Journal of American Folklore* [Online], 121(480), 192–218 [Accessed 16 Oct. 2009].

Howell, D. and Howell, S. 2010a. *Darryl and Sarah – Wallaby Wanderers* [Online]. TravelBlog. Available: https://www.travelblog.org/Bloggers/Darryl-and-Sarah/ [Accessed 4 February 2016].

Howell, D. and Howell, S. 2010b. Darryl and Sarah follows and is followed by... *Darryl and Sarah – Wallaby Wanderers* [Online] TravelBlog. Available: https://www.travelblog.org/Bloggers/Darryl-and-Sarah/social.html [Accessed 4 February 2016].

Howell, D. and Howell, S. 2010c. Happy 9th wedding anniversary [Online]. *TravelBlog* Available: https://www.travelblog.org/Europe/United-Kingdom/England/Staffordshire/Burton-upon-Trent/blog-367830.html [Accessed 26 Apr. 2010].

Howell, D. and Howell, S. 2010d. Hello Norway! [Online]. *TravelBlog*. Available: https://www.travelblog.org/Europe/blog-374477.html [Accessed 26 Apr. 2010].

Howell, D. and Howell, S. 2010e. It's a real mystery. *Darryl and Sarah – Wallaby Wanderers* [Online] TravelBlog. Available from: https://www.travelblog.org/Oceania/Australia/New-South-Wales/Narooma/blog-489630.html [Accessed 2 Feb. 2016].

Howell, D. and Howell, S. 2010f. Needle in a haystack [Online]. *TravelBlog* Available: https://www.travelblog.org/Oceania/Australia/New-South-Wales/Orange/blog-486453.html [Accessed 20 Mar. 2010].

Howell, D. and Howell, S. 2010g. A peak too far [Online]. *TravelBlog*. Available: https://www.travelblog.org/Oceania/Australia/Tasmania/Cradle-Mountain/blog-479978.html [Accessed 26 Feb. 2010].

Howell, D. and Howell, S. 2010h. Such is life [Online]. *TravelBlog*. Available: https://www.travelblog.org/Oceania/Australia/Victoria/Mansfield/blog-489768.html [Accessed 26 Feb. 2010].

Jenkins, O. 2003. Photography and travel brochures: the circle of representation. *Tourism Geographies: An International Journal of Tourism Space, Place, and Environment* [Online], 5. Available: http://www.informaworld.com/10.1080/14616680309715 [Accessed 1 Dec. 2009].

Kennedy, C. 2005. 'Just perfect!' The pragmatics of evalutation in holiday postcards. *In:* Jaworski, A. and Pritchard, A. (eds.) *Discourse, communication, and tourism*. Clevedon, UK: Cromwell.

Landow, G. P. 2006. *Hypertext 3.0: critical theory and new media in an era of globalization*, Baltimore, MD, US: Johns Hopkins University Press.

Lomborg, S. 2009. Navigating the blogosphere: towards a genre-based typology of weblogs. *First Monday* [Online], 14. Available: http://www.uic.edu/htbin/cgiwrap/bin/ojs/index.php/fm/article/view/2329/2178 [Accessed 28 January 2010].

Lovink, G. 2008. *Zero comments: blogging and critical Internet culture*, New York: Routledge.

Munaro, K. 2010a. Day 2 – Amsterdam to Cologne 19/12/09. Cosmos 16 day best of Europe trip Christmas 2009 [Online]. *TravelBlog*. Available: https://www.travelblog.org/Europe/Netherlands/blog-472135.html [Accessed 10 May 2010].

Munaro, K. 2010b. Day 3 – Cologne to Switzerland (Lucerne) 20/12. Cosmos 16 day best of Europe trip Christmas 2009 [Online]. *TravelBlog*. Available: https://www.travelblog.org/Europe/Germany/blog-472139.html [Accessed 11 May 2010].

Munaro, K. 2010c. Day 5 – Lucerne to Venice 'area'. Cosmos 16 day best of Europe trip Christmas 2009 [Online]. *TravelBlog*. Available: https://www.travelblog.org/Europe/Switzerland/blog-472176.html [Accessed 10 May 2010].

Munaro, K. 2010d. Day 6 – Venice 23/12. Cosmos 16 day best of Europe trip Christmas 2009 [Online]. *TravelBlog*. Available: https://www.travelblog.org/Europe/Italy/Veneto/Vittorio-Veneto/blog-472417.html [Accessed 16 February 2016].

Munaro, K. 2010e. Day 8 – Christmas Day in Rome 25/12. Cosmos 16 day best of Europe trip Christmas 2009 [Online]. *TravelBlog*. Available: https://www.travelblog.org/Europe/Italy/blog-472506.html [Accessed 11 May 2010].

Munaro, K. 2010f. Day 9 – Pompeii and Sorrento. Cosmos 16 day best of Europe trip Christmas 2009 [Online]. *TravelBlog*. Available: https://www.travelblog.org/Europe/Italy/blog-472670.html [Accessed 10 May 2010].

Munaro, K. 2010g. Day 10 – Capri 27/12. Cosmos 16 day best of Europe trip Christmas 2009 [Online]. *TravelBlog*. Available: https://www.travelblog.org/Europe/Italy/blog-472697.html [Accessed 10 May 2010].

Munaro, K. 2010h. Day 11 – Sorrento up to Florence 28/12. Cosmos 16 day best of Europe trip Christmas 2009 [Online]. *TravelBlog*. Available: https://www.travelblog.org/Europe/Italy/blog-472842.html [Accessed 11 May 2010].

Munaro, K. 2010i. Day 12 – Florence to French Riviera (Menton) 29/12. Cosmos 16 day best of Europe trip Christmas 2009 [Online]. *TravelBlog*. Available: https://www.travelblog.org/Europe/France/blog-473094.html [Accessed 11 May 2010].

Nakano, S. K. 2010a. *For Mom, love Steve* [Online] BootsnAll. Available: http://www.steveislost.com/ [Accessed 5 Apr. 2010].

Nakano, S. K. 2010b. Day 1797: Walking tour, Mexico City. *For Mom, love Steve* [Online]. BootsnAll. Available: http://www.steveislost.com/blog/day-1797-walking-tour-mexico-city.html [Accessed 5 Apr. 2010].

Nakano, S. K. 2010c. Huehuetenango (way way), Guatemala: The end of Central America. *For Mom, love Steve* [Online]. Available: http://www.steveislost.com/blog/huehuetenango-way-way-guatemala-the-end-of-central-america.html [Accessed 8 Apr. 2010].

Nakano, S. K. 2010d. Mayasa, Nicaragua: Home of tourist crap. *For Mom, love Steve* [Online]. BootsnAll. Available: http://www.steveislost.com/blog/masaya-nicaragua-home-of-tourist-crap.html [Accessed 28 Apr. 2010].

Nakano, S. K. 2010e. What am I doing. *For Mom, love Steve* [Online]. BootsnAll. Available: http://www.steveislost.com/blog/what-am-i-doing.html [Accessed 25 Apr. 2010].

Nardi, B. A., Schiano, D. J., Gumbrecht, M. and Swartz, L. 2004. Why We Blog. *Communications of the ACM: The Blogosphere* [Online], 47(12), 41–46. Available: http://dl.acm.org/citation.cfm?doid=1035134.1035163 [Accessed 29 Feb. 2011].

O'Reilly, C. C. 2005. Tourist or traveller? Narrating backpacker identity. *In:* Jaworski, A. and Pritchard, A. (eds.) *Discourse, communication, and tourism.* Clevedon, UK: Channel View.

Pringle, R. 2005a. *Broken Hill – it begins* [Online]. TravelPod. Available: http://www.travelpod.com/travel-blog/technotrekker/overland05/tpod.html [Accessed 25 Apr. 2010].

Pringle, R. 2005b. *Global roaming: overland from Sydney to Scotland, via a wintry Siberia* [Online]. TravelPod. Available from: http://www.travelpod.com/travel-blog/technotrekker/overland05/tpod.html [Accessed 25 April 2010].

Pringle, R. 2005c. Pangandaran and the Green (Emerald) Canyon. *Global roaming: overland from Sydney to Scotland, via a wintry Siberia. Looks like I've found a new home!* [Online]. TravelPod. Available: http://www.travelpod.com/travel-blog/technotrekker/overland05/tpod.html [Accessed 28 Apr. 2010].

Pringle, R. 2005d. Technotrekker's traveler profile. *Global roaming: overland from Sydney to Scotland, via a wintry Siberia. Looks like I've found a new home!* [Online]. TravelPod. Available from: http://www.travelpod.com/travel-blog/technotrekker/overland05/tpod.html [Accessed 4 Mar. 2016].

Pringle, R. 2005e. Up the road to Mandalay without a paddle. *Global roaming: overland from Sydney to Scotland, via a wintry Siberia. Looks like I've found a new home!* [Online]. TravelPod. Available: http://www.travelpod.com/travel-blog/technotrekker/overland05/tpod.html [Accessed 28 Apr. 2010].

Pringle, R. 2005f. Want to go somewhere today? *Global roaming: overland from Sydney to Scotland, via a wintry Siberia. Looks like I've found a new home!* [Online]. TravelPod. Available: http://www.travelpod.com/travel-blog/technotrekker/overland05/tpod.html [Accessed 15 March 2010].

Pringle, R. 2005g. Why is it so (and freaks of the week). *Global roaming: overland from Sydney to Scotland, via a wintry Siberia. Looks like I've found a new home!* [Online]. TravelPod. Available: http://www.travelpod.com/travel-blog/technotrekker/overland05/tpod.html [Accessed 15 March 2010].

Pringle, R. 2007a. Canal boat cruising – grey nomad style. *Global roaming: overland from Sydney to Scotland, via a wintry Siberia. Looks like I've found a new home!* [Online]. TravelPod. Available: http://www.travelpod.com/travel-blog/technotrekker/overland05/tpod.html [Accessed 9 June 2010].

Pringle, R. 2007b. Life on the Fringe. *Global roaming: overland from Sydney to Scotland, via a wintry Siberia. Looks like I've found a new home!* [Online]. TravelPod. Available: http://www.travelpod.com/travel-blog/technotrekker/overland05/tpod.html [Accessed 15 March 2010].

Pringle, R. 2016. *The longest way home* [Online]. Available: http://www.thelongestwayhome.com/blog/ [Accessed 15 February 2016].

Pühringer, S. and Taylor, A. 2008. A practitioner's report on blogs as a potential source of destination marketing intelligence. *Journal of Vacation Marketing* [Online], 14(2), 177–187 [Accessed 7 October 2009].

Robinson, M. and Picard, D. 2009. Moments, magic, and memories: photographing tourists, tourist photographs, and making worlds. *In:* Robinson, M. and Picard, D. (eds.) *The framed world: tourism, tourists, and photography.* Farnham, UK: Ashgate.

Scarles, C. 2009. Becoming tourist: renegotiating the visual in the tourist experience. *Environment and Planning D-Society and Space* [Online], 27(3), 465–488 [Accessed 19 May 2010].

Schmallegger, D. and Carson, D. 2008. Blogs in tourism: changing approaches to information exchange. *Journal of Vacation Marketing* [Online], 14. Available: http://jvm.sagepub.com/cgi/content/abstract/14/2/99 [Accessed 15 May 2009].

Schmidt, J. 2007. Blogging practices: an analytical framework. *Journal of Computer-Mediated Communication* [Online], 12. Available: http://dx.doi.org/10.1111/j.1083-6101.2007.00379.x [Accessed 24 Feb. 2011].

Serfaty, V. 2004. *The mirror and the veil: an overview of American online diaries and blogs,* Amsterdam: Rodopi.

Sontag, S. 1977. *On photography,* New York: Farrar, Strauss, and Giroux.

Stewart, G. 2010. The paratexts of Inanimate Alice: thresholds, genre expectations, and status. *Convergence* [Online], 16(1), 57–74 [Accessed 22 Mar. 2010].

Syverson, B. 2007. Meaning without borders: *likn* and distributed knowledge. *Leonardo* [Online], 40. Available: http://www.mitpressjournals.org/doi/abs/10.1162/leon.2007.40.5.433.

Timson, L. 2006. *Put it in the family blog* [Online]. Sydney. Available: http://www.smh.com.au/news/web/put-it-in-the-family-blog/2006/06/14/1149964603505.html [Accessed 4 May 2010].

Urry, J. and Larsen, J. 2011. *The tourist gaze 3.0,* Los Angeles, CA, US: Sage.

Walker Rettberg, J. 2014. *Blogging,* Cambridge, UK: Polity.

Warschauer, M. and Grimes, D. 2008. Audience, authorship, and artifact: the emergent semiotics of Web 2.0. *Annual Review of Applied Linguistics* [Online]. Available: http://dx.doi.org/10.1017/S0267190508070013 [Accessed 1 Mar. 2010].

Wenger, A. 2008. Analysis of travel bloggers' characteristics and their communication about Austria as a tourism destination. *Journal of Vacation Marketing* [Online], 14. Available: http://jvm.sagepub.com/cgi/content/abstract/14/2/169 [Accessed 27 Oct. 2010].

Woodsy79. 2010. *Woodsy79's traveler profile* [Online]. TravelPod. Available: http://www.travelpod.com/members/woodsy79 [Accessed 4 Feb 2016].

4 With the reader in mind

Self-presentation and the independent travel blog

Individuals who host their blogs independently on their own websites generally enjoy access to a greater variety of formal features and consequently have more freedom of expression. This suggests they should have greater flexibility in presenting the various aspects of their online self. Yet, as Lynn Z. Bloom observes of diarists, an individual's awareness of a reader's presence leads to self-censorship, and the subsequent presentation of the self as a central character in the narrative tends to be audience-oriented (Bloom 1996). It is reasonable to assume that individuals who write publicly accessible travel blogs must likewise be aware of their potential audiences and that they create these narratives with their readers in mind. Such an awareness of the reader is not new to the writing of travel. One only needs look at the journals of Christopher Columbus or the more recent account of Captain Scott's ill-fated Antarctic expedition to recognise that many of the first travel diaries were records of exploratory journeys and voyages and were, as such, worded as public documents for others to read (Columbus 1989; Scott and Allen 1978). Bloom notes that this audience awareness reflects in an author's use of language and in the formal features of a text so that: 'once a writer, like an actor, is audience-oriented, such considerations as telling a good story, getting the sounds and the rhythm right, supplying sufficient detail for another's understanding, can never be excluded' (Bloom 1996, pp. 24–25).

When this presentation of the self occurs online, it owes a good deal to the technical features of the online platforms that individuals use (Merchant 2006). Page design, fonts, and other visual elements are all manipulated in the process of creating a certain impression of the self (Walker 2004). In effect, an individual's presentation of self in any given social situation is strongly linked to the technology he or she uses at the time (Pinch 2010). While this view seems deterministic, it does imply that each formal feature and integrated social tool of a blog is instrumental in the presentation of at least some aspects of an author's self. Moreover, this self-presentation comprises multiple discursive forms as online narratives often employ a variety of multimedia (Nelson and Hull 2008).

Drawing on these premises, this chapter examines how independent bloggers exercise their comparative freedom of expression and employ any available tools to present various aspects of their online self, while being conscious of their wide and varied readership. Recognising that this self-presentation occurs at a number of different levels, the chapter studies individual entries as well as other formal features and paratextual elements such as templates, titles, and user names. By applying Erving Goffman's theory of self-presentation and Mikhail Bakhtin's concept of speech genres to independently hosted blogs, it analyses the contribution of each of these features to the overall self-presentation of the travel bloggers (Bakhtin 1986; Goffman 1969). The chapter also analyses narrative techniques employed in paratexts, posts, comments, and blogrolls to determine how these blogs negotiate the tensions between travel and tourist discourses, while conveying the impression that the author is an authentic travel blogger and, more often than not, an authentic traveller.

Behind names and titles

Paratexts such as titles, banners, and pseudonyms are crucial to the initial presentation of an author's self as a central character in the independently hosted travel blog and they can help to position the narrative as an account of travel as opposed to tourism. Although the primary functions of a title are identification and description, it also has a 'connotative value' in that the meaning of its constituent words and the style in which they are used may have 'echoes' of other texts (Genette 1997, p. 91). A title may bring to mind a particular genre and subject matter, a similar author, or a historical period. These associations help to build an impression of the author and the text. To some extent, titles like *Traveling Savage* signal the nature of the roles played by a blogger's online self. User names – particularly if they are pseudonyms such as 'Nomadic Matt' of the eponymous travel blog – could have a similar semantic effect and bring into play certain associations. In this respect, both titles and user names may be viewed as utterances whose contexts contribute to a blogger's performance of self. Furthermore, they can supplement the positions indicated by an author in the page, usually labelled 'About Me', which introduces the author and describes the purpose of the blog.

Tracking titles

In general, titles of independently hosted travel blogs incorporate either or both the author's name and the theme of the narrative. So, it is possible to find titles similar to *Nomadic Matt*, such as *Adventurous Kate*, *Heather on her Travels*, or *Wayne on the Road*, that clearly identify both the author and the subject matter of their blogs (Cowper 2010; McCulley 2010; Stadler 2010). Alternatively, a title may indicate the blogger's position, as is the case with *Legal Nomads* (Ettenberg 2016a) or *foXnoMad* (Polat 2016a). They may focus on a particular approach to travel, as in *A Wandering Sole* (Walker 2016a) or *Everything Everywhere* (Arndt 2016a) or hint at the nature of the travel experience as in *Pause the Moment* (Gargiulo 2014). Titles may refer to themed travel, as is the case with the culinary reflections of *The Road Forks* (Patrick and Akila 2009) and *Forks and Jets* (Rees and Rees 2008a). Still others are comparatively offbeat, humorous, or cryptic, such as *Hole in the Donut Cultural Travel* (Weibel 2016a) and *Killing Batteries*

(Pettersen 2010). Alternatively, a title may allude to the blogging process as in *I Should Log Off* (Tobias and Tobias 2015).

This is hardly an exhaustive list of the kinds of titles independently hosted blogs may have, but it goes some way towards illustrating how bloggers initially positon themselves. For the most part, the titles of these blogs, as well as others listed on their blogrolls, contain words that are suggestive of travel experiences that are free, unrestricted, and exciting such as 'adventure', 'nomadic', 'roaming', or 'wandering'. Presenting the authors of these narratives as wanderers and nomads implies that they are not itinerary-driven tourists, but rather independent travellers. While this may be the principal position occupied by these bloggers, it is often just one of many others occupied in a blog. On the whole, however, themes, names, and positions indicated in the title are characteristically personal and orient the blog towards travel rather than tourism.

Visual elements supplementing these titles often support the positions indicated in the titles. Frequently, title banners utilise a background, typeface, and integrated images with a travel theme or concept relevant to the title or user name. Typography, a main component in logos, can convey a particular effect or mood and so shape 'identity' (Ryan and Conover 2004, p. 73) and the choice of typeface can influence a reader's impression of the online self they encounter in the narrative. Two distinctive typefaces reinforce the ideas implicit in *Traveling Savage* (see Figure 4.1). The black stencil font of 'Traveling' is remarkably similar to the lettering that may be seen on a packing crate. On the face of it, this image is touristic – the journey of a packing crate is probably carefully scheduled, organised, and routed to a specific destination, predictable and lacking the spontaneity of travel. In the context of Dann's framework, the very fact that this touristic design spells the word 'traveling' inserts an element of discursive tension here. Conversely, the thick red brush-stroke 'Savage', with the rough and somewhat primitive lines hinting at untamed savagery, is at variance with the clean lines of first half of the title and reinforces the idea of 'exploring' Scotland as stated in the banner's tag line (Savage 2016a).

Visual elements in the title banner of *A Wandering Sole* (Walker 2016a) likewise reiterate the themes implied by the title. The banner displays a panoramic view of mountains and canyons, with a woman seated with her back to the camera in the foreground. Against the image are superimposed a series of words enumerating Laura Walker's various roles as an explorer, traveller, and entrepreneur, among others. The words are carefully arranged on separate lines, as

Figure 4.1 Screenshot of title banner of *Traveling Savage*

if to indicate the need to balance perhaps opposing aspects of Walker's online self – the explorer and the refugee advocate, the entrepreneur and the humanitarian. It seems telling that the ultimate role is that of a traveller, the last word in the list, positioned on a line of its own emphasising the idea of solitude even in its display. The image itself with its blue skies and uninhabited landscape associates the narrative with journeying off the beaten path in search of new unexplored horizons. Notwithstanding this allusion to the spontaneity of travel, the simple and neat presentation of Walker's various roles in a capitalised serif font is testament to her background in design (Walker 2016b). There is a tension here between the idea of wandering and the constructed nature of its visualisation. The button in the centre of the banner that invites readers to 'scroll down' suggests that the experience of the blog itself is one that is organised and positions the reader as a tourist who will be guided through the narrative.

There is also a wealth of meaning in the use of 'sole'. On the one hand, it refers to Walker's marathon running – an activity that involves the company of others, while on the other it reiterates the concept of travel as a solitary pursuit, reinforcing Walker's presentation of herself in the banner image as an independent and adventurous traveller. There is also a spiritual connotation here between the words 'sole' and 'soul', suggesting an experience characterised by inner reflection. The author is 'seeking meaningful connection', as expressed in the small-print tag line below, rather than advocating a superficial consumption of place.

As with *A Wandering Sole*, the visual elements of the title banner in Anil Polat's *foXnoMad* also allude to the central themes of his narrative (see Figure 4.2). The left-hand corner bears the image of a fox standing on a globe. There is an allusion here to the Firefox browser logo, which similarly displays a fox wrapped around a globe. The image cleverly represents two aspects of Polat's online self – the digital expert and the world traveller. For readers who associate the fox with intelligence, this is also a simple visualisation of the blog's tagline of 'Travel Smarter' (Polat 2016a). Unlike Ettenberg, Savage, and Walker, Polat makes it clear that he is willing to place advertising on his banner. The right-hand half of the banner is occupied by an advertisement generated by Google's AdSense program. By inviting sponsors to fund his travel, Polat presents his blog as a marketable commodity. Admittedly, those who use ad-blocking software may not see this advertisement. If present, the advertisement jars with the surrounding elements of travel discourse. If absent, the banner appears incomplete, suggesting that both tourist and travel discourses are necessary to complete the blog and the self-presentation of its author. Whatever the case may be, the advertising sponsorship underwrites Polat's position as a traveller and a blogger of some

Figure 4.2 Screenshot of title banner of *foXnoMad*

repute. On the one hand, the inclusion of advertising is testament to Polat's skills as a digital traveller able to monetise his narrative. Nevertheless, while this commercialisation validates his role as a digital expert, the promotional discourse simultaneously undermines the positioning of the blog as a narrative of travel.

In comparison with other blogs discussed here, the title banner for *Everything Everywhere* says little about the blogger's online self, apart from giving the sense that he has simple tastes. The only image alongside the blue and orange title is a stick figure in the same colours. The banner indicates where the author, Gary Arndt, is on any given day, but does not have a tagline or any travel-related images. At first glance, therefore, the simple phrasing and design does not suggest any obvious discursive tension. A title like *Everything Everywhere* does not specify any one location but suggests a flexibility that can be associated with the concept of travel. Yet, the accompanying text that locates Gary Arndt in a particular place has a destination focus that may be viewed as touristic. There is an underlying implication here that the presentation of the self as a travel blogger ultimately involves negotiating between both travel and tourist discourses.

A similar tension is inherent in *Legal Nomads* whose block-letter title forms a stark contrast to the blurred image in the background of the title banner. This unfocused image, perhaps connotative of an uncharted landscape is at variance with the starkly demarcated lines of the title phrase. Indeed, these last appear to reflect the rigidity of the legal profession. This title is underscored by an apparently handwritten tagline that reads, 'telling stories through food' (Ettenberg 2016a). Ryan and Conover (2004) suggest that such handwritten typefaces also have a more personal touch. Certainly, there is a degree of realism in a handwritten typeface that emphasises writing naturally, the cursive strokes resonating with wandering and nomadic travel; however, ironically, this is produced both artificially and deliberately by using a computer. There is in fact a tension between living spontaneously as a traveller should and the practice of blogging, which requires careful consideration and a good deal of time spent stationary at a computer, consequently preventing further travel. This concept is explored by Nomadic Matt in his own blog, which will be analysed later in this chapter.

Regardless of whether they refer mainly to the author's position or themes in the text, title banners with all their accompanying elements display a tension between the discourses of travel and tourism. The titles themselves differ from those of blogs found on commercially sponsored travel blog hosting sites in several ways. Independent travel bloggers usually possess their own domain name, and, as a result, the URL of their blog, that is to say the address of the website, does not include the name of the blog hosting service. Instead, their blogs generally have domain names that are identical to their blog titles. While commercial webhosts frequently manipulate title bars and URLs to emphasise the destination being described in the travel blogs that they host, this is generally not the case with independently hosted blogs. Although independent travel bloggers are free to coin blog titles that mention destinations, for the most part user names and titles refer to an aspect of the blogger's personality or the nature of their travel experience and have little to do with where they are going. These narratives are more likely to interpret the experience of travel described therein to support a presentation of an online traveller (or tourist) self rather than comment on any given destination. This is a major point of difference with both commercially-sponsored blogs on travel-specific webhosts as well as with texts such as *Tony Wheeler's Travels*. Furthermore, this has implications for tourism marketing researchers who conduct content analyses of travel blogs with the assumption that this will reveal what consumers think of a destination.

Exploring names

User names, whether real or pseudonyms, are important cues in a blogger's self-presentation. Gary Arndt clearly identifies himself as the author of *Everything Everywhere*, listed in *Time* as one of the best blogs of 2010 (Arndt 2016b; Snyder 2010). In contrast, Nomadic Matt does not divulge his full name and always signs his posts with his user name. It may be argued that the authenticity of a narrative improves when its author uses his or her real name, and that using a pseudonym could undermine the credibility of *Nomadic Matt*. That said, a blogger's pseudonym can make a certain impression on an audience (Trammell and Keshelashvili 2005). In being 'nomadic' the author is an adventurous traveller rather than a guidebook-toting tourist. This in turn lends an aura of authenticity to his travel blog, indicating that it is a narrative about real travel experiences. Therefore, a user name may signal a particular aspect of an independent blogger's online self, strengthen the positions he or she occupies in the travel blog, and validate the narrative.

In general, blog titles are personal in that they display authors' first names rather than last names. For example, Kate McCulley writes *Adventurous Kate*, in a fairly straightforward positioning of the self as an intrepid traveller. Such first-name titles suggest an intimacy and emphasis on the personal that is in keeping with travel discourse. An interesting exception is Keith Savage, who uses his last name in the title of his blog, *Traveling Savage*. The same phrase heads the About page of Savage's blog, in which he describes himself as a man who has given up humdrum routine to become 'A hunter, oft-stubbled and bleary-eyed, driven by an insatiable hunger for exploration and experience…' (Savage 2016b). The title ingeniously plays on his legal name and reinforces this blogger's presentation of himself as a person who forsakes civilisation to become a savage, in the sense of someone who is a 'hunter' and a 'native' (Savage 2016b). Perhaps, it also alludes to his appearance – Savage posts a profile picture of his 'oft-stubbled' self to match his description. This is not necessarily always the case, as both the description and photograph can be changed by a blogger at any time. For now, this title indicates two aspects of the blogger – the person named Keith Savage as well as that of a travelling 'savage'. In a sense *Traveling Savage* is both the narrative and the blogger, reinforcing the notion of the blog as a form of self-presentation.

The wide range of names and titles seen in these blogs indicates that these bloggers enjoy a greater freedom to be creative in their self-presentation as compared to individuals who use commercially sponsored travel-specific web hosts. So authors have greater control over the content they create and provide to their audiences. A second point to note is the similarity of some of the titles and user names in these independently hosted blogs. Independent travel bloggers who call themselves 'nomads' or 'wanderers' may link to blogs with similar titles or whose authors have similar user names. So for some independent travel bloggers, user names and titles serve as a badge of membership in the travel blogging community. Furthermore, a number of independent travel bloggers also rely on the contexts suggested by words such as 'adventurer', 'wanderer', or 'nomad' to present themselves as travellers rather than tourists. Although at first glance it seems that travel discourse is predominant in the titling of independent travel blogs and the presentation of authors, there are touristic elements present in the accompanying visual elements, indicating that both discourses play a significant role.

Introducing the author

Although titles and user names convey a good deal about the author and the narrative, the textual feature that best facilitates a presentation of an online self is probably the 'About' page of a blog, which typically provides an overview of the themes of the text and specifies the different positions an author occupies in the narrative. In some cases, this description distinguishes between an author's past self – life as it was before the individual became a traveller or blogger – and a present blogging and travelling self. It is often this space that manifests a blogger's awareness of the travel blog as a platform for presenting the self and of himself or herself as a narrator of a travel experience. As such, this page comprises the specific utterances and discourses authors use to indicate the online roles they occupy and authenticate their position as independent travel bloggers.

Though the About page offers the most complete self-description of the author, a number of bloggers begin their introduction on the home page of their travel blogs. Often, this takes the form of a box containing a short, 30–40 word summary and a thumbnail photograph of the author. Concise as this is, the summary clearly identifies the authors and the positions they assume for readers of their text. Both summaries and About pages are often integrated in default blog template. Therefore, technical features play some part in styling the self-presentation.

On the independent travel blog titled *Traveling Savage*, a boxed-in description paints author Keith Savage as 'A hunter, oft-stubbled and bleary-eyed, driven by an insatiable hunger for exploration and experience' (Savage 2016a). The brief word portrait complements the title, itself a play on the author's name, and cues the position he occupies in his narrative (a point examined in greater depth in the following section). This style of phrasing in the introduction is by no means unique to Savage's blog; *foXnoMad* author Anil Polat is equally succinct about the purpose of his blog and the aspects of self that he wishes to present: 'The blogger and computer engineer who writes *foXnoMad* while on a journey to visit every country in the world' (Polat 2016a). Readers are encouraged to find out more about the bloggers by clicking on a link to the About page. In *A Wandering*

Sole, the statement is even more concise. Instead of a boxed summary, the home page displays a full-screen title banner bearing tags that proclaim the author, Laura Walker, to be a, 'A wandering sole. Storyteller. Explorer. Refugee advocate. Entrepreneur. Humanitarian. Traveler.' (Walker 2016a). In each of these blogs, the initial descriptions indicate for readers the aspects of self these authors wish to emphasise in their capacity as travel bloggers. In *foXnoMad*'s case, for example, it positions the author as a flashpacker and the blog as a guide that will show readers how to 'travel smarter' (Polat 2016a).

The About page expands this initial introduction and establishes who the authors are. Although this description may run into several paragraphs, the initial statements alone are usually enough to give a sense of the self that the authors wish to present to their audience. In addition to this, authors are generally quick to indicate various narratorial positions, often arrived at through a transformation of the self. The assumption of different discursive roles within a single narrative is not new to the blog format or to travel-related texts. Individuals who write personal blogs sometimes vary their positions across their narratives (Hermans 2004; Hevern 2004; Sanderson 2008). For example, Sanderson's analysis of a sports celebrity's blog demonstrates how a single individual discursively constructs the self as a critic, a staunch Christian, and a dedicated player within the same blog. Holland and Huggan observe a similar diversity of narrative roles, ranging from adventurers to clowns, in their study of travel books (1998, p. 16). Likewise, television travel hosts have been known to play both traveller and tourist to describe destinations (Dunn 2005). A similar switching of narratorial roles is evident in a number of independently hosted travel blogs and this is often indicated through the use of various narrative techniques.

In general, bloggers begin by stating their name and describing their profession or the positions they occupy in their narrative. Providing details such as an author's name, age, profession, and cultural background is characteristic of the online self-presentation in personal home pages (Walker 2004). In the case of travel blogs such information is displayed both in the boxed summaries and profile pages. Laura Walker of *A Wandering Sole* writes about her work as a job coach for refugees and lists her interests, which include travel, running, hiking, and outdoor activities, thus explaining the title of her travel blog. However, she notes that both she and her blog have transformed across the years, and she presents her current self as opposed to her 'former self', a design graduate with a passion for running (Walker 2016b). Writing under a pseudonym, independent blogger Nomadic Matt describes a similar transformation of self into a traveller as well as a change of lifestyle and life goals inspired by travelling around the world. His profile on *Nomadic Matt's Travel Site* introduces him as a bestselling author and a seasoned traveller. Nomadic Matt, the reader learns, has made the transition from growing up as a 'sheltered middle-class suburban kid' into a full-time traveller who, upon completing an MBA, has exchanged his 'cubicle job' for a life centred around travel (Nomadic Matt 2016a). This name-vocation-transformation style of introduction is paralleled in *foXnoMad*'s About page. Anil Polat, the 'blogger and computer engineer' describes the shift from being a full-time computer security consultant to a permanent traveller, a lifestyle that requires him 'to minimize my belongings, adapt to frequently changing environments, and make the most out of my tech gadgets', this last affirming his position as a flashpacker and a digital expert who offers travel advice.

Having described the transformation of the self into a traveller, which is usually the rule rather than the exception, the About page in many cases, goes on to reinforce this position by creating a strong and clear association with travel as opposed to tourism. Profiles in the independently hosted blogs mentioned here integrate the same narrative techniques employed by individuals who describe themselves as travellers suggesting a dissociation with touristic discourse. For the most part, the bloggers use words and phrases related to independent travel rather than guided tourism. Their descriptions support the concept of wandering, the idea of travel as not bound by itineraries, as suggested in the titles such as *Legal Nomads*. Contextualising the narrative in references to adventure and exploration further enhances its association with the concept of travel. Nomadic Matt, for example, is on 'an adventure around the world' (Nomadic Matt 2016a). For *Forks and Jets* authors Eva and Jeremy Rees, travel is an escape: 'We are Eva & Jeremy Rees and we are going to escape. We are escaping the 9 to 5, the 40 hour work week, the daily commute, cable television, apartment rent, owning furniture.' (Rees and Rees 2008b). The authors also add that they are exchanging a comfortable lifestyle for a more frugal and difficult existence as travellers:

> We had well-paying careers, nice toys like motorcycles and a classic car, and we were working on our investments and retirement. We are going to miss our 50 inch plasma TV and our shows on HBO and Showtime. Even for this trip we look more like a North Face ad than vagabonds, and our major concerns include kidney theft and sunburn. We're still trying to figure out what some of the straps on our packs are for.
>
> We don't want to be content with two-week vacations once a year, sitting in front of a computer monitor and buying a home, mowing the lawn. Sometimes you have to escape the box completely to think outside it. (Rees and Rees 2008b)

For Eva and Jeremy Rees, the traveller position they occupy is carefully constructed through the discourse of travel. First, this involves a distancing of the way they lived before setting off on their journeys. Prized possessions become 'nice toys' and daily routine is a confining 'box' that must be escaped. Property and practices that tie them down, such as 'owning furniture' or 'paying rent' must be given up if they are to be rootless nomads. Mindful of the need to be seen as 'vagabonds' the authors discuss their unfamiliarity with this experience with self-deprecating humour – they are not yet real travellers, but they are trying. The About page of *Forks and Jets* indicates a need to differentiate between a dissatisfied past self (indicated in the past tense) and a present travelling self (described in present tense) that is enlightened and fulfilled by experience.

For Keith Savage, becoming a traveller means exchanging his passive past (tense) self for one that is active, alert, and liberated in the present (tense). In the About page of *Traveling Savage* he writes:

> I was cowering beneath the covers. I was a complicit zombie.
>
> … life was lavish and lazy and full up with things weightier than any ship's anchor if I'd taken the time to notice the pull or the gradual slouch creeping into my posture. There was no destination and no path, just one foot in front of the other…
>
> And then one frigid December night everything tipped over.
>
> The responsibilities and routines and reasons scattered like bugs from beneath a rock. They looked as minuscule and ugly as bugs, too. The feeling? Like catching up on all the sleep you've lost over the course of your life or the sudden unlatching of a Succubus from your mind. It was levitation. It was levity.
>
> … Time will be the storyteller of what lies beyond these familiar confines. But I am awake.
>
> I am clear-eyed and brimming.
>
> I am the me I wanted to be.
>
> (Savage 2016b)

Laura Walker's initial experience of travel as outlined in *A Wandering Sole* involves a similar surrender of a purportedly unenviable past life. Referring to this 'former self' and the origins of her travel blog, she describes this initial transformation into a traveller when, following her graduation, she went on a trip to Africa. Feeling 'antsy' upon her return, she has now changed her approach to life, taking it 'one day at a time and seeing what adventures/trouble I can get into' (Walker 2016b). The fact that she has since become a successful business person and has found her vocation as a job coach for refugees suggests that the 'adventures' have been fulfilling, inspiring, and transformative. Likewise, Barbara Weibel has exchanged a past self that was 'like a donut – a wonderful outer shell with an empty, hollow inside' for a more satisfying existence as the author of *Hole in the Donut Cultural Travel*. Her blog now fills the emptiness of her past self, by describing the 'inner journey' and 'never-ending spiritual lessons that come from travel' (Weibel 2016b).

In each instance, travel is distinguished from the passivity of tourism by its vivacity and spirit of adventure and exploration. *Traveling Savage* and *A Wandering Sole* discursively construct this idea of being active when its authors occupy a traveller role. The lassitude of Savage's 'cowering' zombie is replaced by the energy of a 'clear-eyed' person who, as 'the me I wanted to be', is his true self. The unadventurous stability of Laura Walker's life is replaced by the comparatively dangerous thrill of 'taking life one day at a time' and a subsequent transformation into a successful entrepreneur. It can be argued that her newer role managing a business venture in East Africa is just as active and adventurous. Even the authors of *Forks and Jets* contrast their present active selves as engaged in relatively difficult yet spontaneous undertakings and having a less than comfortable lifestyle with past selves that passively followed daily routine.

The very fact that the traveller role is generally described in the present tense is significant, given Graham Dann's association of this tense with the narration of travel experiences as opposed to tourism promotion. Nevertheless, the change from an earlier unfulfilled self to a recent revitalised one is also a concept integral to tourist discourse (Dann 1996). Tourism advertising frequently uses 'temporal contrast' – indicated by a change of tense – to suggest that individuals can cast off an earlier state of dissatisfaction with the mundane routine and enjoy a more pleasant and pleasurable experience at a tourist destination at a later time simply by travelling there (Dann 1996, p. 200). On the other hand, while the transformation of self is itself a touristic concept, the change described in these About pages is usually from a mundane but comfortable routine to a more difficult, unpredictable situation rather than a pleasant one. Such skilful rendering of temporal contrast works, therefore, to associate the experiences described therein with travel as opposed to tourism.

Addressing the reader

About pages are generally addressed to the reader, and the audience is often directly and explicitly acknowledged. 'Come along with me,' writes Keith Savage, in a clear invitation to the reader to engage with his narrative (Savage 2016b). Using the second person voice, as Savage does, generally indicates an author's audience awareness. Frequently, authors engage with readers in order to explain the purpose of their blog. Nomadic Matt aims to 'help others like you to realise their travel dreams' and 'give you tested tips, advice, and suggestions so you can see more for less and make your dream trip a reality' (Nomadic Matt 2016a). Meanwhile, Jodi Ettenberg of *Legal Nomads* undertakes to 'to help others with [coeliac] disease travel safely and with less fear' (Ettenberg 2016b). On the face of it, these statements tell readers what to expect from the blog – posts on how to travel, usually by using methods recommended by the author. On another level, they position the authors and set the tone of their relationship with the audience. As persons who will show others how to travel, Nomadic Matt and Jodi Ettenberg become mentors and experts, who will provide valuable advice based on their own experiences.

Such statements tend to be monologic, and bring to mind what Dann refers to as 'tourism's unidirectional discourse', a narrative style that encourages neither response nor interaction (Dann 1996, p. 64). On the whole, such discourse is marked by the presence of an unidentifiable speaker and an equally indistinguishable addressee, in terms of age, gender, or economic and social background (Dann 1996). Indeed, extrapolating from Dann's theories, it can be argued that the audience remains largely unknown, even if the message is intended specifically for readers interested in cheap and independent travel. According to Dann, for the most part 'the speaker speaks, and the listener listens' (1996, p. 64). This creates the impression of a speaker who is better informed and more experienced than the reader. Although Nomadic Matt and Ettenberg are hardly anonymous, they do present themselves as having greater knowledge and expertise than their readers, which they will impart via the blog. However, this necessitates a change from a first-person voice to a second-person one that emphasises 'you' the reader and effectively distances the author with its impersonal tone. This narrative technique allows authors to acknowledge a reader's presence, a recognition that lends conviction to their position as bloggers as it signals their willingness to engage with audiences. Yet, in doing so it also positions readers as potential tourists and creates a perhaps unlooked for association with commercial tourist discourse.

Authors are nevertheless careful to outline the exact nature of their blogs' association with discourses of tourism. Jodi Ettenberg clearly states that she reviews books that are sold via Amazon, which pays her a commission if a sale is made through her website. As for advertising and sponsored content she is emphatic in her refusal to include this: 'No no no. No ads, display or otherwise' and promises to disclose anything written within her role as a brand ambassador with travel company G Adventures (Ettenberg 2016b). The About page suggests that there is some connection between the blogger and promoters of tourism, despite its clear disavowal of anything commercial. While there is an implication a few entries may be of a promotional nature, the narrative is presented as being authentic and up front about its inevitable links with touristic discourse. Schmalleger and Carson observe that in order to be credible and successful, a travel blog must not have obviously promotional content but employ a discursive style that is distinct from tourism marketing (2008). Perhaps Ettenberg is conscious of this as well for she maintains the 'integrity' of her blog with this disclosure:

> I chose not to monetize Legal Nomads via advertising or sponsored content, and have kept the site ad-free. Any affiliate links are products I have used or can vouch for and am comfortable attaching to my reputation online. I will continue to maintain this integrity and treat readers with respect, as I would want to be treated online.
>
> (Ettenberg 2016b)

Implicit in the content and the narrative techniques of Ettenberg's message to her readers are two different positions that she occupies in her blog – that of a traveller and that of a promoter of tourism. The implication that the text is a genuine travel blog simply because it is honest and thus different from conventional marketing discourse reassures readers who expect genuine accounts of her travel experiences. This disclosure is self-focused and written in first-person voice, indicating her affinity with her readers and establishes her as a credible blogger as opposed to a commercial writer of touristic content. The fact remains, however, that she occupies several roles in the blog, including that of brand ambassador, conference speaker, and freelance writer for travel publications. These positions depend on her position as a travel blogger and independent traveller. Ettenberg must appear to be a genuine traveller to attract readership and also to attract opportunities to write or speak, situations where her position as a travel blogger and the authenticity of her narrative is a selling point. At the same time, she also needs to be seen to dissociate herself from tourism to retain her audience and validate her position as a travel blogger. In defining different aspects of online self, Ettenberg must negotiate between discourses of both travel and tourism.

From a blogger's perspective, it is necessary to establish a rapport with readers and so draw their attention to the presentation of the self as a traveller and the narration of travel experiences. Blog readers, in their turn, often expect to be allowed to interact with authors and an author's willingness to respond is regarded as essential to blogging practices (Schmidt 2007; Papworth 2009). The display of the conversation that occurs between blogger and reader on the About page may well strengthen the former's position as an authentic travel blogger (Walker 2004). Several bloggers use the second person voice when they encourage readers to contact them or leave comments on their blog. Laura Walker of *A Wandering Sole* writes, 'I'm a bit slow to respond to blog emails, but I promise I have every intention to respond, and I would love to hear from you!' (Walker 2016b). According to Dann, this is touristic in its singling out of the readers to invite an intimate interaction – a point examined in greater depth later in this chapter with reference to readers' responses to posts. Nevertheless, Walker's apologetic promise to write personalises the statement and removes any authoritarian tone. For now, it is enough to recognise that this touristic style of discourse acknowledges the reader's presence, and consequently solidifies Walker's position as a blogger.

Recognition of the reader's presence is not limited to the comments function alone. In fact, a number of other tools also facilitate and invite audience interaction. Many blogs provide Really Simple Syndication (RSS) feeds or email updates, enabling readers to share the blog's content via services such as *Twitter*, *Facebook*, or *StumbleUpon* and display an email address for contacting the author. These strategies work towards strengthening a blogger's self-presentation in several ways. First, the apparent selection of currently popular tools, implying a sound knowledge of social media, lends conviction to his or her role as a blogger. The term 'apparent' is used deliberately here, as most blogging services freely provide a wide range of tools that authors can use to distribute the blog or embed content from other platforms such as *Flickr* or *Delicious* (Du and Wagner 2006; Schmidt 2007; Nomadic Matt 2016a). Second, while the display of an easily recognised and perhaps popularly used service may be unintentional, it indicates an association with a certain culture. Like the references to brands and products in personal home pages, which are a self-presentational strategy that says something about the author (Schau and Gilly 2003), links to well-known services such as *Twitter* or *Facebook* suggest that authors share similar preferences with readers who also use these platforms. Inviting greater reader engagement may well strengthen authors' credibility as bloggers (Schmidt 2007). Furthermore, such practices improve the visibility of the blogs, indicating an author's desire to present their narratives to a large audience.

A personal tone and the narration of travel experiences validate the presentation of self as a traveller and as an author of a narrative of travel. A monologic style of address also places the author in a position of some authority and strengthens his or her position as an expert on matters related to real travel as opposed to tourism. In most cases, it is difficult for readers to establish whether these authors consciously manipulate the contextual differences between travel and tourism to present themselves as travel bloggers. Yet, at least some authors refer to these discursive distinctions. Jodi Ettenberg, for example, uses her consciousness of this difference as a self-presentational tool to position herself as a credible blogger and suggest that *Legal Nomads* is not merely marketing spiel. Similarly, for Nomadic Matt, Polat, Walker, and Eva and Jeremy Rees, the manipulation of a discursive style associated with tourism cements their position as experts on travel and genuine bloggers willing to engage with their audiences. Therefore, discourses of both travel and tourism play a significant part in adding conviction to an author's presentation of self to readers and adding credibility to a travel blog.

The voice of the post

Bloggers have been known to show a degree of self-awareness and reflect on the practice of blogging and their role as authors (Serfaty 2004; Trammell and Keshelashvili 2005). If bloggers create their posts with an eye to their readership, audiences in their turn expect bloggers to write in their 'own personal voice' and 'be open for dialogue' (Burg and Schmidt 2007, p. 1413). Such expectations may well shape discursive style as authors incorporate various forms of language whose contexts will reinforce and validate their position as travel bloggers. For readers, these narrative forms and techniques are the cues by which they recognise the nature of the author and the text. In Bakhtinian terms, each post is an utterance whose discursive contexts and narrative techniques help identify the author as a travel blogger and the text as a travel blog. However, as authors reflect on the practices of travel and travel blogging, it becomes clear that the two are sometimes viewed as antithetical. For Anil Polat of *foXnoMad*, travel interferes with blogging so that, 'the more you travel the more difficult it is to keep writing. Blogging requires sitting in front of a computer on a regular basis and traveling removes you from that medium' (Polat 2006).

For other authors, it is blogging that proves an obstacle to travel. Nomadic Matt associates being a traveller with a certain spontaneity that conflicts with his travel blogging:

> This website often doesn't give me the flexibility to make crazy changes in my plans like I used to be able to do…
>
> As a digital nomad, I think it's easy … to get trapped in the job. The Internet will always take as much time as you give it. I get stuck behind my computer and stuck in my itinerary, and I feel that I have to go here or I have to do that. I've forgotten how travel is always at its best when it isn't planned.
>
> (Nomadic Matt 2011)

For Nomadic Matt, the practice of blogging imposes a schedule on unplanned travel, turning it into something like tourism. The need to write episodes on certain themes or destinations requires him 'to go here' and 'do that' removing some of the spontaneity associated with real travel (Nomadic Matt 2011). Nomadic Matt and Anil Polat's frustration with the regularity demanded of blogging draws attention to a discursive tension that the authors themselves may be unaware of. Travel is generally associated with timelessness and this reflects in the narrative style used by writers of travel books (Dann 1999). By contrast, tourist discourse is concerned with time and this is indicated in techniques such as the manipulation of tense in advertisements and brochures or the chronological organisation of a tourist itinerary (Dann 1996, pp. 51–52). By styling themselves as 'nomads', Nomadic Matt and Anil Polat suggest that they travel without regard for time and that their descriptions of their journeys may reflect the timelessness of travel (and not tourist) experiences. Nevertheless, the blog format organises these into time-stamped episodes, imposing a touristic temporality, which is nonetheless important for conveying a sense that the narrative is an authentic travel blog.

Another characteristic feature of the narration of travel experiences, as opposed to touristic ones, is the description of the difficulties faced on the journey. A post in *Legal Nomads*, tagged 'Adventures in Transportation' describes author Jodi Ettenberg's travels through Laos by *songthaew*, a form of local transport. She is accompanied by 'irate chickens', 'dirt-covered', vomiting children, and cardboard boxes filled with nails. Still, the discomforts provide an escape from touristic experience:

> Careening past towering karst cliffs, past the emerald green river snaking between them, across bridges with incomparable vistas, we (me and the 37 other people – yes, I counted) were catapulted into an alternate universe, away from the dust and dirt of Luang Prabang, away from the tourists and the touts.
>
> (Ettenberg 2011b)

Ettenberg does not simply drive through the country. She is 'careening', 'catapulted', and 'trundled' across northern Laos, words that seem calculated to impress, upon the reader, the dangers of travel. Even the river she passes is 'snaking' between 'towering' cliffs. Although travel is generally conceived as a solitary experience, having to endure the company of thirty-seven other persons and animals in a confined space makes the journey all the more difficult, thus defining it as a real travel. Finally, with a travel writer's appreciation for the journey rather than the destination, she concludes: 'Arriving in Nong Khiaw was rewarding: a tiny town nestled between limestone cliffs and seemingly frozen in time. But the ride to get there? Even more memorable' (Ettenberg 2011b). This then is the narration of travel – adventurous, energetic, and characteristically uncomfortable.

Mike Robinson observes that it is narrative style that sets apart the discourses of travel from those of tourism, so that 'What is largely missing from travel guide books and is central to travel writing is the distinctive presence of the author's voice' (Robinson 2004, p. 309). Travel writing is also often self-focused and has a distinct personal voice (Blanton 2002), a feature that is discernible in Ettenberg's entry. In comparison, tourist discourse is comparatively impersonal and 'unidirectional' in addressing an audience (Dann 1996, p. 64). Often, this involves 'ego-targeting', a narrative technique that promotes tourism by directly addressing the audience, engaging them in conversation, and encouraging their participation in touristic activities (Dann 1996, pp. 185–188). This parallels a blogger's use of either an obvious or implied 'you', which recognises the reader and establishes the author's role as an expert traveller. Viewed within this theoretical context, *Traveling Savage*'s observations on Scotland's taverns appear fraught with discursive tensions:

> I associate Scottish pubs with traditional Scottish folk music, but pubs didn't always welcome the sound of reels and strathspeys within their walls. Stop in to so-called "traditional pubs" like The Bow Bar or The Abbotsford and you'll find them noticeably lacking music. It seems the conjoining of pubs with traditional music came into its own during the 1960s folk revival, though I would welcome confirmation on this point. Today, folk music is common in pubs, and listening to it is like an umbilical cord to the past, like the culture audibilized.
>
> Perhaps it's only natural for the soul to show when you throw folks in a warm room and plop some pints in their hands.
>
> (Savage 2011a)

Here, the paragraph constantly switches between first and second person voices as he expresses personal opinion and experiences, acknowledges the readers' presence, and invites their participation. The focus on the self and the experience of travel gives way to a monologic and authoritative description of pub culture. The post directly targets its readers and engages their participation in its description, by asking them to verify Savage's description. At a superficial level, this can read like a touristic text. The difference lies in the fact that unlike the faceless sender of the touristic message, the author of this text presents a recognisable online self.

The tensions so produced owe something to the practices intrinsic to writing a blog. As Walker Rettberg points out, blogging is 'a first-person form of writing' (Walker Rettberg 2014, p. 34), and the use of 'I' is a key indicator of the personal nature of the narrative. However, it is also a style of writing that acknowledges and engages the audience and perhaps encourages their participation (Schmidt 2007). This requires a constant shift of focus between the authorial 'I' and the 'you' of the implied reader. The authorial 'I' of the blogger describes what Scottish pubs mean to him and, by addressing 'you' the reader, he engages with the audience. This changing voice, manifested by both travel and tourist discourses, is essential to the presentation of Savage as a blogger.

Including factual content and employing a largely impersonal and a monologic style of address enables authors to place themselves as experts on travel – a position of authority and knowledge that is often claimed by the speaker of tourist discourse.

This discursive style comes to the fore in some paragraphs of the same entry on Scottish pub culture:

> Since Roman times, pubs, or tabernae as they were known, have played an integral role as the gathering place for communities as well as the accommodation for passing travelers. In some pubs I've visited, like The Abbotsford, there is a cloying sense of accumulated history seeping from the very walls, like the ghost of cigarette smoke. In Edinburgh, as in other parts of Scotland, many pubs have been in business for hundreds of years and have provided the background scene for royalty, famous artists, and infamous criminals. Pubs are generally proud of this heritage, and many showcase pictures, paintings, informational plaques, and the original fittings.
>
> (Savage 2011a)

But for the mention of Savage's own visit to The Abbotsford, this paragraph could easily have come out of a guidebook or tourist brochure. Nevertheless, the largely impersonal description is momentarily personalised in the metaphoric first-person description of Savage's travel experience of Abbotsford. This reminder that the text is a personal narrative validates a post that would otherwise be associated with discourses of tourism. The switching of voices here is similar to that seen in *Tony Wheeler's Travels*.

Keith Savage's acknowledgement of his readers, while expected of an authentic blogger, is similarly touristic when he recommends a trip to Scotland: 'Now it's time to consider where, in this incredibly varied country, you should spend your hard-earned vacation' (Savage 2011b). The conversational style, the suggestion of personalised advice, the promotion of an 'incredibly varied country', and the encouragement to consume Scotland, all involve ego-targeting. However, the sentences that follow lack the euphoria that is so characteristic of tourist discourse:

> I won't sugarcoat it; you won't be able to see it all. Not in one trip at least. Planning your destinations in Scotland is at once a horrible war of attrition and some of the most fun I've ever had trip planning. Difficult decisions are ahead. Prepare yourself.
>
> (Savage 2011b)

Having to make 'difficult decisions' suggests the trip is not undertaken easily, an idea more in keeping with the concept of travel rather than tourism. This shift in discursive style suggests the post is not merely promotional, that the destination is not merely a tourist attraction, and that it offers a travel experience. The touch of realism in narrative style may add to the credibility of the text and its author.

When readers respond

Audience engagement is more direct when authors invite comments from readers, thus initiating a dialogue between the two. *Traveling Savage* often ends entries with a question that encourages a discussion of its themes. Concluding a post on Edinburgh, Keith Savage asks, 'Have you explored Edinburgh's underground? Do you have tips for me or suggestions for things I should explore?' (Savage 2011c). In actual fact, most of his respondents offer few suggestions, preferring instead to share their own experiences of Edinburgh or simply to express an appreciation of the post. Nevertheless, this provides an opportunity for Savage to address readers personally. Answering a comment describing a 'ghost tour', he writes, 'Agreed about the spookiness, but it was fun. Did you do any other ghost tours? My wife and I went on one that took us to the Covenanters' Prison in Greyfriar's Kirkyard and it scared the pants off us' (Savage 2011c).

On the whole, such personal interaction fulfils audience expectations with regards to the narrative and its author. Comments, such as these, addressed specifically to a certain reader, written in the first person voice, and describing a personal experience, highlight the authorial voice that, for Mike Robinson, sets forms like travel writing apart from commercially-oriented texts such as guidebooks (Robinson 2004, p. 309). At the same time, the 'singling out process', which positions a reader as a 'confidante' with whom the travel destination and its attendant experiences are shared, is a technique often used in tourism advertising (Dann 1996, pp. 186–187). It allows Savage to strengthen his relationship with his audience and lends conviction to his own position as an authority on Scotland. These statements stop short of openly promoting Greyfriar's Kirkyard as a tourist destination, but nonetheless reflect an intimacy not unusual in a touristic style of address. The addition of a personal anecdote facilitates a manipulation of such touristic discourse towards the presentation of a traveller self.

There is a reversal of this process when readers address the authors and recommend destinations. Replying to a post on travelling in Northern Laos from Jodi Ettenberg in *Legal Nomads*, blogger Andy Jarosz of *501 Places* (Jarosz and Jarosz 2011) writes:

> Looking forward to reading about your northern Laos adventures Jodi – particularly what you did and where you ate in Nong Khiaw. It was my favourite spot in the whole of Laos, not only for the breathtaking scenery but also because we found the most delicious freshly home-baked key lime pie!
> (Ettenberg 2011a)

This comment is both a personalised recommendation that targets Ettenberg and an acknowledgement of the larger audience of blog visitors. Although it describes personal memories, it also incorporates the sort of euphoric testimonial that is typically touristic, according to Dann. As Jarosz engages her in conversation, he describes Nong Khiaw in the 'positive and glowing terms' characteristic of tourist discourse (Dann 1996, p. 65). The food is 'delicious', and the views 'breathtaking'. His promotion of the attractions of the region is almost worthy of a tourist advertisement, and the touristic style places Jarosz in a position of authority as he shares his own experiences with Ettenberg and other readers.

In the ensuing dialogue, both Ettenberg and Savage become confidantes and recipients of recommendations from readers who respond to the ego-targeting techniques of their entries. However, when individuals reply, they address not the unknown promoter of tourism, but the self as traveller that these authors present. Likewise, as the conversation develops between authors and specific readers, the ego-targeting becomes a personal dialogue that adds conviction to the author's position as a traveller. These conversations indicate a genuine polyphony where both authors and readers speak in multiple voices.

Sometimes, tensions arise when readers who assume such a touristic position of authority question the travel discourse in the post. One reader's reaction to Anil Polat's post in 2010 on 'What It's Like to Travel in Northern Iraq' is one such example. Much like Ettenberg in her Laotian post, Polat often refers to the difficulties of travel – the looming threat to the 'eggshell security' of the region and the scarcity of luxury accommodation are principal themes (2010). Although the entry receives a number of positive and admiring comments, one anonymous user takes exception to this description. Having criticised the post and its accompanying photographs, the visitor simply known as 'Onlooker' writes, '… your writing is pretty useless and inaccurate, and missing a lot of information, please do us all a favor and don't visit us again' (Polat 2010). As if to emphasise this, this individual follows this up with links to web pages advertising hotels and sights that Polat has neglected to mention. This is ego-targeting of a different kind. Like Jarosz in *Legal Nomads*, Onlooker engages not Polat alone, but also other readers of this post. Despite having a username, this visitor is something of an unknown sender who assumes a position of touristic authority by recommending other websites, which according to him (or her) describe the authentic Iraq. Onlooker's more positive portrayal of northern Iraq is also comparatively touristic, and readers are invited to participate in this Iraq instead of the Iraq of *foXnoMad*. Polat's travel voice and his credibility as a travel blogger are the targets here.

Here, comments are a strategically controlled self-presentational space. Bloggers usually have the option of deleting or not displaying comments they dislike and the resulting display may be limited to what is useful to the blogger. Therefore, it is difficult to establish whether this conversation appears in its entirety. However, Polat displays enough of the dialogue to drive home his own message about Northern Iraq and chooses instead to defend the accuracy of his post. He refers to the fact that he was travelling in the company of another blogger, suggesting that his version can be corroborated by others and that writing of his trip to Iraq as a travel experience – adventurous and possibly dangerous – is important to the credibility of his narrative. Indeed, as the conversation progresses, it transpires that Onlooker is residing in London, although he/she writes as an authority on northern Iraq.

Polat also assumes control over the dialogue by pointing out that, 'Commenting anonymously on a blog doesn't make you an authority on anything' (Polat 2010). He then goes on to remind Onlooker of the etiquette expected of visitors to *foXnoMad*. 'I'd appreciate it if you'd stop trolling around on my *YouTube* page', he writes, finally asserting that 'I've tried my best to be objective' (Polat 2010).

For other visitors, this display of comments, indicating a willingness to engage with readers, regardless of their opinions, may reinforce Polat's own position of authority. His actions, as much as the substance of his defence, support the presentation of the self not only as a real traveller but also as an authentic blogger.

In most cases, the conversations that develop out of comments from readers and responses from authors constantly shift between discourses of travel and tourism. The resulting discursive tension is a dynamic one, changing as authors write authoritatively recommending certain experiences, and so positioning readers as potential tourists, or offer intimate insights that establish the online self as a traveller. These conversations are essential to blogging practice and consequently validate the positioning of the self as a travel blogger. Nevertheless, they demonstrate that these narratives can never be complete blogs about travel as opposed to tourism, even if the author occupies a traveller role. Indeed, the credibility of this position is often maintained only through the manipulation of narrative techniques that are generally associated with touristic discourse. If these discourses collapse into each other, they are nonetheless essential to sustain an author's presentation of various aspects of his or her online self and for the narrative to work convincingly as a blog.

I link, therefore...

Typically, blogs are online narratives that link to internal content – other pages, an author profile, photographs, and archived posts – and to external content hosted on other websites. In particular, linking to other similar blogs is generally regarded as an essential practice in blogging. Not surprisingly, these narratives have been described as 'link-driven sites' (Blood 2000). In independently hosted travel blogs, links to external content fall broadly into two categories – those that lead to content created by the same bloggers on other social media platforms and those that lead to content by other authors or organisations. The former usually consists of links to a page on a social networking site such as *Facebook*, a microblogging service like *Twitter*, a bookmarking service, or a photo-sharing website such as *Flickr*. In the case of the latter, these could be links to similar travel blogs or other travel-related online resources such as accommodation or flight booking websites or travel forums.

Such linking increases the visibility of blogs, and bloggers select links both carefully and deliberately, creating relations between persons and texts (Reed 2005, p. 235; Serfaty 2004, p. 26). Both internal and external linking allow authors to give readers a sense of who they are through the associations they have with other individuals, organisations, or other online content, a strategy that Donath and boyd refer to as a 'public display of connections' (2004). This practice forms an essential part of positioning and presenting various aspects of an online self for, as Geert Lovink notes, 'Without the right links and tags, you are non-existent. Thus, your self-performance is identical to linking' (Lovink 2008). Therefore, as a reflection of the personal choices and relationships that these bloggers want to encourage, links are essentially self-presentational.

In general, links to other blogs often appear alongside entries in the form of a blogroll, a sidebar of links. The blogroll usually consists of a blogger's personal selection of links, generally to other personal narratives in the form of blogs. In effect, the content of a blogroll presents the blogger. Some independent travel blogs – *Hole in the Donut Cultural Travel* is one such example – allocate a separate page, in place of a blogroll, for external links to other similar blogs and/or travel-related websites. This allows authors to segregate content they have created themselves, such as entries, from links to content outside the blog created by others. The display style on this page reflects the actions of the authors and can provide useful insights into their self-presentation. For example, a dedicated links page in *foXnoMad* categorises its links under labels that reflect Anil Polat's personal interests and the goals and positions expressed in his About page. It should also be noted that linking to other similar blogs creates an association with personal narratives whereas linking to websites that promote travel services connects the blog with the commercial discourses of tourism. When an independent travel blog has links to both personal and commercial content within a single page, the inherent contextual differences create discursive tensions in their self-presentation.

Linking in blogs, says Lovink, is mainly about indicating that 'I share your culture' (2008, p. 252). This is often evident in independently hosted travel blogs, whose authors can be quite discerning when it comes to displaying their affiliations. For instance, the Links page on Barbara Weibel's *Hole in the Donut Cultural Travel* lists other independent travel blogs, usually by authors who have a similar content and purpose for their texts. The sites *501 Places* and *Legal Nomads*, both on Weibel's list, display the authors' professional portfolios and awards in the same style as Weibel's blog. Displaying her association with these individuals positions Weibel as a member of a larger community of travel bloggers that shares a similar vision of how travel blogging is practised.

Both the blogroll and the links page also represent a connection with other forms of personal discourse, often specifically discourse that a reader may associate with travel as opposed to tourism. Furthermore, they connect authors with the travel blogging community and validate their performance as bloggers. In addition to this, the content of the blogroll itself supplements their initial self-presentation by revealing other aspects of self. In this sense, blogrolls and links pages share the author's culture with others, and do not merely indicate the culture shared with a larger community of bloggers.

A number of the travel blogs discussed thus far have dispensed with the traditional blog roll format. *Forks and Jets* continues to display a conventional list of blogs on its home page, but this probably has something to do with the fact that this is a complete and inactive blog, at the time of writing. Here, some commercial content in the form of advertising appears below the blogroll, which lists similar narratives using words and phrases associated with travel. Likewise, *foXnoMad*'s page of Links provides a space for advertising alongside a list of other travel blogs. In both cases, the very different discursive contexts of these external links set up a tension within the narrative. On the other hand, external links to advertisements can be seen as elements that tie the blog to forms of commercial discourse. Nevertheless, these personal and commercial discourses are interdependent since the advertisements probably sponsor these blogs and in fact support the existence of both the blogroll and the Links page (which in turn provide the authenticity that makes the blog a viable commercial venture).

Instead of a blogroll, many blogs display links to other travel blogs or travel resources on a separate page, a strategy evident in *Everything Everywhere*, *Hole in the Donut Cultural Travel* and *foXnoMad.* Allocating a separate page for such external links allows these independent bloggers to do a number of things with the content. First, they draw a clear line between content that is their own and material that is hosted on other websites. Second, these authors often use the available space to preface their links list, usually with an explanation of their selection criteria. Third, they also use the extra space to provide more links. Some of these authors annotate the links, describing the blogs or indicating the usefulness of a particular online travel resource. Both the choice of links and the accompanying explanations can offer a better understanding of the nature of the self-presentation of these bloggers.

Both Arndt and Polat preface their links with an invitation to other bloggers to exchange links with them. This serves the twofold purpose of increasing the visibility of their blogs and engaging an audience of other bloggers. Polat goes a step further, grouping his links on the basis of content and format under labels that reflect his interests, such as 'Green Travel' and 'Technology', and other travel-related websites under 'Travel Resources' (Polat 2016b). These last may represent tourist discourse, but by categorising these, Polat authenticates his own position as an expert on travel. Moreover, the categories solidify his position as a technology enthusiast with an interest in the environment. The blog also advertises travel-related services, and Polat's personal selection of links is offset by commercial advertising along the left-hand margin of the page. As a consequence, some tensions may exist between the different sets of external links – the advertisements are provided by Google AdSense and change according to a visitor's location and interests.

On the other hand, Arndt's 'Travel Blog Directory' is free of commercial advertising and is arranged alphabetically, apart from a few listed as being the 'Best of the Best' for which Arndt provides annotations. The language of his annotations is impersonal of tone and yet the statements themselves indicate a personal connection and firsthand knowledge of the bloggers mentioned. Of *Legal Nomads*' Jodi Ettenberg, he writes: 'I first met Jodi Ettenberg in 2010 in Bangkok. I've since met her in many other countries all over the world. She loves soup' (Arndt 2016c). The annotations place Arndt in an authoritative position, much like the Dann's speaker of tourist discourse, and validate his position as a blogger of some repute by demonstrating a close connection with similarly successful bloggers. Yet, the links themselves represent personal narratives of travel.

Nomadic Matt uses both annotation and categorisation in a page dedicated to travel-related resources. Like Arndt and Polat, he positions himself as something of a travel advisor. The annotations often begin in a style that is impersonal and even imperative, much like the tourist discourse described by Graham Dann, as is evident in this description of *Rail Europe*: 'If you are going to visit Europe and plan on taking a lot of trains, get a rail pass. You will save money a lot of money' (Nomadic Matt 2016b). There is more than a hint of authoritarianism and an implied promotion of an easy and therefore touristic mode of travel. However, the website appears to merit inclusion as, by using a mode of transportation suited to budget travel, the blogger has 'saved hundreds of dollars'. A similar touch of touristic euphoria as well as more advice follows in a description of the *Couchsurfing* website:

> This website allows you to stay on people's couches or spare rooms for free. It's a great way to save money while meeting locals who can tell you much more about a city than you will find out in a hostel/hotel.
>
> (Nomadic Matt 2016b)

Despite the narrative style of the annotation that is akin to promotional discourse, the *Couchsurfing* concept, where travellers are guests of local residents who are willing to offer a bed, suggests an accommodation style that is an alternative to tourist hotels. Some of the descriptions indicate his contempt for guided tourism and the need to be a 'nomadic' and independent traveller. If Nomadic Matt does advocate the use of a tour company – *Walks LLC* is one such example – this is only because of the travel experience it offers in the form of 'behind the scenes tours that give you access to places no one else can get you' (Nomadic Matt 2016b). In the midst of tensions between the contexts of these websites and the annotations, Nomadic Matt engages the attention of his audience and positions himself as a proponent of travel, as indicated in his About page.

Many of the authors mentioned here also use their blogs to promote their professional interests. To this end, they display awards won by their narratives and provide links to portfolios of their work. The 'Portfolio' page of Barbara Weibel's blog allows readers to download and read articles she has published in a wide range of magazines and websites. This association with recognised publishers validates her work and her position as a writer of narratives of travel. In a similar manner, Jodi Ettenberg's 'Speaking and Freelancing' page features her speeches, presentations, and video clips, testifying to her position as an authority on travel. For both Ettenberg and Weibel, these links serve to promote their work, and potentially earn them more money. Although each link is personal in the sense that the authors have chosen to include it in the narrative, it represents an aspect that is commercial, it works to brand and promote the online self these women present via their blogs.

The different styles of linking in these independent travel blogs is another indication of the greater flexibility these authors enjoy when presenting themselves, as compared with those who use commercially sponsored travel blog hosts. The use of blogrolls or links pages in various ways also shows how the same features may be used differently as self-presentational tools. Employing strategies such as categorisation and annotation and displaying a portfolio of published works facilitates the positioning of the online self and also helps reinforce the notion of a culture that is shared with other blogs. Regardless of the technique used, links ultimately reinforce the positions stated in the authors' About pages, including usually that of a traveller self that is underwritten by both travel and tourist discourses.

The shape of the independent travel blog

The personal voice of blogger is more easily identified in independent travel blogs than it is in *Tony Wheeler's Travels* or the travel blogs on advertising-sponsored, travel-specific webhosts. One principal difference between these blogs and those found on sponsored web hosts is that authors enjoy access to a greater variety of features while crafting the presentation of their online self, with the result that their roles are defined not just in the language of their entries but also in visual elements. Here, paratextual elements indicate a greater individualism, as do the About pages and links that build on the self initially constructed in these elements. Indeed, individual features such as the blogroll and the comments box, both of which are widely regarded as essential to blogs, are developed to a greater extent than they are in *Tony Wheeler's Travels* and in the blogs on *TravelPod*, *TravelBlog*, and *BootsnAll*. The resulting presentation of the online self is much more complex and textured than anything found on commercial web hosts.

If the self as independent travel blogger finds greater expression because of this flexibility, then so do the discursive tensions between travel and tourism. The main difference is that the tensions in sponsored blogs arise in part from the relationships between the authors, webhosts, sponsors, and readers. Simply put, the nature of the publisher plays an important part in the discursive tensions. Furthermore, independently hosted blogs allow for greater interaction between authors and readers and this in turn results in a narrative that is highly audience-oriented. In independent travel blogs, a good deal of the tension between travel and tourist discourses grows out of an author's awareness of the reader and the need to indicate various positions that support the presentation of self as a traveller and as a blogger of travel experiences. An author's manipulation of narrative techniques central to tourist discourse enables him or her to acknowledge and address these readers. Both discourses are therefore integral to engaging the audience and placing the blogger in a position of authority and defining the relationship between bloggers and their audiences.

The discourses of travel and tourism are variously integrated in these features so that the tensions between these discourses play out differently in each blog. However, the analysis is as yet incomplete as it does not consider the content created by the authors on other social media platforms. Visual elements contribute significantly to the online presentation of self, but this chapter has not discussed the role of photographs. Accordingly, the following chapter considers the notion that these other online platforms disperse the content of the independent travel blog and extend the self-presentation of its author. The penultimate chapter then examines the photographs hosted both in independent travel blogs as well as on other photo-sharing services.

References

Arndt, G. 2016a. *Everything Everywhere* [Online]. Available from: http://everything-everywhere.com/about-me/ [Accessed 26 February 2016].

Arndt, G. 2016b. About. *Everything Everywhere* [Online]. Available from: http://everything-everywhere.com/about-me/ [Accessed 1 March 2016].

Arndt, G. 2016c. Travel blog directory. *Everything Everywhere* [Online]. Available from: http://everything-everywhere.com/about-me/ [Accessed 7 March 2016].

Bakhtin, M. 1986. *Speech genres and other late essays,* Austin, TX, US: University of Texas Press.

Blanton, C. 2002. *Travel writing: the self and the world,* New York: Routledge.

Blood, R. 2000. *Weblogs: a history and perspective* [Online]. N.p. Available: http://www.rebeccablood.net/essays/weblog_history.html [Accessed 1 Sept. 2010].

Bloom, L. Z. 1996. 'I write for myself and strangers': private diaries as public documents. *In:* Bunkers, S. L. and Huff, C. A. (eds.) *Inscribing the daily: critical essays on women's diaries.* Amherst, MA, US: University of Massachusetts Press.

Burg, T. N. and Schmidt, J. 2007. *Blogtalks reloaded: social software – research and cases*, Vienna: Social Software Lab.

Columbus, C. 1989. *The diary of Christopher Columbus's first voyage to America, 1492–1493*, Dunn, Oliver and Kelley, James E. (eds.) Norman, OK, US: University of Okhlahoma Press.

Cowper, H. 2010. *Heather on her Travels* [Online] N.p. Available: http://www.heatheronhertravels.com/ [Accessed 25 Aug. 2010].

Dann, G. 1996. *The language of tourism: a sociolinguistic perspective,* Wallingford, UK: CAB International.

Dann, G. 1999. Writing out the tourist in space and time. *Annals of Tourism Research* [Online], 26. Available: http://www.sciencedirect.com/science/article/B6V7Y-3VS7VK0-8/2/644ebe6402ad134ca201678b33b3afc4 [Accessed 30 Mar. 2009].

Donath, J. and boyd, d. 2004. Public displays of connection. *BT Technology Journal* [Online], 22(4), 71–82. Available: http://link.springer.com/article/10.1023/B:BTTJ.0000047585.06264.cc. [Accessed 8 Oct. 2010].

Du, H. S. and Wagner, C. 2006. Weblog success: exploring the role of technology. *International Journal of Human-Computer Studies* [Online], 64. Available: http://www.sciencedirect.com/science/article/B6WGR-4K3D386-1/2/46da3e41acfe8024cec06b9f60f7a539.

Dunn, D. 2005. Venice observed: the traveller, the tourist, the post-tourist and British television. *In:* Jaworski, A. and Pritchard, A. (eds.) *Discourse, communication, and tourism.* Clevedon, UK: Channel View.

Ettenberg, J. 2011a. Exploring northern Laos. *Legal Nomads* [Online]. Available from: http://www.legalnomads.com/about [Accessed 3 March 2016].

Ettenberg, J. 2011b. It's not a proper bus ride without a chicken or two. *Legal Nomads* [Online]. Available from: http://www.legalnomads.com/2011/02/its-not-a-proper-bus-ride-without-a-chicken-or-two.html [Accessed 24 Feb. 2016].

Ettenberg, J. 2016a. *Legal Nomads* [Online]. Available from: http://www.legalnomads.com/about [Accessed 26 February 2016].

Ettenberg, J. 2016b. About me and Legal Nomads. *Legal Nomads* [Online]. Available from: http://www.legalnomads.com/about [Accessed 24 February 2016].

Gargiulo, R. 2014. *Pause the moment* [Online]. Available: http://www.pausethemoment.com/ [Accessed 16 May 2016].

Genette, G. 1997. *Paratexts: thresholds of interpretation,* Cambridge, UK: Cambridge University Press.

Goffman, E. 1959. *The presentation of self in everyday life,* London: Allen Lane.

Hermans, H. J. M. 2004. Introduction: The Dialogical Self in a Global and Digital Age. *Identity: An International Journal of Theory and Research* [Online], 4. Available: http://www.informaworld.com/10.1207/s1532706xid0404_1 [Accessed 28 June 2010].

Hevern, V. W. 2004. Threaded identity in cyberspace: weblogs and positioning in the dialogical self. *Identity* [Online], 4(4). Available: http://www.tandfonline.com/doi/pdf/10.1207/s1532706xid0404_2 [Accessed 17 Mar. 2009].

Holland, P. and Huggan, G. 1998. *Tourists with typewriters: critical reflections on contemporary travel writing,* Ann Arbor, MI, US: University of Michigan Press.

Jarosz, A. and Jarosz, S. 2011. *501 Places* [Online]. Available: http://www.501places.com/ [Accessed 7 Mar. 2016].

Lovink, G. 2008. *Zero comments: blogging and critical Internet culture,* New York: Routledge.

McCulley, K. 2010. *Adventurous Kate* [Online]. N.p. Available: http://www.adventurouskate.com/ [Accessed 25 Aug. 2010].

Merchant, G. 2006. Identity, social networks and online communication. *E-Learning and Digital Media* [Online], 3. Available: http://dx.doi.org/10.2304/elea.2006.3.2.235 [Accessed 1 Sept. 2010].

Nelson, M. E. and Hull, G. A. 2008. Self-presentation through multimedia: A Bakhtinian perspective on digital storytelling. *In:* Lundby, K. (ed.) *Digital storytelling, mediatized stories: self-representations in new media.* New York: Peter Lang.

Nomadic Matt. 2011. *Learning to go with the flow* [Online]. Available: http://www.nomadicmatt.com/travel-blogs/going-with-the-flow/ [Accessed 15 Mar. 2011].

Nomadic Matt. 2016a. *About Nomadic Matt* [Online]. Available: http://www.nomadicmatt.com/ [Accessed 24 February 2016].

Nomadic Matt. 2016b. *Travel resources* [Online]. Available: http://www.nomadicmatt.com/ [Accessed 7 March 2016].

Papworth, L. 2009. *No comments, no engagement* [Online]. Available: http://laurelpapworth.com/non-engagement-seth-godin/ [Accessed 13 Nov. 2009].

Patrick and Akila. 2009. *The Road Forks* [Online]. Available: http://theroadforks.com/ [Accessed 25 Aug. 2010].

Pettersen, L. 2010. *Killing Batteries* [Online]. N.p. Available: http://killingbatteries.com/ [Accessed 25 Aug. 2010].

Pinch, T. 2010. The invisible technologies of Goffman's sociology from the merry-go-round to the Internet. *Technology and Culture* [Online], 51(2), 409–425r. [Accessed 19 July 2010].

Polat, A. 2006. Keep your travel blog going with a weekly posting goal. *foXnoMad* [Online]. Available: http://foxnomad.com/2009/02/05/keep-your-travel-blog-going-with-a-weekly-posting-goal/ [Accessed 15 Mar. 2010].

Polat, A. 2010. What it's like to travel in Northern Iraq. *foXnoMad* [Online]. Available from: http://www.foxnomad.com/2010/12/09/what-its-like-to-travel-in-northern-iraq/ [Accessed 3 Mar. 2016].

Polat, A. 2016a. *foXnoMad* [Online]. Available: http://foxnomad.com/ [Accessed 22 Feb. 2016].

Polat, A. 2016b. Links. *foXnoMad* [Online]. Available: http://foxnomad.com/links/ [Accessed 7 Mar. 2016].

Reed, A. 2005. 'My blog is me': texts and persons in UK online journal culture (and anthropology). *Ethnos* [Online], 70. Available: http://dx.doi.org/10.1080/00141840500141311 [Accessed 6 Jul. 2010].

Rees, E. and Rees, J. 2008a. *Forks and Jets* [Online]. Available from http://forksandjets.com [Accessed 26 Feb.2016].

Rees, E. and Rees, J. 2008b. About us. *Forks and Jets* [Online]. Available from: http://forksandjets.com/about/ [Accessed 24 Mar. 2016].

Robinson, M. 2004. Narratives of being elsewhere: tourism and travel writing. *In:* Lew, A. A., Williams, A. M. and Hall, C. M. (eds.) *A companion to tourism.* Malden, MA. US: Blackwell.

Ryan, W. E. and Conover, T. E. 2004. *Graphic communications today,* Clifton Park, NY, US: Thomson/Delmar Learning.

Sanderson, J. 2008. The blog is serving its purpose: self-presentation strategies on 38pitches.com. *Journal of Computer-Mediated Communication* [Online], 13. Available: http://dx.doi.org/10.1111/j.1083-6101.2008.00424.x [Accessed 11 Aug. 2010].

Savage, K. 2011a. The nexus of Scottish culture...pubs? *Traveling Savage* [Online]. Available from: http://www.traveling-savage.com/2011/02/03/nexus-scottish-culture-pubs/ [Accessed 3 Mar. 2011].

Savage, K. 2011b. Planning a trip to Scotland, part 2. *Traveling Savage* [Online]. Available from: http://www.traveling-savage.com/ [Accessed 3 March 2016].

Savage, K. 2011c. What lies beneath Edinburgh's Old Town?. *Traveling Savage* [Online]. Available from: http://www.traveling-savage.com/2011/02/10/what-lies-beneath-edinburghs-old-town/ [Accessed 15 March 2011].

Savage, K. 2016a. *Traveling Savage* [Online]. Available from: http://www.traveling-savage.com/ [Accessed 22 February 2016].

Savage, K. 2016b. The traveling Savage. *Traveling Savage* [Online]. Available from: http://www.traveling-savage.com/ [Accessed 24 Feb. 2016].

Schau, H. J. and Gilly, M. C. 2003. We are what we post? Self-presentation in personal web space. *The Journal of Consumer Research* [Online], 30. Available: http://www.jstor.org/stable/3132017 [Accessed 22 Jun. 2010].

Schmallegger, D. and Carson, D. 2008. Blogs in tourism: changing approaches to information exchange. *Journal of Vacation Marketing* [Online], 14. Available: http://jvm.sagepub.com/cgi/content/abstract/14/2/99 [Accessed 15 May 2009].

Schmidt, J. 2007. Blogging practices: an analytical framework. *Journal of Computer-Mediated Communication* [Online], 12. Available: http://dx.doi.org/10.1111/j.1083-6101.2007.00379.x [Accessed 24 Feb. 2011].

Scott, R. F. and Allen, P. 1978. *Scott's Antarctic diary,* [Audiobook]. Kent, UK: Pinnacle.

Serfaty, V. 2004. *The mirror and the veil: an overview of American online diaries and blogs,* Amsterdam: Rodopi.

Snyder, S. J. 2010. *Best blogs of 2010* [Online]. Time. Available: http://www.time.com/time/specials/packages/article/0,28804,1999770_1999761_1999748,00.html [Accessed 18 Jun. 2010].

Stadler, W. 2010. *Wayne on the Road* [Online]. N.p. Available: http://www.wayneontheroad.com/ [Accessed 25 Aug. 2010].

Tobias, D. and Tobias, J. 2015. *I should log off* [Online]. Available: http://ishouldlogoff.com/ [Accessed 26 February 2016].

Trammell, K. D. and Keshelashvili, A. 2005. Examining the new influencers: A self-presentation study of A-list blogs. *Journalism and Mass Communication Quarterly*

[Online], 82(4), 968. Available: http://jmq.sagepub.com/content/82/4/968.short [Accessed 11 Sept. 2010].

Walker, K. 2004. "It's difficult to hide it": The presentation of self on internet home pages. *Qualitative sociology* [Online], 23. Available: http://link.springer.com/article/10.1023/A:1005407717409 [Accessed 14 Feb. 2011].

Walker, L. 2016a. *A Wandering Sole* [Online]. Available from: http://www.awanderingsole.com [Accessed 24 Feb. 2016].

Walker, L. 2016b. About. *A Wandering Sole* [Online]. Available from: http://www.awanderingsole.com/about-laura-walker [Accessed 24 Feb. 2016].

Walker Rettberg, J. 2014. *Blogging,* Cambridge, UK: Polity.

Weibel, B. 2016a. *Hole in the Donut Cultural Travels* [Online]. Available: http://holeinthedonut.com/ [Accessed 26 Feb. 2016].

Weibel, B. 2016b. About Barbara Weibel. *Hole in the Donut Cultural Travels* [Online]. Available: http://holeinthedonut.com/ [Accessed 24 February 2016].

5 Beyond the borders of the blog

The networked self of the independent travel blogger

Writing about online narratives, George Landow observes that 'The edges of the blog, like the borders of any document on the Internet, are porous and provisional at best' (2006, p. 82). This view still holds true for independently hosted travel blogs. Indeed, it is difficult to determine where the boundaries of these narratives lie, as they extend their descriptions of journey experiences to other online platforms such as social networking services, microblogging services, photo-sharing platforms, and video-sharing sites. For the most part, this involves linking with social networking site *Facebook* and microblogging service *Twitter*. In addition to this, many travel blogs also display a connection to image-sharing tools such as *Instagram* or *Flickr*, visual bookmarking service *Pinterest* and, in some cases, video-sharing platform *YouTube*. Such blogs may be easily described as possessing what Anne Helmond refers to as a 'distributed nature' (2010, p. 7). Generally, links to these other platforms are either embedded in the blog or accessed via a sidebar comprising buttons known as 'widgets'[1]. This last usually graces the top of the home page of most of the travel blogs discussed in the previous chapter.

This distribution of content has led to the recognition that the online presentation of self is likewise dispersed across different social media (Helmond 2010; Nabeth 2009; Reed 2005). In fact, Helmond sees widgets as something of an anchor that helps to 'embed the scattered self in one place' (2010, p. 7), suggesting that a blogger's self-presentation extends beyond the borders of the blog, which acts as a focal point or a central node. Her use of 'the scattered self', however, implies disorder and fragmentation. An alternative to this would be to regard this as a 'networked identity performance' resulting in the presentation of a 'networked self' as proposed by some social media researchers (boyd and Heer 2006; Papacharissi 2009). The idea of a networked self is useful for examining how authors re-present and enhance positions stated in their blogs – such as travel blogger, travel expert, or travel enthusiast – by using the specific affordances available to them across other online platforms. Each independent travel blog can have a very different mix of social tools, the selection of which has some bearing on the self he or she wishes to present to an online audience. For example, *A Wandering Sole* does not link to *Instagram* or *LinkedIn*, whereas *Traveling Savage* does. Admittedly, there is ample scope for research in this area, but it is beyond the ambit of this book to do justice to an analysis of a blogger's self-presentation across all the aforementioned platforms. This chapter must perforce focus its attention on two social tools that many independent travel bloggers use and have used for some time – an online social networking service (*Facebook*) and a microblogging service (*Twitter*). Bloggers use various affordances of these platforms to network various aspects of the self already presented in their travel blogs. This requires a further and continuous negotiation of the discursive tensions between travel and tourism. Another key feature of these blogs is the travel-related photographs that supplement the narrative in the posts, sometimes via a link to *Instagram*, but these will be examined in a subsequent chapter.

There are two dimensions to the networked self. Not only is it situated in a network of social media surrounding the blog (technological), but also displayed via networking between individuals (social). One of the principal means by which individuals articulate a networked self is by connecting to other people online (Baym 2010; Papacharissi 2010). Describing the style of self-presentation on social networking sites as implicit rather than explicit, Zizi Papacharissi writes, 'individuals use the tools at hand to present themselves in "show not tell" mode by pointing and connection to individuals, groups, or points of reference' (Papacharissi 2010, p. 141). A second point to note here is that a presentation of the networked self ultimately involves 'tools at hand', suggesting that individuals utilise the various specific affordances and formal features of online platforms to position themselves online. Social media allow users to structure information about themselves in different ways (Walker Rettberg 2009). Moreover, as Trevor Pinch notes, the same technical features of an online platform can be used variously by different authors as self-presentational elements (2010). According to Papacharissi, the architecture and tone of a social platform indicates how users should 'condition their self-performances' (Papacharissi 2009, p. 211). She concludes that applications provided by a website like *Facebook* can, in fact, shape the presentation of self: 'the network provides a wider set of props or applications to assist in self-presentation.... [they] facilitate multiplicity, showing audiences the many 'faces' of one's identity and simultaneously negotiating and presenting identity to a variety of audiences' (Papacharissi 2009, pp. 211–212).

Based on this research, it can be argued that formal features of *Facebook* can be self-presentational elements. An individual's selection of the applications available on a single platform has significance as well. For example, the very fact that a blogger uses a *Facebook* page instead of a profile influences the extent and intimacy of social interaction.

The information shared across these social media platforms can also reveal a great deal about these authors. By constructing 'controlled performances', individuals can ensure that they present only what they intend an audience to see (Papacharissi 2009, p. 210). In the case of social networking sites, this means deciding who can access the content created by bloggers or restricting interactivity. On a *Facebook* profile, this could involve adding an individual to one's 'Friends List' or limiting access to items posted on the 'Timeline'. Authors may also use specific narrative techniques to reinforce the themes and positions they present in their blogs. Thus, both the content of web pages hosted on other platforms as well as specific practices followed in order to distribute this content have some bearing on an independent travel blogger's presentation of the online self.

Several factors must be considered in a discussion of the 'networked self' in independent travel blogs. First, the way in which specific tools are used for networking the self as travel blogger is important. Keeping this in mind, this chapter discusses how various formal features of *Facebook* and *Twitter* are employed in the presentation of the online self of independent travel bloggers. A second important factor is the manner in which both *Facebook* and *Twitter* are used to connect with people and display this connection to others. It is necessary to examine the implications of these connections. A third factor to be considered is authorial decisions regarding display of information. What is *not* said on these platforms can be as informative as the content that is created and made available to an audience. It should be noted that the travel experiences narrated on these platforms and the independent travel blog itself may form just a small part of an individual's online performance of self. Content on these platforms may reveal aspects to a blogger's personality that have little to do with the self of the blog. However, this chapter is concerned with how self-presentation on *Facebook* and *Twitter* relates to the travel experience and the author as a blogger of travel.

Find me on *Facebook*

By and large, *Facebook* is the social networking service of choice for the independent travel blogs included in this study. Some blogs also link to *Google Plus*. Perhaps the decision to link to *Facebook* is strategic. *Technorati*'s 'Digital Influence Report' of 2013 ranks the social networking service alongside blogging as an influential platform with consumers looking for trustworthy sources of information (Swartz 2013). *Facebook* is highly popular, with over a billion daily users (Facebook 2016). Creating and sharing relevant content by means of a *Facebook* page or a *Facebook* profile enables bloggers to reach out to this vast global audience and potentially improves the visibility of a travel blog. Given that having a link to *Facebook* is a practice observed by many travel blogs, it is possible that connecting to this website is in itself a self-presentational strategy that validates an individual's position as a genuine blogger. Authors have been known to capitalise on the symbolic meaning of a brand to enhance their online self-presentation (Schau and Gilly 2003). Displaying a connection to *Facebook* can, consequently, enhance the impression of the self as networked. Furthermore, by appearing to use this service, bloggers claim an affinity with other *Facebook* users within their audience. They imply, 'I'm like you, I use *Facebook* too. Follow me, "Like" me.' Therefore, the link to *Facebook* both expands the blog's audience by extending the narrative to another platform and simultaneously draws on the contexts of the service to demonstrate that the self is networked simply because an individual uses a noteworthy social media brand.

Several different techniques are used to display this link, each offering its own advantages as a self-presentational strategy. Often, this connection takes the form

Figure 5.1 Screenshots of widgets on *Traveling Savage*

of a button-like widget on a sidebar, as is the case with *Traveling Savage*, *Hole in the Donut Cultural Travel*, *Forks and Jets*, *foXnoMad*, *A Wandering Sole* and *Legal Nomads* (see Figure 5.1). These button widgets are a clear visualisation of the 'distributed nature of the blog' and the travel blogger as having a networked self. Also, the style of the button itself ensures that the *Facebook* symbol is distinctly visible, and makes obvious the author's affiliation with the brand. Alternatively, and sometimes additionally, a section of the *Facebook* page may be embedded within the home page of the travel blog – a style employed by *Traveling Savage* and *Hole in the Donut Cultural Travel*, for example – showing visitors thumbnail pictures of users who 'Like' the blogger's *Facebook* page. While button widgets visually present the travel blogger self as networked across various platforms, the embedded page section locates this blogging self within a network of other *Facebook* users. *Traveling Savage* also uses both widgets and embedded pages, thus giving the sense of Keith Savage as a travel blogger who is networked across platforms and networking with people. Most blogs also incorporate social media sharing buttons under each entry. Readers of blogs connected to *Facebook* can click on a button to share entries with other users of the latter platform, effectively distributing content from these blogs across the social networking site. As a consequence, an author can potentially extend their self-presentation to a wider audience beyond the blog through a network of connections made by various means with other *Facebook* users.

The decision to distribute a travel blog via *Facebook* in this manner essentially requires balancing two different aspects of the online self – that of the traveller and that of the blogger – that are presented in these blogs. Although travel is generally presented as an experience that is solitary, blogging is by nature communal. The writing of a travel blog requires a balancing of the presentation of a self in the company of other social media users, while also retaining the position of a solitary traveller. In the process of networking the online self of their travel blogs, individuals begin to demonstrate a professional approach in addressing mass audiences that is comparable to that of tourism promoters who use social media to increase awareness of their brand. *Lonely Planet*'s *Facebook* page, for example, promotes articles published on the company's website and engages visitors in conversation in much the same way that independent travel bloggers address audiences and promote blog posts on their *Facebook* pages.

What friends are for

Facebook is eminently suited for the creation and presentation of an online self via a publicly visible profile. There is ample evidence to show that the making and displaying of connections to other individuals is integral to this self-presentation. By definition, *Facebook* and other similar social networking sites are, according to danah boyd and Nicole Ellison,

> web-based services that allow individuals to (1) construct a public or semi-public profile within a bounded system, (2) articulate a list of other users with whom they share a connection, and (3) view and traverse their list of connections and those made by others within the system.
>
> (2008, p. 211)

The definition implies that a 'semi-public profile' and a 'list of connections' are the main features of a social networking site, with an emphasis on the latter. In another study, Donath and boyd similarly focus on connections as crucial to self-presentation, observing that: 'people create a self-descriptive profile and then make links to other people they know on the site, creating a network of personal connections….their network of connections is displayed as an integral piece of their self-presentation' (Donath and boyd 2004, p. 72).

Although individuals may link their travel blogs to either a personal profile on *Facebook* or to a *Facebook* page, most bloggers favour the latter. Regardless of their choice, a display of links to other users, labelled either 'People' or 'Friends', features in both pages and profiles respectively. Writing from the theoretical perspective of Erving Goffman's work on self-presentation, Papacharissi argues that such linking is fundamental in an online performance of the self,[2] which is validated by displaying an individual's 'circle of association' that enables those who encounter this performance to make assumptions about his or her interests and likes or dislikes (2009, p. 210). Visitors to a page may interact with a number of other users who 'Like' its content, while those viewing a profile may (if the privacy settings permit) see an author's 'Friends', that is to say persons whose profiles they link to. Other associations are made and exhibited as well – links to other pages 'Liked by this Page', links to other websites created by the same author, and links to other online content of interest to the author. The platform itself provides a section containing links to other pages that 'People also Like', consequently situating the page in a network of other similar *Facebook* pages. On the face of it, the connections displayed indicate a blogger's personal interests and the kind of associations he or she wishes to make. However, *Facebook* utilises its user preferences to locate each page among others that it believes share a similar culture, consequently implying an affinity that may not be foreseen or desired by these bloggers. To some degree, therefore, the self that bloggers present via *Facebook* pages is subject to the particular affordances and tools of the platform and may have aspects to it that are unintentional or which set up a discursive tension within the page.

Connecting with profiles

Both *Forks and Jets* and *foXnoMad* link to the personal *Facebook* profiles of their authors, Eva Rees and Anil Polat respectively. In *Forks and Jets* the connection is made via a widget at the bottom of the home page. In a more unusual style, *foXnoMad* links to both a *Facebook* page and the author's personal profile via a page in the blog titled 'Facebook'. Here Polat explains the purpose of each link:

> To get more from foXnoMad on Facebook, meet other foXnoMad readers, and learn more about me, "Like" foXnoMad on Facebook using the widget below. […] You can add me on Facebook. This is my personal profile, not one for the site if you want to keep up with me there as well. I look forward to being your digital friend.

Polat's dedication of an entire page to promote his *Facebook* connection is a complex self-presentational strategy. By indicating that his personal profile on

Facebook is different to the one on his blog, Polat suggests that the former is more authentic and complete, offering a glimpse into the real Polat, the person behind the travel blogger. On the one hand, the invitation to go behind the scenes suggests that the travel blog itself is a performance and, by extension, the blogger but an actor playing a part. At the same time, its intimacy strengthens the rapport between Polat and his reader and validates his position as a blogger. Implicit in this invitation to 'learn more about me' is the presentation of a self that extends beyond the blog and onto *Facebook* (Polat 2016c). Polat's personal profile reinforces this idea by incorporating the title of his blog in the URL for the same (http://www.facebook.com/foxnomad), effectively suggesting that the *Facebook* self of Anil Polat is but an extension of the blogging self of *foXnoMad* (Polat 2016b).

It is worth noting that the latest post on the Timeline of Polat's personal profile, a feature that displays his public posts in a reverse-chronological list, is dated 13 May 2014. By contrast, the *Facebook* page for his blog 'FoXnoMad: travel smarter' is active, at the time of writing. The underlying implication here is that the *Facebook* page offers readers a better means of connecting with Polat and so the reader can 'get more' (Polat 2006). However, despite the apparent inactivity of the Timeline, other elements of his profile support his presentation of the self as an authentic travel blogger. That Polat's *Facebook* profile largely reinforces themes and positions expressed in the blog is manifest in links to other pages on *Facebook* as well as links to other *Facebook* users via a Friends list. Polat indicates his various interests by linking his profile to *Facebook* pages for his favourite music (Michael Jackson and The Beatles), movies (*Star Trek*), and television shows (*Dexter*). However, it is in his more extensive list of 'Likes' that the travel theme comes to the fore. This consists mainly of links to the *Facebook* pages of other independent travel blogs such as *Traveling Savage*, *Nomadic Matt*, and *Legal Nomads*. Also listed are links to travel-related *Facebook* pages ('Budget Your Trip', 'Hostelworld', *et al.*) as well as blogging-related *Facebook* pages ('Travel Writers Exchange' and 'World Bloggers Day') among others.

Listing one's interests in this manner is often characteristic of the self-presentation that takes place on social networking sites (boyd and Ellison 2008; Liu 2007). Titles such as 'Hostelworld' draw on the contexts of cheap and independent travel and reinforce Polat's position as an advocate of budget travel. Similarly, the titles of pages related to writing, as well as links to pages of other bloggers, locate the self in a community of other online writers. To that extent, positions presented in his travel blog are reiterated and networked across Polat's *Facebook* profile. Furthermore, the list of interests reads almost like *foXnoMad*'s blogroll, mirroring and reinforcing the connections made via the blog and the blogger's association with the independent travel blogger community. From a Bakhtinian point of view, for an audience that is familiar with *foXnoMad* and the other travel blogs, each of these names is an utterance contextualised in discourses of travel. More importantly, these parallels serve to demonstrate that the same blogging self is networked across other platforms. Ultimately, while the links reveal new aspects to Anil Polat, for the most part they reiterate positions and discourses of *foXnoMad*. Polat the 'digital friend' who can be found on *Facebook* is not necessarily distinct from the Polat the blogger of *foXnoMad*.

Eva Rees's personal *Facebook* profile is distinctly different in a number of ways. Like the Polat profile, there is a wealth of information here on this blogger's personal interests and her list of 'Friends' is extensive. Yet, few of these links are related to travel, and Rees does not appear to have a connection with other travel bloggers and, barring a few *Facebook* pages for travel agencies, most of the other pages she links to have little to do with travel. Instead, these indicate her liking for design, and fashion, and her tastes in film, literature, and music (Rees 2016). Links to pages such as 'Pixels', 'Fonts', and 'Photography', testify to her professional interests – she works in design – rather than her position as a travel blogger (Rees 2016).

This is not to say that Rees's self-presentation on *Facebook* has little relevance to the traveller self of her blog. *Forks and Jets* describes itself as 'the true story of a couple of amateur foodie traveloguers going around the world' (Rees and Rees 2008a), and this is borne out by the Timeline of her profile, which displays a series of travel photographs showing Eva Rees visiting restaurants, hiking, or simply posing against iconic sights, this last much as a tourist would do. Yet, barring links to *Facebook* pages for various restaurants and breweries, the connections displayed via her 'Links' present aspects of Eva Rees that are not obvious on *Forks and Jets*, suggesting that on this platform Eva Rees the person and the professional designer takes precedence over Eva Rees, 'traveloguer'. Perhaps the clearest indication of this is the URL of the profile (http://www.facebook.com/evarees), which includes the author's name rather than the blog title. What needs to be recognised here is that some elements of a *Facebook* profile may supplement rather than reiterate aspects of self that individuals present on their blogs. One could also argue that, by providing greater insights into Rees's personal and professional life, the links reveal the real person behind the online self of the blog. Albeit the function of the profile is to validate the online self of the blog, this apparently authentic *Facebook* self as suggested by the connections displayed only serves to indicate the performative nature of *Forks and Jets*. In comparison, Polat's reiterative profile suggests that the blogging self of Anil Polat is the real self.

The 'Check-ins' page on Rees's *Facebook* profile (see Figure 5.2) is the principal indicator of her traveller self. This application consists of an interactive world map dotted with markers showing the places Rees has visited. Thus, it is a visualisation of what the authors of *Forks and Jets* hope to achieve, 'escaping our small corner of the world, known as Los Angeles, because we believe there is a bigger world out there' (Rees and Rees 2008b). The theme of escape is repeated several times in the *Forks and Jets* 'About Us' page, referring to the notion of travel as something adventurous. In this respect, the pin-dotted map extends the self that is described in the travel blog onto Rees's *Facebook* profile. The map itself is associated with both travel and tourism, and the contexts of the application introduce some degree of discursive tension. It is a point of convergence of two aspects of Rees's online self – that of the traveller occupying *Forks and Jets* and that of the person presented on *Facebook*.

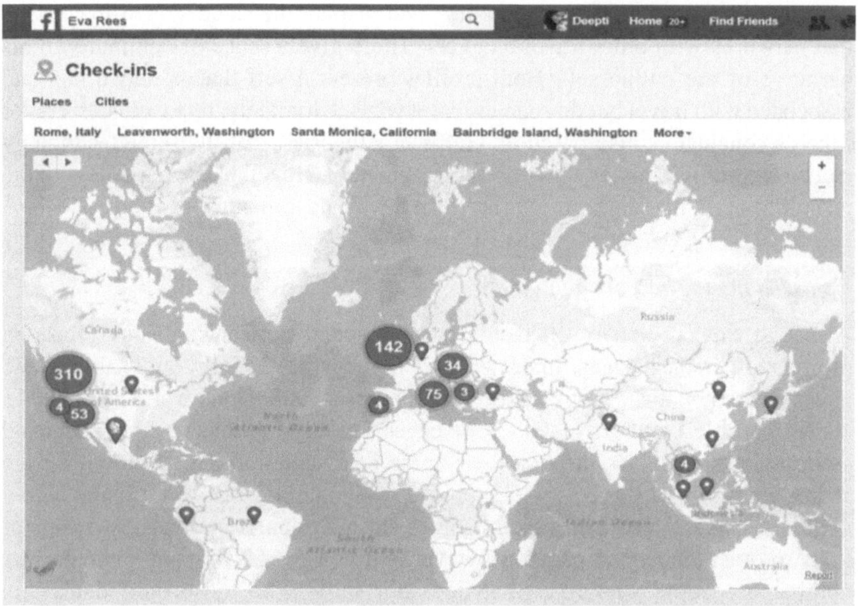

Figure 5.2 Screenshot of Check-ins tool

On the face of it, the map is evidence that the bloggers did escape their 'small corner' as intended, and its various pins testify to the range of their travels into 'a bigger world' (Rees and Rees 2008b). At the same time, however, these travels are effectively captured as the pins inscribe a path across the map and geographically locate each travel experience. Each virtual pin indicates the number of photographs taken and places visited at each destination. Such a capturing of sights is itself a touristic practice (Sontag 1977), although the photographs themselves may depict a travel experience and position the bloggers as travellers. Furthermore, each place mentioned has a corresponding *Facebook* page. In effect, the pins pave the way for tourists in that they are virtual guidebooks that show a potential visitor what to see and do in any given destination. Consequently, the traveller self of Eva Rees who has travelled the globe collapses into a touristic self that promotes certain places and guides future visitors.

Polat and Rees's profiles affirm Goffman's theories on the performance of self in several ways. Zizi Papacharissi suggests that the various applications on *Facebook* 'facilitate multiplicity' and allow users to present 'the many "faces" of one's identity' to a number of different audiences (Papacharissi 2009, p. 212). Certainly, the 'Check-ins' application, which Rees uses but Polat does not, allows Eva Rees to show her audience her traveller face, while the Likes page displays other aspects of self, a number of which have little relevance to the traveller self. The links listed here may be viewed as utterances drawn from a variety of discursive contexts – professional, personal, travel, and tourism – some of which lie in opposition to each other. By contrast, many links on Polat's profile duplicate connections he makes through his blog and display the same self of *foXnoMad* that networks with other travel bloggers. These give a sense of continuity to his narrative of the online self. Both profiles present a self that is networked and associated with travel but do so in different ways. Ultimately, this validates Trevor Pinch's conclusion, also based on Goffman's theories, that the same technology can be used differently as a self-presentational tool. Nonetheless, regardless of the technique used, the same tensions between travel and tourism appear on *Facebook*.

Connections in the **Facebook** *page*

Although the previously cited analyses of social networking sites focus on profiles rather than pages, many of their findings are equally applicable to the pages created by these bloggers (boyd and Ellison 2008; Donath and boyd 2004). As with profiles, authors of *Facebook* pages can display links to other users and so describe themselves through their circle of associations. In addition, a page shares a number of features with a profile – a Timeline, an 'About' page, photo galleries, and a list of Likes that displays an individual's interests by means of links to other *Facebook* pages. However, while a *Facebook* page indicates the number of people who like it, it does not show who these individuals are. Generally speaking, *Facebook* pages tend to be less personal than profiles. Connections to individuals via a profile are easily displayed, whereas most users who like a *Facebook* remain anonymous to other visitors unless they choose to post messages on the Timeline. Anyone can 'like' a page, but individuals must have a blogger's approval to be listed as a 'Friend' on his or her profile. Consequently, there is more anonymity and perhaps less intimacy in the interaction that takes place between a blogger and visitors to the *Facebook* page. Employing a *Facebook* page instead of a personal profile is a self-presentational strategy that has something in common with the promotion of tourism. A number of tourism organisations, including publishers such as *Lonely Planet*, use *Facebook* pages rather than profiles as promotional tools. Nevertheless, a *Facebook* page can be very effective in promoting the blog as a narrative of travel experiences and enhancing the author's position as a traveller.

Most independent travel blogs in this study, including *Traveling Savage*, *Hole in the Donut Cultural Travel*, *Legal Nomads*, *Nomadic Matt*, and *A Wandering Sole*, link to *Facebook* pages by the same titles (Ettenberg 2016b; Walker 2016b; Weibel 2016c; Nomadic Matt 2016b; Savage 2016b). The repetition of each blog's title in their corresponding *Facebook* pages lends continuity to the narrative of travel experiences begun in these blogs and signals that the authors remain in character, as independent travel bloggers. Gérard Genette's theory of the connotative value of titles based on phrases from other texts suggests that this naming technique allows the two texts to support each other (Genette 1997, p. 91). Certainly, for visitors who are familiar with the blog, using the same title on *Facebook* provides a context for the page, reaffirms the travel theme, and indicates the distributed nature of the blog. All the same, linking to profiles focuses on the self as travel blogger, while linking to pages shifts audience attention to the narrative within the blog. A profile bearing the author's real name can convey the impression that the text is more private, the discourse more personal, and that a different aspect to the author is being revealed. By contrast, a blog-titled page is less intimate and distances authors from their audiences. Bloggers such as Barbara Weibel of *Hole in the Donut Cultural Travel* and Jodi Ettenberg of *Legal Nomads* have *Facebook* pages to which their blogs link, as well as personal profiles under their own names. However, both authors choose to link their blogs to pages rather than their profiles. In Ettenberg's case, for example, her 'Legal Nomads' page on *Facebook* displays a public self as travel blogger to a large audience, while her personal profile has little public information and presents a private Ettenberg accessible only to those she accepts as a Friend. In general, therefore, pages place emphasis on the blog rather than the blogger.

Although connections on social networking sites are often based on an individual's offline social networks, the 'friends' linked to via these sites are not necessarily personal acquaintances of the author (boyd 2006; boyd and Ellison 2008). This is especially true of *Facebook* pages due to the nature of the technology. A *Facebook* page lists users instead of Friends. Furthermore, anyone may click on the Like button of a page and receive notifications about updates to content, whereas becoming a Friend on a profile requires an author's approval. Authors of *Facebook* profiles can, if they choose, make their Friends list publicly visible but the author of a *Facebook* page cannot similarly make its users known to others. Consequently, a blogger such as Anil Polat, who opts for a profile, has more control over connections made to other people and can use 'friendship links' to independent travel bloggers as 'identity markers', to quote boyd and Ellison, to present the travel aspect of his personality (2008, p. 220).

As *Facebook* pages do not have a similar list feature, this poses some challenges for authors wishing to express their affiliations and aspects of their personality via links to other people. For example, 'Hole in the Donut Travels', the *Facebook* page for *Hole in the Donut Cultural Travel*, listed 6,740 users at the time of writing (Weibel 2016c). Visitors to the blog itself will see a portion of the *Facebook* page embedded there, displaying links to just six user profiles below this number (Weibel 2016a). Visitors to the *Facebook* page will be able to view the names of those who post comments on the Timeline. Not all bloggers choose to embed their *Facebook* page on their blogs in this manner. However, for those who do, this is a useful means of displaying one's connections. There has been research to suggest that the number of friends indicated on a profile can influence a visitor's impression of the author (Utz 2010). It is possible that indicating the number of *Facebook* users similarly facilitates Weibel's presentation of a well-networked self to readers of her blog.

Bloggers who use *Facebook* pages can, however, articulate the self as travel blogger by indicating their interests via the 'Liked by this Page' feature to establish 'face', as Papacharissi puts it. The 'Hole in the Donut Travels' page links to the pages for *foXnoMad* and *A Wandering Sole* on *Facebook*. These links enable Weibel to express her affiliation with the travel blogging community, a point that is driven home by links to pages for *BootsnAll* as well as *Bloglovin'*. Her interest in travel-related issues is also made clear through links to *Facebook* pages for *Lonely Planet* and *Travel + Leisure* magazine as well as various other publications, travel agencies, and hotels such as the Marriott. These links associate her blog with a larger body of discourse on themes related to travel as well as tourism, supporting two aspects of Weibel's self: the traveller and the writer for magazines that promote tourism. In the process, they also reaffirm the discursive tensions present in her blog. On the one hand, connection with other bloggers' *Facebook* pages demonstrates her affinity with like-minded individuals and listing travel-themed *Facebook* pages reinforces her position as a traveller and the theme of travel in her blog narrative. On the other hand, while links to boutique hotels and tour operators have touristic associations that contrast this travel theme, they strengthen Weibel's position as an authority on travel, capable of judging and filtering the best travel-related resources for her readers. This is similar to the discursive tensions in Weibel's travel blog, where she links to advertisements for travel-related services as well as independent travel blogs.

Talking on the Timeline

By far the best means of displaying connections to other individuals – and therefore, showing the self as networking with others – is via *Facebook*'s Timeline, formerly known as the Wall, an application seen on both pages and profiles. This feature allows both authors and visitors to create and display content on their page or profile. Author-generated content usually consists of comments, links, photographs, and responses to messages posted by visitors. Visitors may post questions, reply to statements from the author, or indicate that they Like something on the page or profile. It may be argued that authors have little control over what others say and cannot use such content to support or maintain the positions that their online self occupies. Nevertheless, both author- and user-generated content have been the focus of academic interest and there is some indication that the conversations and connections that occur via such features give a reliable impression of the individual authoring the page or profile (boyd 2006; Utz 2010; Walther *et al.* 2008). Basically, an individual can use the Timeline to engage with audiences and so emphasise narratorial positions and themes described in their blogs.

In the *Facebook* pages of these travel bloggers, this generally takes the form of announcements of travel plans, questions about travel-related issues directed at readers, or requests for advice. Nomadic Matt often posts questions and updates on his Timeline and invites readers to respond:

> **Nomadic Matt**
>
> 3 November 2010
>
> If you could travel with one person (real or imaginary), who would it be? I'd go with Anthony Bourdain.
>
> (Nomadic Matt 2016b)

and

> **Nomadic Matt**
>
> 19 October 2010
>
> is going to Australia today for the next two weeks. I'm going back to Perth after 3 years and going up towards Broome. Very excited to see Western Australia. It's the best part! Where does your next trip take you?
>
> (Nomadic Matt 2016b)

These questions and remarks sustain the travel discourse in *Nomadic Matt* and cement his position as a traveller as stated in his blog. The questions are intended to start a conversation related to travel. Nomadic Matt adopts a reflective tone while sharing personal thoughts, and his comments are utterances are drawn from a travel context. For example, mentioning Anthony Bourdain implies a connection between the author and the television travel show host. Bourdain's television show on the Travel Channel is called *No Reservations*, and the celebrity chef blogged about travel on the show's website. For an audience familiar with the contexts of the name, the association with Bourdain validates Nomadic Matt's own position as a traveller and blogger. Even the name of the television show draws on the concept of independent or adventurous travel, rather than tourism. A discerning reader may find a resonance in being 'Nomadic' and travelling with '*No Reservations*'.

While questions such as these may be meant to invite responses in a similar vein, they can attract unanticipated comments. Some simply indicate that they 'like' the post. Others reply with suggestions of other persons associated with travel such as Richard Branson, Mark Twain, and Ewan McGregor, each of these an utterance that builds on connotations of travel suggested by Bourdain's name and the themes of Nomadic Matt's blog. Still other answers are flippant. Raven Yàw Garcia writes, 'My thoughts exactly. Or Jessica Simpson (For obvious reasons)' (Nomadic Matt 2016b). His response paves the way for similar suggestions.

This is similar to the ego-targeting discussed in the previous chapter. In a subtle tweaking of touristic narrative technique, the author positions the reader as a confidante, but also positions himself as a potential confidante, eager to receive their recommendations. This invitation to engage in conversation positions Nomadic Matt as an individual who is networking with others, a practice that validates and enhances his self-presentation as a genuine blogger. While this is ego-targeting of a sort, it is different in that the reader is invited not to participate in a touristic experience, but instead to speak as an authority on a travel-related matter. There is a subtle manipulation of a discursive style that is touristic to have a conversation about travel. Simultaneously, using the Timeline for this purpose ultimately serves a promotional purpose – to increase the visibility of *Nomadic Matt* where readers may hope to learn more about his upcoming trip.

Another simple technique by which authors promote their blogs is posting a link to the most recent entry on the Timeline. Barbara Weibel's *Facebook* Timeline includes links to her 'New Blog Post' as well as older entries 'From the Archive'. This effectively reminds audiences of her primary and continuing position as a travel blogger. Furthermore, by commenting on entries from other independent travel bloggers on their own Timeline, authors can reiterate their connections to the blogging community and reinforce links made via a blogroll or Links page. Nomadic Matt does this by recommending entries by other bloggers, such as Jodi Ettenberg of *Legal Nomads*:

> **Nomadic Matt**
>
> 25 March 2016
>
> No one can predict what tomorrow will bring. If can't live in fear of the unknown. Awesome article from Legal Nomads!
>
> (Nomadic Matt 2016b)

Similarly, Anil Polat of *foXnoMad* merits a mention by Heather Cowper of *Heather on Her Travels* who writes on her *Facebook* page:

> **Heather on Her Travels**
>
> 31 October 2010
>
> Warning – nervous flyers should not read this article from Anil Polat. But if you have a more pragmatic disposition, you may want to know what to do if the worst happens!
>
> 7 Plane Crash Facts That Could Save Your Life | foXnoMad www.foxnomad.com.
>
> (Cowper 2010)

The recommendation of online content via links is viewed as an essential part of blogging, and is characteristic of filter blogs (Walker Rettberg 2014, p. 20). Readers who are familiar with the practices of blogging may feel that Nomadic Matt and Heather Cowper remain in character as bloggers by sharing links via *Facebook*. As a reflection of a blogger's online interests, the sharing of links has some significance for the presentation of an online self. Furthermore, by linking to other travel blogs, Nomadic Matt and Cowper position themselves within the community of independent travel bloggers and strengthen their affiliations with its members. Through a simple act of networking, they indicate that they too are travel bloggers and this blogging self is networked in both the social and technological senses of the term.

In addition to talking about other travel blogs, authors may also link to websites where their own blog has been mentioned as in this post from Jodi Ettenberg on her *Facebook* page for *Legal Nomads*:

> **Legal Nomads**
>
> 3 November 2010
>
> Wow. Klout's top online travel influencers list came out and I'm listed at number 8. Very flattering! List is updated daily but it's a great start.
>
> (Ettenberg 2016b)

Nomadic Matt's preface to a link for a post on *Buzzfeed* is similar in tone and content:

> Buzzfeed did a great piece on travel blogging this weekend (and even used a photo of my book collection!). There's advice from lots of experts so if you're a travel blogger or want to be a travel blogger, check out this post!
>
> (Nomadic Matt 2016b)

The post itself is titled *Here's How to Become a Successful Travel Blogger*. What really strengthens the position of these authors as experts on travel and as travel bloggers is the one-line article summary that appears with the link itself. This allows Jodi Ettenberg to present herself as one of the 'top online travel influencers' and Nomadic Matt to suggest that he is successful at blogging. The recommendations of others may be viewed as being more credible than any form of self-promotion. Moreover, such references from other websites locate these blogs in a larger body of discourse on issues related to travel or tourism. On the one hand these connections serve to establish these bloggers' credibility and to potentially expand the readership for their blogs. However, the notion of connecting and being seen everywhere online sits at odds with travel's association with experiences that are solitary and off-the-road, so to speak.

Facebook *and photographs*

A travel blogger's *Facebook* page displays several types of photographs: those that are usually sourced from the blog, a profile photograph of the author, a cover photograph that forms a banner across the top of the page, and thumbnail pictures of visitors who post comments on the Timeline. Photographs sourced from the travel blogs generally feature a travel destination and invite readers to read the corresponding blog post, although this is not necessarily always the case. For example, a photograph of a tree-lined street in Argentina is accompanied by a caption that invites readers to read more about budget travel to this destination in *Nomadic Matt*:

> **Nomadic Matt**
>
> 24 March 2016
>
> Argentina doesn't have to be an expensive country to visit! After spending a month there, here are my 10 ways to save money on any visit to this wonderful land of steak, wine, nature, and tango!
>
> (Nomadic Matt 2016b)

A link to the blog appears below this. By presenting links to resources, posts, and pages on the blog, the caption turns the written narrative into an area to be explored and discovered. In previous years, this *Facebook* page also featured a weekly captioned photograph. By and large, both recent and older photographs suggest the kind of solitude, timelessness, and lack of focus on destination that is characteristic of a travel experience. They do not depict easily recognisable tourist icons and could, in fact, have been shot in a number of locations. This lack of emphasis on destination in the image creates an association with travel. Yet, the accompanying descriptions are impersonal, and even authoritative in their exhortation to visit certain sights, experience particular modes of travel, and read the books or guides written by Nomadic Matt. In a caption for an image of Sydney's beaches, Nomadic Matt writes euphorically and somewhat imperatively:

> Bondi Beach in Sydney. What an awesome (albeit busy) beach! So much sand! Be sure to do the Bondi to Coogee costal walk. It takes about 2 hours. Bring lots of sunscreen as it's totally exposed. Along the way, stop at Bronte Beach, which was my favorite of all of them!
>
> (Nomadic Matt 2016b; see Figure 5.3)

Figure 5.3 Screenshot of Bondi Beach post

The narrative style of tourist discourse is thus skilfully turned to the presentation of the blog and the narrative of travel contained therein.

Gary Arndt's travel photographs similarly function as a promotional element for his blog *Everything Everywhere*. Arndt's *Facebook* page is different in that it is named for the author rather than the blog and identifies him as a travel photographer. The focus here is on the individual rather than the narrative and on the roles occupied by Arndt's online self. His photographs of scenes in Ethiopia shot in March 2016 authenticate the travel plans announced via blog posts earlier in the year. These images link either to his travel blog, acting as promotional elements for this narrative or to his album on *Instagram*, extending the networked self to other platforms. Here again, each photograph functions principally as a feature that distributes the content of the blog and serves to reinforce the self as a traveller who explores vistas and locales that are exotic and off the beaten path. At the same time, each photograph testifies to a skill that has been commercialised and supports his professional self as a travel photographer. Furthermore, the capturing of sights is in itself touristic and paves the way for potential tourism to destinations that may not be otherwise viewed as tourist hotspots.

Also prominent is the thumbnail profile photographs of individuals who contribute content to a page, usually in the form of comments responding to posts on the Timeline. There is ample evidence to suggest that such images help an audience form an impression of the profile or page's owner (Donath and boyd 2004; Utz 2010). There is, as Papacharissi points out, a general assumption that it is possible to judge an individual by the company he or she keeps (Papacharissi 2009, p. 210). Viewed from this perspective, the profile pictures of the persons a blogger connects to via *Facebook* become important self-presentational elements, leading researchers such as Sonia Utz to conclude that 'To make a good impression, it is not enough to carefully construct one's profile; it is also wise to carefully select one's *friends*' (Utz 2010, p. 329). Although bloggers have greater control over connections made via a profile rather than a page, it can be argued that both types of connections represent the community they engage. The photographs of those who interact with these bloggers via *Facebook* contributes to their public display of connections and consequently the self they present online.

It is beyond the scope of this study to analyse, as Utz does, exactly how these audiences interpret the images of other users or visitors to a *Facebook* page. As a result, it is difficult to determine to what extent these photographs offer a sense of the different aspects of self a blogger wishes to present. Visitors can be quite diverse and it is very likely that they will update their photographs frequently. A profile picture whose contexts and connotations have little to do with travel can introduce discursive tensions in the text. Yet, at least some of the photographs of visitors to the 'Legal Nomads' *Facebook* page, at the time of writing, resembled Jodi Ettenberg's own profile picture. Resting a cursor over each thumbnail photograph displays a larger profile photo and cover page of the user commenting on the page. Many of the visitors to Ettenberg's page display similar cover pages depicting landscapes and outdoor locations. For example, at the time of writing, paralleling Ettenberg's blurred image of a street strewn with petals is John

Cavendish's cover photograph of a narrow street in Da Lat, visible next to his comments on her eighth-anniversary post (Cavendish 2016). Given that this is content generated by users other than Ettenberg herself, it may be difficult to view these images as a self-presentational element. Here, inadvertently, the thumbnails work to Ettenberg's advantage, forming a display of connections to persons who are travellers, who visit similar destinations, and who have similar travel experiences. Although she does not consciously control the content of these photographs, the images show Ettenberg's affiliation with a community of travellers. Such is the nature of the tool that it can, although not necessarily, enhance the presentation of her position as a traveller and as a travel blogger.

Putting a name to the face

Several studies of social networking sites suggest that profile photographs are an important element in self-presentation and provide valuable clues to the author's personality (boyd and Heer 2006; Ellison *et al.* 2006; Siibak 2009). Indeed, boyd and Heer suggest that photographs are 'the most noticeable component of Profile [sic] identity performance and active users update their photos regularly to convey various things about themselves' (2006, p. 8). This is borne out by Ellison *et al.*'s study of online dating sites (2006) and Siibak's analysis of photograph selection by teenagers on social networking sites (2009), which concludes that profile owners may deliberately select and display images that best represent what they want to say about themselves. Ellison *et al.* also observe that profile photographs can be used to support textual statements and descriptions. Admittedly, these findings are based on analyses of profiles where the self-presentation is directed at very different audiences – potential dates or peers. However, it can be argued that profile photographs may well have a similar function on pages related to travel blogs, and it is worth considering how authors use profile photographs to indicate that they are travellers and bloggers.

Of the two *Facebook* profile owners mentioned here – Anil Polat and Eva Rees – only Rees uses a photograph that hints at her position as a traveller. The photograph shows her posing on against a giant boot, a landmark in south Seattle. The image is touristic in its framing of Rees against what is no doubt an iconic sight that is part of Seattle's history – the boot was once part of a cowboy-themed gas station. Moreover, it provides a link to the self she presents in her travel blog, and is a good contextual clue. By contrast, Polat's photograph shows the author in a domestic setting, holding a bottle of wine. Although this does nothing for Polat's position as a traveller or a technology expert, it fulfils his promise (in the blog) that the profile will offer 'more about me' (Polat 2016c). Ultimately, both profile photographs support aspects of the self these individuals reveal in their travel blogs. It should be said, however, that this may change each time these bloggers update their images.

By and large, profile photographs on *Facebook* pages reinforce the title and themes of the blog. Sometimes, this is achieved by using graphic elements from the travel blog in place of a picture of its author. The *Facebook* page for *Traveling Savage* displays the same packing crate and bottle of whisky that features on the blog's banner, while the author's photograph is placed prominently as a cover photo. In this instance, the profile photograph does not identify Keith Savage, the author, but it functions effectively as a link to his blog and provides a context for his *Facebook* page. Barbara Weibel of *Hole in the Donut Cultural Travel* uses the same photograph of herself on both her blog as well as her *Facebook* page, clearly implying that the same self is networked across the two texts (Weibel 2016c). Similarly, the green silhouette of a backpacker that features in Nomadic Matt's profile photograph on *Facebook* also marches across the top of his blog's home page (Nomadic Matt 2016b). This does not necessarily mean that all *Facebook* pages will have a photograph with a clearly defined link to the corresponding travel blog. In general, however, photographs of both *Facebook* profiles and pages create a connection with the contexts, positions, and self that are presented in the blog.

Although the features and applications of *Facebook* pages and profiles are used in different ways, they share a common purpose: to distribute the blog and present a networked self. Both pages and profiles allow for a deeper audience engagement, although the level of intimacy varies between pages and profiles and between profiles. Both pages and profiles allow for a display of connections with individuals and online resources, both of which function as a self-presentational strategy for reiterating positions that these authors occupy in their blogs. That said, the tensions between travel and tourism on pages and profiles play out variously. Some bloggers manipulate narrative techniques associated with the promotion of place to the promotion of their blogs as an online destination that offers a travel experience. In other instances, the connection to online resources related to tourism creates a commercial association that nevertheless serves to validate the author's position as an authority on travel and a discerning consumer. Similarly, while authors reiterate connections with other travel bloggers, they also engage audiences in conversation using techniques similar to those used by tourism organisations such as *Lonely Planet*. As a consequence, the presentation of the self as networked and networking with others requires a negotiation of the discourses of both travel and tourism.

To tweet is to travel

Microblogging platforms such as *Twitter* are often defined against blogging as a form of communication characterised by brief blog-like posts or updates published on the Web via a computer or mobile media (Java *et al.* 2007; Oulasvirta *et al.* 2010). The posts are generally self-presentational in nature because the messages work in two ways:

> (1) through creation of the sender's persona in the eyes of others similar to Goffman's' notion of self-presentation…or at least keeping him or her "alive" as a poster who is interesting enough to be followed, and, secondly, (2) via the deepening interest followers find in his or her life.
>
> (Oulasvirta *et al.* 2010, p. 248)

The underlying implication is that individuals may use *Twitter* posts to 'create' the self as a blogger who plays the role of a traveller, travel guide, or tourist, as the case may be. Second, by posting frequently, an individual who uses *Twitter* to re-present his positions occupied in the travel blog can keep the same 'alive' for readers. Understanding how travel bloggers achieve this using *Twitter* requires an examination of how conventions and techniques such as 'retweeting' a message, using the '#' or hashtags, and the '@'or at signs to start a conversation, ultimately figure in the presentation of self as a travel blogger or in the distribution of the content of the travel blog.

There are a number of parallels between the content and narrative style of the post and other forms of travel-related discourse such as holiday postcards and travel books. *Twitter* allows users to include links to multimedia. Consequently, as in postcards, a message may be accompanied by a photograph which can be viewed within the *Twitter* page. Chris Kennedy's examination (Kennedy 2005) of the discursive features of messages on holiday postcards indicates that they have much in common with tweets with respect to content, function, and narrative technique. These include a lack of detail regarding destinations, the description of everyday activities, and the overall brevity and public nature of the message. This supports Oulasvirtas *et al.*'s findings, based on a study of messages on microblogging service *Jaiku*, which describes the distinguishing characteristics of microblogs posts as 'I-centred' content, the 'mundane… reporting of ordinary, predictable, and repetitive life events,' and 'an illusion of real-time connection' (2010, p. 238). The sense that a travel experience is occurring in the present time or is timeless is also typical of travel books where, according to Graham Dann:

> [The] traveller/travel writer is to present what tourist is to past and future.… it is in the act of promotion that tourist becomes cast into the past tense...the travel writer's account is often framed as if actually taking place in the eternal "now."
>
> (1999, p. 169)

This suggests the discursive style of microblogging – self-centred, focused on routine activities, and creating the sense of a real-time connection – suits the narration of travel.

Despite this implication that *Twitter* is best suited for a networking and presentation of a traveller self, this chapter demonstrates how certain conventions of *Twitter* as used by travel bloggers can, in fact, incorporate tourist discourse. To this end, it analyses the content and style of *Twitter* posts, considering in particular references to the travel blog, the author as blogger, and the narration of the travel experience. Following is a discussion of how titles, formal features such as profile pictures, user names, and links, and the conventions of *Twitter* messages are relevant to self-presentation. As with *Facebook*, links to other people and online content reiterate themes and connections of the travel blog but also introduce a touristic element in the narrative. Ultimately, the networked self of the travel blogger and the dispersed content of the blog are negotiated in the discursive tensions between travel and tourism as seen on their *Twitter* pages.

Titles and profiles on Twitter

As with *Facebook*, the link to *Twitter* is often indicated by a widget on the blog – a style used in travel blogs such as *A Wandering Sole*, *Traveling Savage*, and *Legal Nomads*. The clearly visible *Twitter* logo enhances the impression of a travel blogger as networked and of the travel blog as having distributed content. The button also demonstrates brand affiliation, in the same manner as a *Facebook* button. Bloggers reap the benefits of being seen as tech savvy and having an affinity with other users, especially if they choose, like Laura Walker of *A Wandering Sole*, to go a step further and embed their *Twitter* stream in the home page of their travel blog. This strategy enables her to indicate that she is in the process of networking with others. While some of the tweets displayed are posts by Walker, there are also a number of retweets, messages posted by others that Walker has shared via her own *Twitter* page (Walker 2016a). The resulting display of connections allows Walker to position herself as a blogger who is networked and also networking with others. Moreover, this strategy is self-presentational in that it enables Walker to indicate an association with a community on *Twitter* that shares her interests. It also suggests that, at least for Laura Walker, displaying a connection to *Twitter* and presenting herself as a *Twitter* user is integral to the presentation of the self as travel blogger.

Twitter allows its users to display both a personal name and a user name on their pages. This personal name forms the page title, followed by the user name in the format personal name @user name. In general, the independent travel bloggers in this study adapt this feature to create several title styles ranging from impersonal and blog-oriented to personal and self-oriented. Nomadic Matt of *Nomadic Matt* and Eva and Jeremy Rees of *Forks and Jets* use their blog title as a personal name and as a username. The resulting titles read Nomadic Matt @nomadicmatt, or Forks and Jets @ForksandJets respectively (Nomadic Matt 2016a; Rees and Rees 2016). The style is remarkably similar to that employed by commercial tourism organisations to emphasise corporate identity on their own *Twitter* pages. Guidebook publisher *Lonely Planet*, for example, is Lonely Planet @lonelyplanet on *Twitter* (*Lonely Planet* 2016). While a repetition of the blog title clearly identifies the context of the messages and keeps the blog alive for any visitor, for an audience familiar with this and similar *Twitter* pages such as Frommer's @ Frommers, or Virgin Atlantic @VirginAtlantic, the title creates an association with commercial tourist discourse. In increasing the visibility of their blogs, these authors ultimately engage in a narrative style that is touristic, while the presentation of self as a travel blogger becomes secondary.

Most other independent travel bloggers in this study use their personal names as their *Twitter* titles, followed by the name of their blog as a user name. Titles such as Laura @awanderingsole, Jodi Ettenberg @legalnomads, Keith Savage @ travelingsavage, or Anil @foxnomad give prominence to the authors, but also contextualise the page and call attention to their position as travel bloggers (Ettenberg 2016a; Polat 2016a; Savage 2016a; Walker 2016a). This technique neatly locates the page within the extended narrative of the travel blog. However, titles may focus solely on the author as an individual, as is the case with Heather Cowper @ heathercowper, the travel blogger who writes *Heather on Her Travels*. While this style is more personal, suggesting an intimacy suited to the discourses of travel, it does not appear to be popular with the bloggers discussed here. Indicating that the *Twitter* page is an extension of the blog narrative is a paramount concern.

Profile descriptions often refer to an individual's travel blogger role, recapture themes of the blog, and end with a link to the blog. Barbara Weibel, for example, 'Ran away from corporate life to be a travel writer [and] photographer' (Weibel 2016b). Likewise, Anil Polat (2016a) is a 'Digital nomad traveling the world indefinitely' while Jodi Ettenberg (Ettenberg 2016a) is a 'Former lawyer from Montreal now telling stories through food on the award-winning Legal Nomads' – terms that reflect the titles and profile descriptions of their blogs *FoXnoMad* and *Legal Nomads*, respectively. Both Weibel and Ettenberg refer to an escape from routine and secure jobs and describe themselves as writers, creating an association with experiences of travel that reiterate themes of their blogs. Polat's presentation of himself as a 'digital nomad' (2016a) is particularly significant for its reference to travel as nomadic, or in other words, timeless and not bound to destinations of a tourist itinerary. By calling himself a digital nomad, he clearly draws on the contexts of travel, and indicates that he is a traveller. Yet, the same term also implies that this self is also nomadic in a 'digital' sense – not limited to the travel blog, but extended or 'networked' across various digital platforms. He travels 'indefinitely' not just in the offline world, but online as well.

In general, independent travel bloggers use the same photograph on their *Twitter* pages and blog profiles. The effect of this technique is twofold. It extends the self as travel blogger to another platform and keeps it alive for the audience. In addition to this, it signals a discursive style that is personal and consequently, more in the context of travel than tourism. Keith Savage's *Twitter* profile photograph, for example, is identical to the one he uses in *Traveling Savage*, thus sustaining the self as travel blogger. Those who do not use a personal photograph – and there are few such users in the sample selected for this study – may use visual elements from their blog. *Forks and Jets* authors Eva and Jeremy Rees do not have a photograph of themselves but instead use a logo based on their initials 'EJ' in a font that is identical to the one in their blog title. The 'EJ' logo also appears as a URL icon or favicon in the blog. The 'Forks and Jets' page is impersonal in its reiteration of the blog's title, and the sparse description that identifies the authors merely as 'a couple of amateur foodie traveloguers' (Rees and Rees 2016). Having a logo rather than a personal photograph can seem touristic, when seen in the context of tourism-related pages such as guidebook publishers Lonely Planet and Frommer's or even Virgin Atlantic that use similar visual elements on their *Twitter* web pages. Yet, the allusion to Eva and Jeremy Rees, indicated in the initials that make up the logo, personalises a touristic style of presentation and refers, however obliquely, to the self as travel blogger.

Figure 5.4 Screenshot of Nomadic Matt's *Twitter* page

Another alternative to using a personal photograph is to have an image that reflects the themes of the blog. Nomadic Matt's *Twitter* profile picture depicts Uncle Traveling Matt, a character from the television show *Fraggle Rock*, who sends postcards and tells stories of his travels (Figure 5.4). Nomadic Matt explains that he first chose this image as a joke; it has since 'sort of become how people recognize me' (Nomadic Matt 2016c). The resemblance of names makes the Uncle Travelling Matt avatar an ideal choice as a profile photograph. Moreover, the connotations of the character's name act in the same manner as Gérard Genette's 'pseudonym effect' (Genette 1997, pp. 48–50). Genette suggests that a name may be chosen deliberately, with an eye to its meaning and contexts, in the hope that a reader will recognise the connotations and contexts it is associated with. This induces an effect in the reader's mind and influences his or her idea of the author and the work itself (Genette 1997, pp. 48–50). This holds true for the image of Uncle Traveling Matt. As an adventurous explorer, Uncle Matt is associated with travel rather than tourism. As a teller of stories, he symbolises the narration of travel. Thus by referring to Uncle Travelling Matt, the author skilfully uses the contexts and connotations of the image to present the self as travel blogger without resorting to using a personal photograph.

Another simple way of extending the themes of the blog is to use the same visual elements on both the blog and its corresponding *Twitter* page, which generally permits some customisation of its background. The same donut with the world map as its icing that features in *Hole in the Donut Cultural Travel* appears in banner across the blog's corresponding *Twitter* page, as does Barbara Weibel's profile photograph. This indicates the distributed nature of the blog, provides a context for the audience, and implies that the same self as travel blogger is networked across these platforms. However, not all bloggers who use *Twitter* pages achieve such uniformity of theme. Anil Polat's page on *Twitter* indicates a connection with the blog, but displays a different profile photograph of the blogger. The content of the tweets and the link to *foXnoMad* give a sense of the page as a travel-related text, but the connection to the blog is not as obvious as in Weibel's page, as it does not share visual elements with the blog itself.

Connections, conventions, and conversations @ Twitter

Twitter users connect with each other in several ways. Individuals may link to others on the platform and 'follow' them. They may, in turn, have 'followers'. Users can use the '@' symbol to engage others in conversation (Gilpin 2010; Honeycutt and Herring 2009). They may also 'retweet' information or comments from other users (boyd *et al.* 2010). One popular convention is to use the hashtag '#' followed by a specific key word to start, contribute to, or follow a conversation surrounding a particular topic (Zhou *et al.* 2010). The bloggers studied here also employ technical features such as lists and conventions such as @, @user name, RT @user name, and hashtags to connect with others and present various aspects of their online self through the networking that takes place in these connections and conversations.

Each *Twitter* page displays the number of persons its author follows and is following. However, the follower count on *Twitter* is a poor indicator of how interesting or popular an independent travel blogger is. Nomadic Matt had 98,846 *Twitter* followers at the time of writing and Gary Arndt's *Twitter* page displayed 160,275 followers. While this may seem impressive to some visitors, others may be aware that some of these followers may in fact be web bots or spiders gathering data about certain topics (Teutle 2010). Evidently, the number of followers is a poor self-presentational element. However, a person may follow any number of users, and this allows an individual to display interests and affiliations within the *Twitter* community through the use of a number of different strategies (boyd *et al.* 2010).

One feature that is useful for doing this is the Lists function on *Twitter,* used to good effect by travel blogger and photographer Gary Arndt of *Everything Everywhere* and Jodi Ettenberg of *Legal Nomads.* Both bloggers categorise the users they follow using travel-related themes that reflect those of their blogs and support their profile descriptions. For example, Ettenberg's lists of gluten-free cuisine and legal resources attests to her position as a former lawyer with an interest in foods that are coeliac-friendly who is now, according to her *Twitter* profile, 'telling stories through food' (Ettenberg 2016a). On Arndt's *Twitter* page this includes lists of hotels, official tourism organisations, photography, and other travel bloggers. Interestingly, 'A comprehensive list of travel bloggers/podcasters on Twitter' is differentiated from 'People involved in travel related public relations and marketing' (Arndt 2010b). This implies that, in Arndt's eyes at least, the discourse of travel bloggers is distinct from the discourses of tourism marketing or public relations. The bloggers list also supports Arndt's position as a travel blogger and places him in a network of similar authors. The second list positions him as an authority on the best online resources on travel and tourism.

Dawn R. Gilpin (2010) argues that follower counts on *Twitter* are not as significant as the connections displayed when users communicate with each other. Conversations and interactions that take place on *Twitter* are essential to 'identity construction' (Gilpin 2010, pp. 233–234). Most *Twitter* conversations are prefaced by the @ symbol and user name, and this is displayed in each message (Honeycutt and Herring 2009). As a result, by simply addressing comments to other bloggers, an individual can indicate an association with the travel blogging community on *Twitter*. Take, for example, this exchange between Nomadic Matt and another travel blogger, Backpacking Matt:

> backpackingmatt @Matt Kyhnn 17 Nov 2010
>
> Found a bungalow in Koh Phi Phi just in time for the clear blue skies to turn into a proper monsoon
>
> nomadicmatt @Nomadic Matt 17 Nov 2010
>
> @backpackingmatt weren't u just in Bali?
>
> (Nomadic Matt 2016a)

Although the tweets are in a travel context, they can hardly be regarded as distributing the content of the travel blog. However, the user names (identical to blog titles or pseudonyms) clearly identify this as a conversation between two bloggers for anyone familiar with the travel blogging community. If the audience does not recognise the authors' user names, clicking on the message displays a description of Backpackingmatt as a 'Travel blogger exploring the world' (Kyhnn 2016), which clearly indicates Nomadic Matt's affiliation with the travel blogging community.

It should be noted here that this conversation is only visible to those who visit the *Twitter* pages of these bloggers and click on the post itself to expand it. Such is the nature of the technology that a person who follows either only Nomadic Matt or Matthew Kyhnn will not see any conversation between them that begins with the @username syntax on his or her (the follower's) own page. However, a travel blogger can deliberately make such conversations more easily visible to their audience and so display the connection with similar authors by using a different narrative technique that places the @username later in the message, as Keith Savage does in this post from 5 December 2010, where he writes, 'Having a brainstorm session with @globetrooper and @thefutureisred in #Argentina' (Savage 2016a). The tweet works as a self-presentational element by showing Savage as networking with other travel bloggers (both offline and on *Twitter*) and validating his position as a traveller through the mention of Argentina. The hashtag is also significant, and this will be examined in greater detail presently.

Bloggers often use the RT @user syntax or simply click on a button to retweet a message from another user. They may retweet a post to attract attention, indicate loyalty, or to publicly agree with someone or validate their thoughts (boyd *et al.*

2010). As the source of the retweet is usually easily visible, regardless of narrative technique, authors can indicate engagement with other travel bloggers, gain attention for themselves, show support for this community of travellers, and so remind visitors that they are travel bloggers and that they occupy particular roles online. For example, Gary Arndt's retweet on 25 November 2010 of Jodi Ettenberg's post, 'RT @legalnomads: New post: an afternoon in Paris' Montmartre http://su.pr/1DsMRu #travel #lp,' identifies the context of this conversation as travel blogging and shows his connection with another travel blogger (Arndt 2010a). He further strengthens his ties with this community by promoting Ettenberg's new blog post, indicated in the link. In this case, the "#travel" and the mention of Paris also emphasises the travel theme. Retweeting a retweeted message also enhances presentation of a networked self via a display of several connections, especially if the original author's name is retained.

When bloggers #travel

Hashtags are used in *Twitter* messages to engage in a more public conversation on a particular topic. The hyperlinked keyword used with the hashtag indicates the topic of the tweet and links to a public listing of all *Twitter* messages on the same subject. Therefore, hashtags related to travel or blogging can link a user to a public conversation around these themes and may be used to present the self as an independent travel blogger. Jodi Ettenberg's message on her new post, mentioned as a retweet by Gary Arndt, uses #travel with the link to her blog post in a clear indication of its themes and to join the larger conversation on *Twitter* surrounding issues related to travel (Arndt 2010a; Ettenberg 2016a). For Arndt, retweeting a message containing this hashtag allows him to capitalise on the visibility this offers and direct potential visitors to his own blog. The #Argentina used by Keith Savage fulfils a similar purpose. It disseminates the tweet to a large and unknown audience interested in Argentina, beyond the one consisting of his followers. In this sense, the message that is personal in its mention of fellow bloggers also takes on a touristic quality in addressing a largely unknown audience to promote the blog and its author.

Guidebook publisher *Lonely Planet* encourages visitors to its *Twitter* page to use the #lp in any post they would like to have retweeted. Jodi Ettenberg, whose blog is listed in the publisher's *Pathfinder* page, uses this hashtag extensively to promote her blog posts. In using #lp, Ettenberg associates herself with the touristic discourse represented by *Lonely Planet*, relying on the brand name to validate her message and promote her blog. She also uses #MatadorN, creating an association with Matador Network, an independent travel media organisation to much the same effect. The #lp, in particular, associates her tweets with a brand name whose touristic contexts of guidebook-directed sightseeing are quite different from the 'nomadic' style of travel suggested by *Legal Nomads.* Conversely, the #lp allows *Lonely Planet* to curate and provide access to a large amount of travel-related content created by travel bloggers. This has implications for self-presentation – *Lonely Planet* positions itself as an arbiter of taste, picking out content that is genuine and proving itself capable of recognising the unique and extraordinary, that is to say what is travel-like, in destinations that have become clichéd or touristic. By retweeting Ettenberg's posts, the company manipulates the content of a personal message – in this case the link to the *Legal Nomads* – and draws on the reputation of the bloggers to enhance its own brand image. At the same time it potentially sells travel-related products and services, and thus paves the way for tourism to the places described therein. This is by no means a one-sided relationship; such recognition from *Lonely Planet* reinforces Ettenberg's position as an expert on travel.

It is not uncommon for marketers to manipulate trending topics for their own purposes. In their study of *Twitter* use during the 2009 Iranian elections, Zhou *et al.* (2010) observed that spammers used #IranElection to advertise their own websites. Similarly, many posts using #travelblog are generated by commercial entities such as Destination Canada, Gap Year Travel Store and Dook Travels. Although #travelblog seems to be the obvious choice as a self-presentational element, it was in fact rarely used by travel bloggers at the time of writing. However, there was some use of #travelblogger in combination with #travel, suggesting that at least some bloggers are keen to avoid #travelblog's association with commercial tourist discourse but nevertheless highlight their blogging activities. This validates the observation that, while 'many marketers wish to be in conversation with their consumers, not all consumers are looking to be in conversation with marketers' (boyd *et al.* 2010). Ironically, it is in *not* using #travelblog that these authors refer to their narratives and network these across *Twitter*. At present, it seems unlikely that this hashtag will prove useful in distributing the content of travel blogs.

Linking to the blog is perhaps the most straightforward technique for presenting the self as travel blogger and increasing the visibility of the blog via a post. In the period between July and November 2010, Eva and Jeremy Rees had three tweets, all of which distributed the content of their travel blog:

> ForksandJets @Forks and Jets 3 Aug 2010
>
> Team Rees puts their beer caps on in Colorado http://bit.ly/aL9ydJ new on www.forksandjets.com
>
> ForksandJets @Forks and Jets 28 Jul 2010
>
> Some thoughts about moving to Denver, CO http://bit.ly/b7mKj2 on www.forksandjets.com
>
> ForksandJets @Forks and Jets 22 Jul 2010
>
> Is British food boring and gray? http://bit.ly/cm2CCv Team Rees Investigates on forksandjets.com.
>
> (Rees and Rees 2016)

It is possible that there were other posts during this period that were later deleted. Even so, it is significant that the Reeses use tweets to present themselves as bloggers, and point audiences to their travel blog.

There are a number of other lesser used strategies for indicating the travel theme. Tweets may also link to content on travel-related websites and while these do not necessarily refer to the blog or the author as travel blogger, they are valuable contextual clues. Authors may also share links that are not travel-related or blog-related, thus revealing personal interests and aspects of self that have no relevance to the travel blog as in this tweet from Jodi Ettenberg on 7 December 2010: 'The neuroscience of magic: http://bit.ly/fQfpPH' (2016a).

Twitter and the discourse of travel

There are a number of striking similarities in the discursive style of tweets and travel discourse, bearing out Nancy Baym's observation that online language blends narrative techniques and formats drawn from other narrative forms and media. Microblog posts are often self-centred, describe daily activities and personal experiences, and are generally written in the present tense (Honeycutt and Herring 2009; Oulasvirta *et al.* 2010). To that extent, they employ the same narrative techniques as travel writing, which is also personal, focused on experience rather than destination, and written as if happening in the present. This is certainly the case with at least some of the posts from independent travel bloggers who use *Twitter* to provide updates about their journey.

Often, as is the case with travel discourse, the tweet focuses on the experience rather than the destination itself. For instance, when Jodi Ettenberg tweets about her trip to Milan on 25 November 2010, she describes how she is, 'Eating roasted chestnuts after climbing the Duomo and soon running off to my meetings. Trying to make the most of my 1 day in Milan' (Ettenberg 2016a). Similarly, Nomadic Matt also tweets on 14 April 2016 that he is 'About to fly @united for the first time in 2 yrs. Not looking forward to 5 hours on a plane w/o power/tv/wifi. Crap compared to AA or Delta' (Nomadic Matt 2016a). Each tweet describes personal experience and is written in the present tense. If Ettenberg mentions her destination, she does not quite describe it. The activity of eating chestnuts takes precedence over the place she is in. The assertion that she is making the most of her trip implies a need to experience travel. Still, the fleeting nature of a day trip suggests a touristic superficiality. Meanwhile, Nomadic Matt highlights the discomforts of his upcoming flight – a theme that is characteristic of a travel experience rather than a touristic one. While he suggests that the journey is arduous, the fact that this hardship results from a lack of access to the Internet while in an aeroplane indicates a need for connectivity with the world that is at odds with the rootlessness implied by being a nomadic traveller. Thus, while using various digital platforms allows him to keep the traveller alive for his audience, it also detracts from the idea of real travel as something of an escape.

There is also much in common between the travel-related tweet and the holiday postcard. Chris Kennedy finds that holiday postcards are generally used as a 'relational' device, meant to strengthen ties between people (2005, p. 228). Messages are usually written without much thought or planning and are essentially public, as anyone may read them. Content is usually general and lacking in detail, with locations mentioned but not described. Noting that the messages usually describe activities, accommodation, or personal physical appearance, Kennedy concludes that the language is generally positive and uses general terms. Although this research is based on a narrow sample, it is hard to ignore the resemblances. A message on *Twitter* is probably as unplanned and is definitely public. The conversations and connections made via *Twitter* clearly indicate the relational aspect of travel bloggers' tweets. In addition to this, the content of the messages is mundane and general in nature.

The postcard-like nature of the message is reflected in Barbara Weibel's tweet on a visit to Thailand on 15 April 2016: 'Laundry day for monk robes at Wat Phan Tao #ChiangMai, #Thailand ow.ly/ZSqTh' (Weibel 2016b). As with the postcard, the tweet presents an exotic scene. The hashtags locate the accompanying image of orange robes draped on clothes lines, functioning much like a postcard caption. Nevertheless, the post offers little comment on the destination, and unlike postcards, this image does not depict an easily recognisable tourist icon but instead displays a mundane activity that could have taken place in a number of other Asian destinations. The tweet and its accompanying image take viewers off the beaten path and show them something different and unique. In so doing, they position Weibel as a traveller who seeks the unrecognisable and the unexplored. The tweet effectively fulfils two functions. First, this exemplifies how authors can manipulate familiar genres to a new form of communication. Second, it indicates how such changes can be self-presentational strategies. Tweets with links to travel-related photographs enhance the traveller position presented by authors in their blogs. At the same time, the hashtags locate the image and the post within a public conversation on *Twitter* about this destination. The solitary travel experience suggested by the image consequently becomes a part of multitude of other messages and images and becomes both familiar and available to a global audience in a manner that is touristic.

Some travel tweets resemble postcard messages in their use of positive language to describe travel experiences. Nomadic Matt enthusiastically tweets of a visit to Bangkok on 19 November 2010, 'BKK is a city you grow to love. There's a ton of great areas in it. It's not a tourist city' (Nomadic Matt 2016a). Even the word 'not' is used in a positive context, highlighting that this is a traveller's destination in being 'not a tourist city' (Nomadic Matt 2016a). Yet, there is also a touch of tourist discourse in the euphoric description of 'a ton of great areas' (Nomadic Matt 2016a). Keith Savage is similarly positive when he tweets of a visit to Scotland on 1 December 2010, 'Have you tried the fish and chips at the Pierowall Hotel in Westray, Orkney? Amazing!' @soultravelers3 @WanderingEds (Savage 2016a). While the relative obscurity of the destination suggests travel rather than tourism, the focus on place and the euphoric exclamation is more suited to promotional tourist discourse. Simultaneously, by hailing fellow travellers, Savage effectively indicates his own position as a traveller. The tweet is both a personal communication between travellers, which effectively indicates Savage's own position online, as well as a touristic endorsement of the hotel in question. The resulting description of the experience is situated in discourses of both travel and tourism.

The networked self of the travel blogger

Central to the argument in this chapter is the idea that the self as travel blogger is networked across multiple online platforms. Each of these tools comes with its own set of affordances that travel bloggers use in various ways to distribute their blogs. This mainly involves making careful choices and controlling the information publicly displayed to audiences. In general, the display of connections to other travel bloggers presents these bloggers as networked and networking with others. At the same time, these connections allow a blogger to indicate their affiliations and interests and, through these, the different roles their online selves occupy. The staging of a blogger's self-presentation is, to a large extent, determined by the how far the affordances of a platform facilitate the display of these connections.

Needless to say, various narrative strategies employed by bloggers who use these platforms are central to and determine the presentation of an online self and distribute the blog. However, it is sometimes the case that the presentation of the blogging self occurs at the expense of the promotion of the narrative. Quite often, a decision that emphasises themes and content of the blog detracts from a sense of the author as travel blogger and vice versa. For example, 'Forks and Jets' on *Twitter* clearly is an extension of the blog narrative, but cannot be said to network the bloggers. Authors such as Anil Polat appear to manage this well, easily incorporating references to both the blog and the self as blogger on both *Facebook* and *Twitter*. Others manage such complexities by using one platform mainly to refer to their blog and another to express themselves as travel bloggers. For example, Keith Savage uses detail from his blog on both his *Facebook* and *Twitter* pages to different effect. The latter places greater emphasis on Savage, the individual while the former clearly links to the narrative he writes. Similarly, bloggers may interact with a more general audience on their *Facebook* page, and refer to the themes and content of their blogs, while using *Twitter* principally to connect with other travel bloggers.

Evidently, there is no single winning strategy, for these individuals employ various techniques to move beyond the boundaries of their travel blog, distribute its content, and express various aspects of their online self. Ultimately, this involves a skilful management of discourses of travel and tourism. Bloggers strive to describe personal experiences of travel and so dissociate themselves from commercial tourism. Nevertheless, they must also strive to gain visibility for their blogs by engaging with global audiences, and validating both their narratives and their position as authentic bloggers of travel often requires a discursive style that is touristic. In the end, networking the self and presenting the travel blog requires a negotiation of the discursive tensions between travel and tourism.

Notes

1 Kruse *et al.* define a 'widget' as 'a simple graphical object such as a pushbutton…or menu that allows users easy interaction with the program' (1993, p. 148). They also identify different types of widgets such as buttons, sliders, and lists. Although this definition is taken from the context of a computer program written for the study of spectrometry, it is equally useful to describe the widgets that appear on the home pages of travel blogs.

2 Papacharissi sees self-presentation as performance. Basing her interpretation on Goffman's *The Presentation of Self in Everyday Life* (1959), she describes the process of self-presentation as 'a performance taking place on a single or multiple stages' (Papacharissi 2009, p. 210).

References

Arndt, G. 2010a. Gary Arndt [Online]. *Twitter*. Available: http://twitter.com/EverywhereTrip [Accessed 18 April 2016].

Arndt, G. 2010b. Gary Arndt: Lists [Online]. *Twitter*. Available: http://twitter.com/EverywhereTrip [Accessed 18 April 2016].

Baym, N. K. 2010. *Personal connections in the digital age*, Cambridge, UK: Polity.

Boyd, d. 2006. Friends, Friendsters, and Top 8: Writing community into being on social network sites. *First Monday* [Online], 11. Available: http://firstmonday.org/htbin/cgiwrap/bin/ojs/index.php/fm/article/view/1418/1336 [Accessed 25 Oct. 2010].

Boyd, d. and Ellison, N. 2008. Social network sites: definition, history, and scholarship. *Journal of Computer-Mediated Communication* [Online], 13(1), 210–230. [Accessed 22 September. 2010].

Boyd, d., Golder, S. and Lotan, G. 2010. Tweet, tweet, retweet: conversational aspects of retweeting on Twitter. *43rd Hawaii International Conference on System Sciences* [Online]. Available: http://ieeexplore.ieee.org/stamp/stamp.jsp?tp=&arnumber=5428313 [Accessed 25 Nov. 2010].

Boyd, d. and Heer, J. 2006. Profiles as conversation: networked identity performance on Friendster. *39th Hawaii International Conference on Systems Sciences* [Online], Vol. 3. Available: http://ieeexplore.ieee.org/xpl/articleDetails.jsp?arnumber=1579411 [Accessed 8 Oct. 2010].

Cavendish, J. 2016. John Cavendish [Online]. *Facebook*. Available: https://www.facebook.com/jgcuk [Accessed 14 Apr. 2016].

Cowper, H. 2010. Heather on her travels [Online] *Facebook*. Available: https://www.facebook.com/Heatheronhertravels/ [Accessed 02 Aug. 2016]

Dann, G. 1999. Writing out the tourist in space and time. *Annals of Tourism Research* [Online], 26. Available: http://www.sciencedirect.com/science/article/B6V7Y-3VS7VK0-8/2/644ebe6402ad134ca201678b33b3afc4 [Accessed 30 March 2009].

Donath, J. and boyd, d. 2004. Public displays of connection. *BT Technology Journal* [Online], 22. Available: http://link.springer.com/article/10.1023/B:BTTJ.0000047585.06264.cc [Accessed 8 October 2010].

Ellison, N., Heino, R. and Gibbs, J. 2006. Managing impressions online: self-presentation processes in the online dating environment. *Journal of Computer-Mediated Communication* [Online], 11. Available: http://jcmc.indiana.edu/vol11/issue2/ellison.html [Accessed 22 September. 2010].

Ettenberg, J. 2016a. Jodi Ettenberg [Online]. *Twitter*. Available: https://twitter.com/legalnomads [Accessed 15 April 2016].

Ettenberg, J. 2016b. Legal Nomads [Online]. *Facebook*. Available: http://www.facebook.com/LegalNomads [Accessed 24 March 2016].

Facebook. 2016. Company Info [Online]. *Facebook*. Available: http://newsroom.fb.com/company-info/ [Accessed 20 March 2016].

Genette, G. 1997. *Paratexts: thresholds of interpretation*, Cambridge, UK: Cambridge University Press.

Gilpin, D. R. 2010. Working the Twittersphere: microblogging as professional identity construction. *In:* Papacharissi, Z. (ed.) *A networked self: identity, community and culture on social network sites*. New York: Routledge.

Goffman, E. 1959. *The presentation of self in everyday life*, London: Allen Lane.

Helmond, A. 2010. Identity 2.0: constructing identity with cultural software. Digital Methods Initiative. *Anne Helmond* [Online]. Available: http://www.annehelmond.nl/wordpress/wp-content/uploads/2010/01/helmond_identity20_dmiconference.pdf [Accessed 22 June 2010].

Honeycutt, C. and Herring, S. C. 2009. Beyond microblogging: conversation and collaboration via Twitter. *42nd Hawaii International Conference on System Sciences (HICSS)* [Online]. Available: https://www.computer.org/csdl/proceedings/hicss/2009/3450/00/03-05-05-abs.html [Accessed 18 Nov. 2010].

Java, A., Song, X., Finin, T. and Tseng, B. 2007. Why we twitter: understanding microblogging usage and communities. *Proceedings of the 9th WebKDD and 1st SNA-KDD 2007 Workshop on Web Mining and Social Network Analysis* [Online]. Available: http://dl.acm.org/citation.cfm?id=1348556 [Accessed 18 Nov. 2010].

Kennedy, C. 2005. 'Just perfect!' The pragmatics of evaluation in holiday postcards. *In:* Jaworski, A. and Pritchard, A. (eds.) *Discourse, communication, and tourism*. Clevedon, UK: Channel View.

Kruse, F. A., Lefkoff, A. B., Boardman, J. W., Heidebrecht, K. B., Shapiro, A. T., Barloon, P. J. and Goetz, A. F. H. 1993. The spectral image processing system (SIPS)--interactive visualization and analysis of imaging spectrometer data. *Remote Sensing of Environment* [Online], 44. Available: http://www.sciencedirect.com/science/article/B6V6V-489S4HM-12/2/d79e18b996e915fccc374dadb8a415e3 [Accessed 7 Oct. 2010].

Kyhnn, M. 2016. Matt Kyhnn [Online]. *Twitter*. Available: https://twitter.com/backpackingmatt [Accessed 18 April 2016].

Landow, G. P. 2006. *Hypertext 3.0: Critical theory and new media in an era of globalization*, Baltimore, MD, US: Johns Hopkins University Press.

Liu, H. 2007. Social network profiles as taste performances. *Journal of Computer-Mediated Communication* [Online], 13. Available: http://jcmc.indiana.edu/vol13/issue1/liu.html [Accessed 26 Oct. 2010].

Lonely Planet. 2016. *Lonely Planet* [Online]. *Twitter*. Available: https://twitter.com/lonelyplanet [Accessed 15 April 2016].

Nabeth, T. 2009. Social web and identity: a likely encounter. *Identity in the Information Society* [Online], 2. Available: http://dx.doi.org/10.1007/s12394-009-0029-z [Accessed 28 June 2010].

Nomadic Matt. 2016a. Nomadic Matt [Online]. *Twitter*. Available: http://www.twitter.com/nomadicmatt [Accessed 15 April 2016].

Nomadic Matt. 2016b. Nomadic Matt [Online]. *Facebook*. Available: http://www.facebook.com/nomadicmatt [Accessed 11 March 2016].

Nomadic Matt. 2016c. You asked so I answered. *Nomadic Matt* [Online]. Available: http://www.nomadicmatt.com/travel-blogs/you-asked-so-i-answered/ [Accessed 18 Apr. 2016].

Oulasvirta, A., Lehtonen, E., Kurvinen, E. and Raento, M. 2010. Making the ordinary visible in microblogs. *Personal and Ubiquitous Computing* [Online], 14. Available: http://dx.doi.org/10.1007/s00779-009-0259-y [Accessed 16 Nov. 2010].

Papacharissi, Z. 2009. The virtual geographies of social networks: a comparative analysis of Facebook, LinkedIn and ASmallWorld. *New Media and Society,* 11, 199–220.

Papacharissi, Z. 2010. *A private sphere: democracy in a digital Age,* Cambridge, UK: Polity.

Pinch, T. 2010. The invisible technologies of Goffman's sociology from the merry-go-round to the Internet. *Technology and Culture* [Online], 51(2), 409–425r. [Accessed 19 July 2010].

Polat, A. 2006. FoXnoMad [Online].*Facebook.* Available: https://foxnomad.com/contact/facebook/ [Accessed 25 August 2010].

Polat, A. 2016a. Anil [Online]. *Twitter.* Available: http://twitter.com/foxnomad/ [Accessed 15 April 2016].

Polat, A. 2016b. Anil Polat [Online]. *Facebook.* Available: http://www.facebook.com/foxnomad [Accessed 23 March 2016].

Polat, A. 2016c. FoXnoMad [Online]. *Facebook.* Available: https://foxnomad.com/contact/facebook/ [Accessed 23 March 2016].

Reed, A. 2005. 'My blog is me': texts and persons in UK online journal culture (and anthropology). *Ethnos* [Online], 70. Available: http://dx.doi.org/10.1080/00141840500141311 [Accessed 6 July 2010].

Rees, E. 2016. Eva Rees [Online]. *Facebook.* Available: http://www.facebook.com/evarees [Accessed 24 March 2016].

Rees, E. and Rees, J. 2008a. *Forks and Jets* [Online]. Available: http://foxnomad.com/contact/facebook/ [Accessed 23 Mar. 2016].

Rees, E. and Rees, J. 2008b. About Us [Online]. *Forks and Jets.* N.p. Available: http://forksandjets.com/about/ [Accessed 24 March 2016].

Rees, E. and Rees, J. 2016. Forks and Jets [Online]. *Twitter.* Available: http://twitter.com/#!/ForksandJets [Accessed 15 April 2016].

Savage, K. 2016a. Keith Savage [Online]. *Twitter.* Available: https://twitter.com/travelingsavage [Accessed 15 April 2016].

Savage, K. 2016b. *Traveling Savage* [Online]. Available: http://www.traveling-savage.com/ [Accessed 24 March 2016].

Schau, H. J. and Gilly, M. C. 2003. We are what we post? Self-presentation in personal web space. *The Journal of Consumer Research* [Online], 30. Available: http://www.jstor.org/stable/3132017 [Accessed 22 June 2010].

Siibak. 2009. Constructing the self through the photo selection: visual impression management on social networking websites. *Cyberpsychology: Journal of Psychosocial Research on Cyberspace* [Online], 3. Available: http://cyberpsychology.eu/view.php?cisloclanku=2009061501&article=1 [Accessed 10 Nov. 2010].

Sontag, S. 1977. *On photography,* New York: Farrar, Strauss, and Giroux.

Swartz, J. 2013. Technorati Media's 2013 Digital Influence Report [Online]. *Technorati Media.* Available: http://technorati.com/report/2013-dir/ [Accessed 17 May 2016].

Teutle, A. R. M. 2010. Twitter: Network properties analysis. *20th International Conference on Electronics, Communications and Computer (CONIELECOMP)* [Online]. Available: http://ieeexplore.ieee.org/stamp/stamp.jsp?arnumber=5440773 [Accessed 6 December 2010].

Utz, S. 2010. Show me your friends and I will tell you what type of person you are: how one's profile, number of friends, and type of friends influence impression formation on social networks. *Journal of Computer-Mediated Communication* [Online], 15. Available: http://onlinelibrary.wiley.com/doi/10.1111/j.1083-6101.2010.01522.x/full [Accessed 24 September 2010].

Walker, L. 2016a. Laura [Online]. *Twitter*. Available: http://twitter.com/awanderingsole [Accessed 15 April 2016].

Walker, L. 2016b. A Wandering Sole [Online]. *Facebook*. Available: http://www.facebook.com/awanderingsole [Accessed 24 March 2016].

Walker Rettberg, J. 2009. 'Freshly generated for you, and Barack Obama': How social media represent your life. *European Journal of Communication* [Online], 24. Available: http://ejc.sagepub.com/content/24/4/451.abstract [Accessed 22 Nov. 2009].

Walker Rettberg, J. 2014. *Blogging*, Cambridge, UK: Polity.

Walther, J. B., Van Der Heide, B., Kim, S. Y., Westerman, D. and Tong, S. T. 2008. The role of friends' appearance and behavior on evaluations of individuals on Facebook: are we known by the company we keep? *Human Communication Research* [Online], 34. Available: http://dx.doi.org/10.1111/j.1468-2958.2007.00312.x [Accessed 12 Oct. 2010].

Weibel, B. 2016a. *Hole in the Donut Cultural Travel* [Online]. Available: http://holeinthedonut.com/ [Accessed 26 February 2016].

Weibel, B. 2016b. Barbara Weibel [Online]. *Twitter*. Available: http://www.twitter.com/holeinthedonut [Accessed 18 April 2016].

Weibel, B. 2016c. Hole in the Donut Cultural Travel [Online]. *Facebook*. Available: http://www.facebook.com/holeinthedonut [Accessed 24 March 2016].

Zhou, Z., Bandari, R., Kong, J., Qian, H. and Roychowdhury, V. 2010. Information resonance on Twitter: watching Iran. *1st Workshop on Social Media Analytics (SOMA '10)* [Online]. Available: http://dl.acm.org/citation.cfm?id=1964875 [Accessed 25 Nov. 2010].

6 Worth a thousand words (or more)

Framing the discursive tensions in travel photographs

Many generic definitions rarely mention photographs as being essential to blogs because earlier forms of this genre were incapable of including images. Nevertheless, travel-related photographs are integral to blogs discussed in this study, appearing alongside entries, as entries in themselves, in photo galleries, and in the form of slideshows. Tourism and photography are inextricably linked to each other, so much so that they are described as 'modern twins' (Baerenholdt *et al.* 2003, p. 69). Moreover, photographs in personal online narratives are generally self-presentational elements that provide a context for the experiences described therein (Nelson and Hull 2008; van Dijck 2008). Indeed, travel photography may be employed in a carefully and deliberately constructed performance of an 'ideal self' (Lo and McKercher 2015, p. 147). Against this background, this chapter examines how photographs in independent travel blogs contribute to the overall presentation of various aspects of the online self of travel bloggers. Some analyses of travel-related photographs identify discursive styles that are either associated with or distinct from tourist discourse (Dann 1996; Robinson and Picard 2009; Urry and Larsen 2011). This chapter draws on these findings to determine how various narrative techniques in these images associate the experience represented within with travel or tourism and examines the discursive tensions that arise as a consequence.

According to Susan Sontag, the practice of tourism is essentially the practice of photography, as tourists 'appropriate' and consume places they visit via the images they capture using cameras (1977, p. 4). In recent years, this has become all the more apparent due to the advances in mobile phone technology and location-based services. Tourists can now photograph destinations using camera phones and share their images, which can then be contextualised in online maps (Bamford *et al.* 2007). This has facilitated photo blogging and the instant sharing of travel-related images via online platforms such as *Flickr* and *Instagram* (van Dijck 2008). Images in advertisements and brochures organise such consumption of place by showing tourists what sights to visit, 'gaze upon', and photograph (Urry and Larsen 2011, p. 6). Indeed, visitors to a place may even find signposts at a monument or tourist site, indicating the best views and ideal backgrounds for taking photographs (Baerenholdt *et al.* 2003; Dann 2003). What follows is a 'circle of representation' (Jenkins 2003) as more images of the destination are created, reiterating themes from tourism advertising and potentially directing the gaze of future visitors. In this sense, photography both produces and is a product of tourism.

Though recent research into travel-related photography is largely based on theories concerned with the consumption and practice of tourism, it still reveals some insights into the nature of tourist discourse. Several studies that test, and for the most part confirm, the validity of the concept of a 'hermeneutic circle of representation' as popularised by Urry and Larsen, (2011, p. 187) suggest that tourists' photographs largely replicate existing images of the destination (Caton and Santos 2008; Garrod 2009; Jenkins 2003). These findings are based on analyses of images captured at tourist sites and do not consider whether tourists also photograph other locations. Still, this suggestion that the subject matter of travel-related photographs is predetermined leaves little possibility for new and original content creation. Furthermore, although Urry and Larsen admit that tourist photographs can at times contribute fresh images of a destination, they go on to add that these in turn inspire commercial photographs that promote the place. The underlying implication is that there is little distinction between the content and style of photographs created for personal purposes and those created for commercial ones. According to Graham Dann, the latter have certain characteristic visual techniques. These include an emphasis on colour in the image and its accompanying narrative, attention to its format (placement, size, shape, content, and structure), the use of 'visual clichés' such as bright sunshine or pristine beaches, and 'connotation procedures' such as specific effects, poses, objects, lighting, sequencing, and artistic composition (Dann 1996, pp. 188–198).

Tourists are far from being the mindless consumers and producers of the tourist gaze suggested by these studies. In fact, individuals often personalise photographs of a place by foregrounding family members and thus ensure that 'it isn't just a postcard' (Baerenholdt *et al.* 2003, p. 90). The attractions they photograph generally remain in the background. In this respect, such photographs are a departure from commercial tourist discourse by not being postcard-like in composition and content. Nevertheless, this 'family gaze' is also carefully choreographed, as individuals strike a suitable pose to demonstrate that they are a family on holiday. The studied nature of such an image – Baerenholdt *et al.* appropriately describe this as a performance (2003, p. 69) – suggests a 'staged authenticity', to borrow a term from Dean MacCannell (2008), albeit in a slightly different context. It is contrived in the manner of tourism rather than spontaneous in the manner of travel, even though the intent of the photographer is often to create an image that is not touristic. This suggests tensions between travel and tourism in the practice of travel-related photography. Such images can have touristic associations without necessarily possessing the characteristics of commercial tourist images.

Robinson and Picard identify two distinct styles in travel-related photographs, based on which they categorise these images as 'the professional travel photograph' and the 'vernacular tourist photograph' (Robinson and Picard 2009, pp. 8–9). The difference between the two lies in the photographic technique as well as the contexts in which they are likely to appear. Echoing Dann's assessment of tourist discourse, they write that the professional travel photograph 'borrows strongly from the techniques of the artist' and features in forms of commercial tourist discourse such as postcards, magazines, guidebooks, and brochures (Robinson and Picard 2009, p. 8). Perhaps in an acknowledgement of Urry's work, the authors add that these photographs are 'reproduced, copied, mimicked, and parodied', thus attracting academic interest (2009, p. 9). In contrast, 'vernacular tourist photographs', which include the holiday snapshot, are

> located largely in the private rather than the public sphere...and linked to their public absence, their social impact is somewhat minimal.... Regardless of various degrees of competency and artistic flair with which the photographer may capture the occasion of travel, and the holiday experience as a series of frames, the process of photography is divested of technical reference points and the holiday photography is almost entirely an amateur object.
>
> (Robinson and Picard 2009, p. 9)

A distinguishing feature of such photographs is their function as storytelling devices, souvenirs, and a means of representing social relationships and constructing identity (Lo *et al.* 2011; Robinson and Picard 2009). Furthermore, they are characteristically spontaneous and 'uncontaminated by technical over-indulgence' (Robinson and Picard 2009, p. 22). Thus, for these authors, the personal and unplanned nature of such photographs sets them apart from commercial tourist images.

This recognition that travel-related photographs are not necessarily reproductions of commercial images owes something to Dean MacCannell's theory of a 'second gaze' (MacCannell 2001). This involves looking beyond the attractions represented in commercial travel-related discourse, seeking out 'openings and gaps....the unexpected, not the extraordinary, objects and events that may open a window in structure, a chance to glimpse the real' (MacCannell 2001, p. 36). If the work of Urry and Dann provides a means of understanding what constitutes tourist discourse in a travel-related photograph, then MacCannell's second gaze offers a means of distinguishing travel discourse in the image. Extrapolating from this, one may argue that photographs that contain travel discourse capture 'real' sights rather than ones indicated by tourist brochures, 'unexpected' events that are not organised specifically as tourist attractions, and on the whole look at places in a new way. Apart from suggesting that those who photograph from this perspective are more discerning, the second gaze may appear to be an ambiguous concept for identifying travel discourse. However, in conjunction with the work of Robinson and Picard, it can be argued that photographs that contain travel discourse are also distinguished by amateur technique, a focus on real and unexpected events or objects that are not part of the designated attraction, and an emphasis on personal experience. Along with their accompanying text, they form part of a larger narrative about the travel experience.

The travel-related photographs in independent travel blogs, however, often resist such neat distinctions. This is in part due to the technology of the blog or the hosting service, as well as the advances in digital photography, one of the latest developments in the increasingly visual turn in tourism, first noted by Judith Adler (1989). As Haldrup and Larsen point out, digital photography has provided tourists with an array of options for performing the self through online narratives of travel (Haldrup and Larsen 2009, pp. 122–153). Digital photographs may be easily edited or altered, and this in turn allows individuals to manipulate their self-presentation in these images (van Dijck 2008, p. 66). The differences between the sophisticated professional techniques associated with tourist discourse and the amateurish style of travel discourse are blurred when individuals use photo-editing software to edit and enhance images either directly on their cameras or on a computer. The discursive distinctions are further complicated when the photograph is displayed online. To begin with, the ability to share images online means that personal travel-related photographs are no longer mainly privately or temporarily displayed. Photographs on a travel blog can be potentially as accessible to a large audience as are tourism advertisements. In addition to this, features like comments and tags enable a constant reinterpretation of the photograph's meaning via the addition of accompanying text (Davies 2007), a phenomenon that is particularly relevant to independent travel blogs that often invite and receive comments from readers. Also, the structure of a photo-sharing website may permit or limit certain display styles, and this in turn can shape the meaning of the image (Davies 2007). Although there is a tendency on the part of both researchers and tourists to differentiate between a photographic style that is associated with commercial tourism and one that is not, technologies of digital photography and online photo-sharing complicate these distinctions, some of which are unclear to begin with.

In light of these issues, this chapter begins with the premise that the tensions between travel and tourism are expressed in the content of travel-related photographs and the manner in which they are presented on the blog. In particular, it discusses the contribution of the accompanying text, particularly captions, comments, and tags to these discursive tensions. In so doing, it extends the argument of previous chapters that identifying destination is but a minor concern when travel bloggers post images. More importantly, photographs shared via services such as *Flickr* and *Instagram* distribute the content and inherent discursive tensions of the independent travel blog and extend the self-presentation of its author.

The photographic post

Travel-related photographs are often discussed in connection with the narrative they supplement or form a part of. Several such studies are based on Roland Barthes' view of text as 'a parasitic message designed to connote…sublimate, patheticize, or rationalize the image' (Barthes 1977, p. 25). For example, Graham Dann's analysis of tourism advertisements considers the relationship between their words and images. Based on their analysis of postcard images, Albers and James (1988) argue that travel photographs are closely intertwined with an accompanying text, without which they would be devoid of any connotative meaning. Others describe personal travel-related photographs as a device that prompts the telling of a story about the travel experience (Robinson and Picard 2009; Walker and Moulton 1989). Generally speaking, photographs shared online also provide a talking point about personal experiences and are employed in self-presentation (Nelson and Hull 2008; van Dijck 2008). Like Barthes, all of these authors argue that text illustrates the image instead of vice versa. So it is possible that accompanying text in the form of captions, comments, and entries that supplements travel-related photographs on blogs contributes to a blogger's presentation of various aspects of his or her online self.

This is not to say that travel-related photographs without captions, entries, or tags, are devoid of meaning. Photographs in themselves validate the travel experience (Sontag 1977, p. 9). Furthermore, images can have 'semiotic autonomy', that is to say that they can still have depth of meaning in the absence of an accompanying text such as a caption (Chaplin 2006; Lindekens as cited in Dann 1996, p. 189). Even though this view opposes Barthes' position, it should be remembered that meaning derives from the contexts the image was previously used in or the texts they previously accompanied. After all, if tourists photograph 'classic sights', this is because they recognise what they see before them from 'markers' in advertisements, brochures, and guidebooks (MacCannell 1976, p. 124; Robinson and Picard 2009, p.16). The image, once captured, will still make sense independent of an accompanying text because of these other existing contexts. This is perhaps something that Barthes himself recognises in his later works, particularly in *Camera Lucida* (1993) where he discusses the meaning of images based on his prior understanding of and familiarity with the contexts of the subject pictured rather than the accompanying text. He acknowledges that the reading of a photograph relies on 'a certain knowledge on the reader's part' (Barthes 1977, p. 28). This is similar to Bakhtin's argument that an individual's knowledge of the social contexts of a message and the connotations of each unit of communication, or utterance, influences how well its meaning is communicated (1986). Travel-related photographs in independent travel blogs are almost always accompanied by words in the form of captions, comments, and the blog entry itself, each of which provides a context that shapes the meaning of the image. The following section discusses how each of these elements contribute to the self-presentation of the independent travel bloggers selected for this study, and considers the tensions between travel and tourism present therein.

The traveller self and the tourist sight

Although travel-related photographs in blogs often illustrate an entry and validate the travel experience described therein, the reverse can also happen – sometimes the entry illustrates the photograph and situates it in discourses of travel and tourism. Some independent travel bloggers construct an entire post around a single photograph. A case in point is the *Traveling Savage* blog that has a series of photo-based posts titled 'Picture This', each of which centres on an image of a location that author Keith Savage describes. One such entry, 'Picture This: The Castle on the Rock' (Figure 6.1; Savage 2011) features a photograph of Edinburgh Castle, described on the *Lonely Planet* website as one of the 'top things to do' in Edinburgh (*Lonely Planet* 2016a). Various elements within the image suggest a tension between travel and tourism, which is enhanced by the accompanying entry.

The picture of Edinburgh Castle posted on *Traveling Savage* closely resembles a similar photograph on the official website for the castle (Historic Environment Scotland 2016), although the latter is taken from a different angle. Both photographs place the Castle in the centre of the composition, clearly showing its position atop a hill, trees in the foreground, and a blue sky behind it. The image is, at first glance, touristic in that it captures an iconic monument rather than an unexpected sight. The similarities with the Edinburgh Castle website image suggest that this picture reproduces tourist discourse and completes the circle of representation that Urry defines as characteristic of touristic consumption of place. This sense of replication is reinforced by the absence of people in the photograph – a characteristic of commercial forms of tourist discourse such as postcard images (Garrod 2009). Yet, the image on the blog is neither impersonal tourist discourse, nor is its author wholly inconspicuous. The bottom right corner of the photograph bears a watermark of a circular buckle, a visual element of the *Traveling Savage* title banner. The watermark is a stamp of the author's ownership and is self-presentational in that it showcases the photo-editing skill of the blogger. Moreover, it enhances the validity of the photograph, the travel experience, and the accompanying travel narrative by differentiating it from similar images in guidebooks or postcards. Savage's copyrighting of his work authenticates the

Figure 6.1 Screenshot of Keith Savage's photograph of Edinburgh Castle as seen from the Sir Walter Scott monument

traveller self he presents online, but at the same time this has an undertone of commercialisation that feeds into promotional tourist discourse and associates him with those who photograph such monuments to sell their images as postcards or for brochures. This is all the more evident when users click on the image and are invited to purchase the same via photo-sharing service *SmugMug* for personal or commercial use.

Various statements in the accompanying entry contextualise the image in discourses of both travel and tourism. Initially, the entry describes the image and the experience it refers to in terms generally associated with travel – as something involving danger and difficulty. It also reveals that the castle is not Savage's intended destination, although it is the subject of the photograph:

> After 297 spiraling steps, I reach the top of Edinburgh's Sir Walter Scott monument. Dizziness from the climb and a sudden sense of vertigo assault me, and for a split second I lament that I hadn't purchased any insurance for travel for this trip. Erratic winds rip at my jacket, blur my vision with tears, and roar in my ears. It's a trial by wind to reach Edinburgh's upper levels.
>
> But the reward is immense.
>
> In all directions the city seems to bow before me. Only Arthur's Seat, in the distance, looks at me with a level gaze. Then, curling around the monument's uppermost and tiny viewing deck, I spot it: **Edinburgh Castle** [sic].
>
> (Savage 2011)

To begin with, the image does not represent the attraction Savage has visited – the Sir Walter Scott monument. Instead, the real tourist destination is framed out of the picture. Apart from a passing reference, it is written out like the tourists that Graham Dann speaks of 'writing out'. As a consequence, in looking beyond the Sir Walter Scott monument and focusing unexpectedly on Edinburgh Castle, the photograph constitutes a second gaze. Subsequent statements draw on the contexts of travel and likewise construct the experience as one of travel – the climb is described as steep and difficult, a central theme in narratives of travel experience as opposed to touristic ones. Savage makes a point of mentioning the number of steps (297), the dizziness and vertigo which 'assault' him, strong winds that 'roar' and 'rip' at his jacket, all of which suggest that the journey is particularly arduous and even dangerous (Savage 2011). This is accentuated by the fact that he braves all of this while travelling without insurance, suggesting the risk and adventure associated with travel. On the face of it, this photograph of Edinburgh Castle may appear to be a touristic appropriation of a well-known monument. In the context of these accompanying statements, however, it is situated not as a touristic destination that is easily accessed, but as a goal achieved at some cost to a traveller who has gone off the beaten path.

Having presented this as a travel experience and himself as a traveller, Savage draws readers' attention to the vivid colours of the scene depicted in the image. He writes that 'It glows in the morning light, fencing with the clouds above it, like some computer-generated fantasy'. This suggestion of artificiality and colourfulness imbues the image with touristic qualities, as does the implication that it is manipulated on a computer. What is more significant, however, is the metaphor employed here. Although similes and metaphors are present in many forms of travel-related communication, they are most often associated with travel writing (Dann 1999). In his profile, Savage describes the blog as a step towards achieving his goal to be a travel writer. Thus, the literary tropes in this entry are self-presentational elements strengthening his position as an amateur travel writer and his travel blog as an example of a travel narrative.

At first glance, the content and composition of this photograph suggest touristic discourse. The Castle is after all primarily a tourist icon. However, a closer look at the photograph reveals that it is not entirely impersonal. The personalised watermark identifies the author, even though he does not feature in the image. The picture is already a reflection of the second gaze for its depiction of the Castle rather than the Scott monument, thus strengthening Savage's position as a traveller who forsakes the beaten path in search of something more authentic. If the accompanying entry draws attention to the touristic qualities of the image, it also constructs it as a product of a travel experience. If by presenting an iconic sight the image locates the experience in discourses of tourism, the same image allows Savage to reinforce his traveller position and validate his blog as a travel narrative. The presence of discourses of travel and tourism create tensions in the narrative, and yet both are necessary to the presentation of blog and its author.

Captions, comments, and conversations

Accompanying text, such as captions, guides a reader's interpretation of an image and so fixes its meaning (Barthes 1977). It plays a large part in the reading of newspaper and magazine photographs (Hall 1981; Westman and Laine-Hernandez 2008). Similarly, comments that readers add to online photographs and conversations that develop when authors reply can alter, emphasise, or undermine existing contexts and meanings (Davies 2007). As noted in earlier chapters, comments are a definitive feature of blogs as is interaction between readers and bloggers. The very presence of comments and a conversation about a photograph affirms the credibility of the text as a travel blog and its author as a blogger. This interaction produces a self that is located in multiple discourses (Serfaty 2004, p. 61). Following from previous studies of the relationship between image and text, it can be argued that captions and comments enable authors to emphasise specific elements of travel and tourist discourse in the photograph that best reinforce the positions they occupy in their blog. Consequently, this accompanying text locates the photograph and the travel blogger in the tensions between these discourses.

Traveling Savage's photograph of the castle has a title, but no caption. However, there are a number of comments from readers, several of which frame the photograph as travel discourse. Islandmomma writes, 'I've never seen a photograph taken of the castle from the monument before', to which Savage replies, 'I can't recall one either' (Savage 2011). Another visitor, Flexicover, echoes this with the observation that 'it's quite rare to see it at that angle'. This emphasis on the rarity – the unexpectedness – of the image, and its apparent difference from existing representations of this monument, place it as travel discourse. Although Savage himself does not emphasise this aspect of the image in his entry, such statements supplement his presentation of the castle as part of a travel experience. The suggestion that he has gone off the beaten path to get this photograph solidifies his position as an exploring traveller and 'hunter' of new experiences.

Other comments question the authenticity of this experience. Fellow travel blogger Backpacking Matt reflects on the more technical aspects of the image: 'This must be photoshopped, the sun never comes out in Edinburgh! :-).' (Savage 2011). The smiley added at the end suggests that this accusation of manipulation is made in jest. Nevertheless, this is a reference to the unrealistic technical perfection of photographs that Dann notes as a feature of tourist discourse, and reiterates Savage's own remark that the photograph seems 'computer-generated' (2011). Savage in his turn assures him, and perhaps others who may read this conversation, that the image is real: 'Matt, more than half of my three weeks in Edinburgh were sunny days!' (2011). Conversely, in reply to another comment from Serena that compares the image to 'a lovely Miazaki cartoon'[1], the author writes 'I can't say you're wrong' (Savage 2011). In both cases, Savage's replies enable him to enhance his self-presentation as a travel blogger. While his affirmation of the cartoon-like quality of the photograph may seem to acknowledge an artificiality and inauthenticity that is associated with tourist discourse, his acknowledgement of the image's stylistic affinity with the works of a renowned animator implies that Savage is similarly talented, even artistic. His rejection of any hint of inauthenticity likewise reassures readers of his credibility as a travel blogger.

Captions and comments are all the more essential to shaping meaning when a photograph is the principal component of a post and has no accompanying paragraphs of description. This is especially true of forms of travel-related communication such as postcards, where a caption can determine the meaning of the image it refers to and locate it in a larger discursive context (Goldsworthy 2010). Although his blog posts are generally accompanied by photographs, Nomadic Matt also shares images via *Instagram*, a photo-sharing website to which he provides a link from the blog. Here, each image bears a brief caption in the form of a comment. This is a clever utilisation of the comments function of this platform to make up for a deficiency of the template, which does not allow for captioning. The platform does, however, encourage users to tag their photographs with hyperlinked hashtags that are similar to those employed on *Twitter*. There is a touristic element in the postcard-style brevity of these one-word labels. However, they allow users to locate images in a destination as well as position the experience as one of adventurous travel. Against a photograph of a mountain trail in Torres del Paine, Nomadic Matt posts the comment: 'Over the river and through the woods to watch some glacier calving at Glacier Frances! Just another day in Torres del Paine!' and follows this with a series of hashtags including #travel #lp #torres #patagonia #chile #backpacking #intrepidtravel #latergram #bbctravel #instatravel #earthfocus #beautifuldestinations

#bestvacations #earthpix @lonelyplanet (Figure 6.2). Some of these are deliberately targeted at travel publishers such as BBC Travel and *Lonely Planet*, thus locating the image in discourses of tourism while also validating his position as an expert on backpacking and travel to 'beautiful destinations'. A more detailed discussion of hashtags follows later in this chapter. For now, it is worth noting that assigning a clear destination to the experience presented in this photograph is also, in light of Dann's theory, a touristic concern. It is this accompanying text that fixes a location – Nomadic Matt's photograph does not depict any iconic tourist marker that indicates the destination and, while it displays a beautiful landscape, the subject is hardly iconic. Nevertheless, the accompanying suggestion that the blogger has literally gone cross-country to capture the image testifies to his being a traveller as opposed to a tourist.

Nomadic Matt, by his own admission, is hardly a professional photographer (Nomadic Matt 2015). Many of the basic rules of composition that usually govern landscape photographs seen on postcards, such as the rule of thirds, leading lines, and the golden rule are barely visible (Long 2012, pp. 215–220). A photograph based on these principles would be more dynamic, whereas Nomadic Matt's image is mundanely amateur. Broadly speaking, however, there is a postcard-like quality to the landscape depicted here – verdant slopes and a snow-covered peak – making its content something of a touristic cliché. However, the skies are a stormy grey rather than a sunny blue and the rock-strewn steam bed is more easily associated with the treacherous terrain explored by a traveller than with touristic activities.

Significantly, the ensuing conversation highlights differing aspects of the photograph and presents contradicting interpretations of the scene. For wholeinthebucket, the scene is 'so awesome' (Nomadic Matt 2016). In contrast,

Figure 6.2 Screenshot of Nomadic Matt's *Instagram* image

for hostelme, the sight is 'Ominus [sic] but beautiful' (Nomadic Matt 2016). It is alwaysasterisk who positions the photograph as a representation of travel, appreciating its being 'Not your typical view!' (Nomadic Matt 2016). The descriptions are at once touristic for their euphoria and yet authentic as personal recommendations of the chosen destination. 'Enjoy this amazing paradise', writes mariemichellb, a comment that she punctuates with handclap emoticons. Although the blogger chooses not to respond to the comments, the displayed conversation provides a context for the image. Text added by both blogger and viewers changes the meaning of the photograph at once associating the experience with travel as well as tourism. By referring to the view as both 'awesome' and 'ominous', the viewers affirm Nomadic Matt's presentation of a traveller self, while the blogger himself employs hashtags that rely on the touristic contexts of Lonely Planet and BBC Travel to authenticate the same experience. Ultimately, the photograph presents a location that is an apparently unique and unexplored destination.

The blogger's own comment-as-caption states his position as a nomadic traveller in search of adventure. Although Nomadic Matt does not affirm interpretations of the destination as being dangerous, it is significant that he does not contradict it either. In this photograph the author's caption directs readers to particular aspects of the photograph. However, it does not fix meaning, but encourages polysemy, or the co-existence of multiple meanings, by generating comments, which shape meaning by referring to contexts of both travel and tourism. Despite the absence of replies from the author, the comments are nonetheless self-presentation for reinforcing positions and themes established in the blog narrative.

The album online

Images from the blog that are shared via services such as *Flickr*, *Instagram*, or *SmugMug* acquire an accompanying text on these platforms that is not necessarily anticipated or contributed by the bloggers. Sequencing and tagging in particular provide contexts that can influence the meaning of a photograph and a viewer's sense of its author (Davies 2007; Richter and Schadler 2009; Van House 2009; Walker and Moulton 1989). A photograph that appears in a blog entry may form part of a sequence of images on a *Flickr* page, some of which may not appear in the blog. Its position in this sequence can add to its meaning. Captions placed on this platform can differ from those in the blog. Authors (and visitors, if the authors and the platform so permit) may also tag photographs, possibly using terms relevant to themes in the blog. Such labelling of images and embedding them on other websites allows authors to distribute content and extend their self-presentation across several platforms (Richter and Schadler 2009). In particular, tagging can locate the photograph in a larger pool of images and a variety of discourses, some of which may have little relevance to the blog. Services such as *Flickr* also enable geotagging and sharing of EXIF (Exchangeable Image File Format) data, which includes such details as camera settings, the time at which the image was captured, and perhaps the geographic location of the scene in the photograph. It is likely that these techniques locate the photograph in discourses of travel and tourism and have implications for the positions authors occupy in their blogs.

Finding meaning in the sequence

Walker and Moulton's extensive analysis of print photo albums has formed the basis of several studies of online travel photography and the sharing of digital photographs online (Lo *et al.* 2011; Van House 2009; Walker and Moulton 1989). Some of their conclusions are especially applicable to the study of travel bloggers' photographs on platforms such as *Flickr*, *Instagram*, and *SmugMug*. First, they argue that a travel photo album is about its creator. As 'a thematic whole' (Walker and Moulton 1989, p. 171) and 'the context for a life' (ibid., p. 173), an album is a self-presentational element whose themes and contexts offer insights into its owner – in this case, the independent travel blogger. Second, they observe that a photograph derives meaning from structural elements such as sequence. So, the position of a photograph among other images in a blog entry or on a *Flickr* page and their arrangement on a page may have thematic significance and say something about a blog and its author. Finally, they conclude that images are consciously selected and displayed to illustrate specific themes. Extending this argument to bloggers' *Flickr* or *Instagram* pages, it can be argued that photographs shared via these services may be chosen to reflect themes in their blogs or the positions occupied by the blogger. Similarly, where only a few photographs from an online album are embedded in the travel blog, it can be argued that this controlled display also says something about the constitution of the blog and its author.

Writing about museums in Europe in an entry titled 'Culture vulture', the authors of *Forks and Jets* post a series of photographs of art galleries, memorials, and museums they have visited (Rees and Rees 2009). Four of these depict the Auschwitz-Birkenau Memorial and Museum near Krakow in Poland. Each image links to Eva Rees's *Flickr* album where it is displayed on a separate page along with captions and tags (Rees 2009a). Readers are invited to post comments, but they rarely do so in this album. The page also provides a link to the EXIF data for the image. In addition to this, a thumbnail of the photograph locates it in a 'photostream', a sequence of other images, some of which do not feature in the blog entry. Clicking on this thumbnail displays the photograph on a separate page among these other images. This last feature is particularly significant to this study. Since the same Auschwitz photograph may be viewed in different sequences, and therefore contexts, in the blog and the *Flickr* album, it can have very different meanings on each platform. This in turn has implications for the presentation of the authors and their blog.

The Auschwitz death camp, where many Poles perished, including a large number of Polish Jews, is generally regarded as an icon of the Holocaust and an epitome of what researchers increasingly refer to as dark tourism, a term that describes the commoditisation of places connected with disasters, genocide, and other such tragic events (Beech 2009; Lennon and Foley 2004; Tarlow 2005;

Auschwitz-Birkenau State Museum 2011). Located in Poland, this was once a Nazi death camp so it is reasonable to view it as a site that evokes considerable angst for those who live there, justifying the blog entry's description of Auschwitz as a place that 'must leave the Poles feeling trapped' (Rees and Rees 2009). It may be argued that such sites are hardly the stuff of superficial tourism, are generally off the beaten path, and encourage a deeper consideration of the cultural and historical importance of the destination. To that extent the photographs extend the travel themes of *Forks and Jets*. Nevertheless, the images are a result of the authors' visit to a recognisable tourist destination, and locating them in the blog does little for the bloggers' self-presentation as travellers searching for 'a new perspective of the world' (Rees and Rees 2008). The iconicity of Auschwitz has special significance in the *Forks and Jets* blog because author Eva Rees mentions her Polish origins here (Rees and Rees 2008). This is reiterated in her *Flickr* profile, where she indicates that she is 'Polish born' and that Warsaw is her hometown, although she currently resides in Los Angeles (Rees 2016). Even though this entry does not indicate whether the image has personal relevance for her, it extends her self-presentation to this platform and readers who view this in the context of her self-description may find additional meaning.

The 'Culture vulture' entry is essentially a column of photographs interspersed with lines of description. The Auschwitz photographs derive their meaning from their place in this series of photographs as well as the position of the sequence as a whole among other elements of the entry. The sequential arrangement reinforces the narrative structure and theme of the entry – primarily a list of recommended European museums and art galleries. The display is easily associated with the narrative style of tourist brochures and appears to be a visual itinerary of things to see and do. In fact, some of the recommended destinations are featured in other notable travel guides. *Lonely Planet* lists the Warsaw Rising Museum and Wieliczka Salt Mines near Krakow, pictured in this *Forks and Jets* entry, among the most popular sights of Poland (*Lonely Planet* 2016b; 2016c). As a thematic whole, the sequence also supports the notion that the authors are 'culture vultures'. The superficiality of a culture vulture may be associated with tourists and occupying this discursive role requires the language of tourism. It is difficult for a reader to establish whether the *Forks and Jets* authors, whose 'About Us' page presents them as 'escaping to a faraway place' (Rees and Rees 2008), use this phrase self-deprecatingly. It could be argued that visiting museums is a passive touristic activity, and that these photographs reflect guided tourist experience rather than spontaneous travel. To that extent, theme and structure locate this sequence in tourist discourse. However, as a selection of the 'few [museums] which we loved' (Rees and Rees 2009) it also reflects the bloggers' personal preferences and does not merely reiterate a tourism advertiser's impersonal recommendation of things to see and do in Europe.

The first of the four Auschwitz photographs, depicting a gallery in the Museum, is the third image in this series and is placed between two similar images taken inside art galleries in Germany and Poland. Here, it is one of several examples of what the authors refer to as 'traditional museums' (Rees and Rees 2009). The remaining three photographs are sandwiched between photographs of Memento Park in Budapest and others of Edinburgh and Berlin, as examples of 'places that have become museums in themselves' (Figure 6.3; Rees and Rees 2009). Thus, the adjacent photographs situate the Auschwitz images in a narrative about travel in Europe. Within the sequence as a whole, these photographs are also located in the impersonal discourses of tourism and in the personal narrative of travel in Europe. The lines of text immediately below the last Auschwitz photograph reiterate this:

> Of course there is the grandaddy of all, **Auschwitz** (sic) outside Krakow, Poland. A massive, unrestored piece of land-locked anguish that must leave the Poles feeling trapped with a place and time that can not be allowed to be forgotten. You can understand how it must feel to be occupied, forced to help in building this monstrosity and then to have this scar never heal, to continue to exist to this day as part of a greater good, and common education.
>
> (Rees and Rees 2009)

If these lines have the impersonal, monologic tone of tourist discourse and address an undefined audience, their content is nevertheless a more personal reflection than a guidebook-style description.

On Eva Rees's *Flickr* pages, the same Auschwitz photographs appear in a different context, occupy a different position, and consequently have a different meaning. Here, each image may be viewed separately on its own page, or among a sequence of other images. Rees's 'photo stream' displays the four blog photographs alongside five more images of Auschwitz, each captioned 'Near Krakow, Poland'. Also on the same web page are photographs of Krakow – featuring restaurants, streets, night life, and local cuisine such as *pierogi* (dumplings) and *miodowka* (honey vodka). On the whole, the page reinforces the themes of *Forks and Jets*, particularly the authors' position as 'amateur foodie traveloguers' (Rees and Rees 2008). It extends Eva Rees's presentation of self, in *Forks and Jets*, as a person of Polish origin. Notably, each caption ends with the line 'Read about our trip around the world at Forks and Jets', directing viewers to the blog narrative. There is also one photograph of author Jeremy Rees and another of an old car, a Trabant, which has special significance for the authors.

By and large, these images capture experiences that could be described as personal and off the beaten path. This is not to say that the *Flickr* page is purely travel discourse – at least some of the destinations shown here, such as Kazimierz and Auschwitz itself, find mention in forms of travel-related communication generally associated with tourism, such as the *Lonely Planet* guide to Poland. Nevertheless, it can be argued that this sequence as a whole tells a travel story that differs significantly from the blog entry. Here, the Auschwitz images are part of a more detailed visual description of the concentration camp, as well as a larger narrative about Polish culture, particularly in the region around Krakow. The gravity of these images is incongruous with the vivacity of photographs of the restaurant scene and night life in this town. The sequencing juxtaposes themes of

Memento Park, Budapest

Of course there is the grandaddy of all, **Auschwitz** outside Krakow, Poland. A massive, unrestored piece of land-locked anguish that must leave the Poles feeling trapped with a place and time that can not be allowed to be forgotten. You can understand how it must feel to be occupied, forced to help in building this monstrosity and then to have this scar never heal, to continue to exist to this day as part of a greater good, and common education.

Figure 6.3 Screenshot of photographs of Auschwitz

life and death, past and present, dark and light. In the context of discourses of travel and tourism, this arrangement signals an apparent insensitivity that is touristic. Although this may be an inadvertent effect of *Flickr*'s photostream feature, to display photographs of a death camp alongside others that depict the authors enjoying a night out on the town trivialises all that Auschwitz symbolises for all that it presents a complex Polish experience. Such are the affordances of this platform that images such as the Auschwitz photographs can appear in a sequence that is at odds with their implicit or explicit meaning.

For a reader approaching the *Flickr* page from the blog, the position of the Auschwitz photographs in the photostream is particularly significant. Only some photographs of the memorial are embedded in the blog and arranged in an order different to that of the *Flickr* page. One of these images shows the concentration camp surrounded by a barbed wire fence, while another displays victims' suitcases. Both of these are symbolic of the site, and perhaps this was a factor that influenced the authors' selection. The *Flickr* album predates the blog entry. A more discerning reader may find some humour in the idea that *Forks and Jets* is something of a 'vulture' that scavenges photographs from Eva Rees's *Flickr* page. In this sense, the different sequencing and the controlled display of only certain photographs reinforces the theme of the blog entry.

Readers may also have the sense that the *Flickr* page takes them backstage, showing them the real story behind the writing of the entry and offering a deeper insight into experiences of the bloggers. With *Forks and Jets*, they get the highlights of the journey, but with Eva Rees's *Flickr* page they can view the complete experience. In both the blog and *Flickr* sequences, the Auschwitz images are situated in discourses of travel and tourism. However, the discourses work very differently on each platform. In the discursive contexts of tourism suggested in the 'Culture vulture' sequence, these photographs are a self-presentational element that supports the theme of the entry and the author's position as an expert on the European cultural experience. Within the elements of travel discourse on the *Flickr* page sequence, they are a self-presentational element that supports the central theme of *Forks and Jets* – culinary tourism. Here, alongside images that have personal significance for the authors, these photographs form 'a context' for Eva Rees's life and offer insights into the positions she occupies in the blog. Thus a photograph's varying location in the discourses of travel and tourism on each platform plays some part in distributing the content of the travel blog and the self-presentation of its author.

Tagging the travel experience

Several aspects of tagging are particularly relevant to the study of photographs on Eva Rees's *Flickr* page. In effect, every tag added to a photograph is itself an accompanying text and brings with it additional accompanying texts. First, as a technical feature, each tag links the image to a larger body of discourse that consists mainly of images added and similarly tagged by other users (Richter and Schadler 2009, p. 174). If an image has multiple tags, it will be linked to multiple image sequences and consequently a variety of discursive contexts. Second, each tag is a word (or a phrase) that comes with a set of connotations that adds meaning to the photograph. David Barton argues that the words or phrases comprising the set of tags accompanying an image also create meaning by relating to each other (2015). In addition to this, tags are self-presentational elements and authors can attract attention to their images by using a common tag that features prominently in the *Flickr* tag cloud (Marlow *et al.* 2006). Tagging an image on *Flickr* heightens its visibility, distributes it to a large audience and situates it, along with its author, across a network of photographs and photographers (van Dijck 2010). In the case of Eva Rees's album, the use of a common tag attracts attention to the blog and her role as a travel blogger. It also potentially connects her to others interested in travel-related photography. The Auschwitz photographs in particular could be located in a larger discourse surrounding the site.

Eva Rees's photograph of a barbed wire fence at Auschwitz is perhaps one of the most iconic of her photographs of this concentration camp. It is simply captioned, 'Near Krakow, Poland', followed by a link to the blog where, viewers are promised, they can read more about the trip. Similar images of the fence feature on the Auschwitz-Birkenau Memorial and Museum's website. Furthermore, clicking on the 'concentration camp' tag leads to a display of images from other users using the same phrase, a number of which are similar in theme. Like the *Forks and Jets* authors, other users also post 'concentrationcamp' photographs of Auschwitz's barbed wire fence, and the discarded shoes of Holocaust victims. *Flickr* user brunoat's photograph in particular is nearly identical in content, except that it foregrounds a section of barbed wire. The photographer, Bruno Abarca, asks viewers to 'please contact me, or buy a print here, but do not use my photographs without my consent', indicating that this photograph has commercial attributes (2007). This can influence the meaning and position of Rees's own photograph for a viewer who sees both images. The replication of a theme from tourist discourse and the parallels with images captured by other users suggests that Rees's photograph is part of the hermeneutic circle of representation and is located in tourist discourse. This also bears out Richter and Schadler's observation that tagging digital photographs has made them 'completely disconnected from authenticity or uniqueness, characteristics that used to go with private photography' (2009, p. 175). What appears to be a unique personal travel-related photograph in Rees's album and on *Forks and Jets* becomes increasingly touristic as the accompanying texts and contexts change in the process of distribution and dissemination via *Flickr*.

Of all the Auschwitz photographs in their *Flickr* collection, the images of the fence and the discarded shoes are the ones that the authors choose to embed in *Forks and Jets*. Although the *Flickr* page predates the blog entry, it is difficult to establish whether the recognisable theme is a factor determining the authors' selection. It is reasonable to argue that having these particular images in the entry is most likely to gain visibility for the blog, particularly as each links to *Forks and Jets*. Ultimately, this travel blog is positioned by the authors as a narrative of travel but is, perhaps unwittingly, also located and disseminated, via this photograph, in discourses of tourism as other users post similar images of what has perhaps become an iconic sight at this destination. Nevertheless, it should be noted that each pool of other images linked to this photograph via its tags is constantly revised as other users add and tag new photographs on *Flickr*. At the time of writing, clicking on the 'concentrationcamp' tag beside this photograph, as well others of Auschwitz with the same tag, also displayed a page of recently uploaded images of the concentration camps at Dachau and Treblinka. Thus, Eva Rees's Auschwitz image is effectively related to a larger body of discourse about concentration camps, and acquires a context and meaning additional to that of the blog and her *Flickr* album. Conversely, recently uploaded images using the 'Auschwitz' tag included photographs of a memorial in Berlin and a tour bus, consequently linking the image to discourses about travel and tourism in Europe. This effectively demonstrates the semantic ambiguities governing tagging systems as well as how photographs constantly change meaning in the process of distribution (Golder and Huberman 2006).

Such is the brevity of the Auschwitz photograph's caption that the accompanying tags play a considerably significant part in describing the image. Chaplin argues that in the absence of captions, viewers will interpret the meaning of an image from the other writing surrounding it. In the context of *Flickr* pages, this surrounding text consists mainly of any tags accompanying in the image, which contribute to its meaning. Indeed, tags are generally used for communication and an individual's audience awareness has some impact on how these tags are used (Oded and Chen 2010). In this sense, they are self-presentational and this is reflected in Eva Rees's choice of tags – Cracow, Krakow, Poland, Polska, Polski, RTW, Us, Slavic, Vistula, Wisla, summer, tourism, urban, walking, history, and Polish history.

The use of both English and Polish destination names (Cracow/Krakow, Polska/Poland, Wisla/Vistula) supports the authors' self-presentation in two ways. To begin with, it ensures a greater connectivity and networking of the *Flickr* album and, in the process, the blog. Moreover, using Polish terms expands on and validates Eva Rees's description of her Polish origins. They also add a depth of meaning to what would otherwise be merely a series of words denoting place names. Using the local language adds a dimension of authenticity to both the image and the author's self-presentation. The extensive use of destination names as tags is therefore at once touristic in its focus on destination, and personal in its reference to the author's roots.

The choice of tags is also self-presentational, as it reveals the authors' awareness of their audience and demonstrates how they publicise their photographs and travel blog. Tags such as 'summer' and 'urban' are generic and are comparatively ambiguous, given the subject of the Auschwitz fence photograph. In particular, 'summer', a word often used in the context of holidaymaking, suggests a superficiality that can be associated with tourism. While this supports the touristic aspects of Auschwitz, and the fact that the photograph is embedded in an entry termed 'Culture vulture' it seems oddly situated among terms that reflect the gravity of the site. Despite this, the words are nonetheless significant. Both feature in *Flickr*'s tag cloud of most popular tags, and consequently their use ensures a greater visibility for the Auschwitz photograph, Rees's album, and *Forks and Jets*. Also generic is 'tourism' which implies that this photograph has a touristic theme. The authors' decision to use 'travel' instead of 'tourism' in other albums is particularly meaningful. The difference may be due to the blog having two authors, but it also indicates the Rees's awareness of their audience and how *Flickr* works. The 'travel' tag is used more extensively on *Flickr* – over 14 million images at the time of writing – and is thus likely to gain better visibility for an image than 'tourism'. Images that display a 'travel' tag are not necessarily viewed as travel discourse. Nevertheless, affixing this tag has touristic implications as it is primarily a promotional strategy meant to distribute the content of the blog and attract the attention of potential readers.

Two tags that particularly reinforce the themes of the blog and the authors' position as travellers exploring the world are 'RTW' and 'Us'. The former refers to a Round-The-World trip and using this for the Auschwitz image highlights the travel theme of *Forks and Jets* and the author's intention to explore the world. The 'Us' tag is self-referential and may serve to organise the photographs or indicate ownership (Golder and Huberman 2006). As Barton points out, tags are not necessarily used to contribute to the public conversation around a theme, but also may be employed individually to denote a meaning specific to a user or an album (2015). On Eva Rees's *Flickr* page, the 'Us' tag draws together a variety of images mostly featuring food from different parts of the world and essentially presents the 'foodie traveloguers' of *Forks and Jets*. It reinforces and extends the bloggers' self-presentation, and validates the central theme of their travel blog.

Lastly, some photographs on Eva Rees's *Flickr* page carry geotags[2], which contextualise each image in a map. Most of her images depict the ruined Mayan city at Palenque in Mexico. One such image is 'Temple of the Inscriptions', indicated on a map as located in a hilly region at some distance from the nearest town (Rees 2009b). Eva Rees's photograph indicates that the temple itself is easily accessed via well-defined paths. However, the map indicates that the destination as a whole may be regarded as being off the beaten path. To this extent, the image as contextualised by its geotag suggests a travel experience. Yet, geotagging allows the authors to present themselves as explorers of the world or as travellers going off the beaten path to a place that has not been publicised by others.

Flickr also displays other users' images of the same location that have the same geotag. The platform indicates that only two other users posted images of the Temple around the same time, some of them taken twenty-eight months prior to the Rees's visit in 2009. Since then, however, many more *Flickr* users have posted images of Palenque, and Eva Rees's photograph is now part of a large collection of similar images captured by visitors to the region. Among the few other images dated at around the same time as their own, the Temple photograph appears unique. It is, in this context, a location that is appropriate for a travel experience as opposed to a touristic one. Within the larger sequence, however, it suggests neither the extraordinary or unique quality of travel, but appears entwined in the circle of representation that characterises tourist discourse. This image functions like the photograph in a brochure that invites tourists to visit the destination. In effect, Palenque is depicted much like a tourist site marked on a guidebook map, indicated as a destination worth visiting. By utilising the geotagging feature, authors validate their position as travellers exploring the world and suggest that they are experiencing travel rather than tourism. In doing so, they also engage in touristic discourse and pave the way for making the destination itself part of a tourist's itinerary.

While putting Palenque on a *Flickr* map reflects the themes of exploration and discovery generally associated with travel, the fact that the entire region has been mapped and reproduced online using satellite imagery suggests that 'real' travel is arguably no longer possible. Although within the map the Temple of Inscriptions appears to be a fairly remote destination, being able to locate it on a map and so 'box' it in suggests that Eva and Jeremy Rees's desire to escape and find 'a new perspective' of the world is not really an achievable goal (Rees and Rees 2008). In the context of the *Flickr* map, particularly at the time when the Temple image was uploaded, Palenque appears to be the kind of destination that would be classified as a travel destination as opposed to a touristic one. This is, in part, due to the scarcity of photographs of the temple displayed on *Flickr* at the time. However, it is worth noting that *Flickr* is but one of many services that allow images to be contextualised in maps. It is quite possible that other services such as Google Maps may display a large number of images of the same Temple. In such different contexts, Palenque may not seem as unique as Eva Rees's photograph suggests.

Much like sequencing, tagging changes the meaning of a photograph and locates it discourses of both travel and tourism. When photograph captions are sparing in detail, as is the case with the Auschwitz photographs on Eva Rees's *Flickr* page, tags provide an additional context for the images they accompany. The presence of tags has implications for the blog in which the photographs are embedded, *Forks and Jets*. As a technical feature, they locate the blog, via the embedded image, in a larger body of discourse about travel and tourism in Poland, particularly with reference to Auschwitz as a tourist site and the Krakow region in general. A large number and variety of tags increases the chances of the image, and consequently the blog, being viewed. As words, tags distribute the themes of the blog to a potentially large audience. In this way, they extend and expand on the authors' self-presentation in their travel blog. At the same time, the different discursive contexts of each word also create tensions between discourses of travel and tourism in the image, and by extension in the blog. Following from authors such as Marlow *et al.*, tags are referred to here as self-presentational elements. However, the term self-presentation suggests that the authors have some control over how tags work, which is by no means the case. Such is the nature of the platform that photographs may shift between various discourses as both the bloggers as well as other users add and tag their own images. Thus, the discursive tension is a dynamic one.

The profile as a frame

Although user profiles are not immediately visible alongside photographs posted on *Flickr* or *Instagram*, they are important as an accompanying text. What is said in a profile can frame the meaning of the album. The template of the profile pages on *Flickr* and the home page of *Instagram* accounts allow users to post a thumbnail photograph or avatar. This is referred to as a 'buddy icon' on *Flickr*. Users can also post a description of themselves and their albums. In this space, *Flickr* users may describe the theme and purpose of their albums. They may also indicate details such as name, gender, relationship status, occupation, current location, hometown, and a link to their website if they have one. Several rows of the user's 'Favorite' images occupy the centre of the page. In addition to this, the profile page also lists other *Flickr* members who the user 'follows' and the *Flickr* groups that he or she belongs to. Thus, the profile is a self-presentational space where individuals may reveal something of themselves and the self they wish to present via their images and their affiliations with others in the *Flickr* or *Instagram* community. This self-presentation is shaped to some extent by the template provided by these platforms, which according to Trevor Pinch (2010), is often the case where technology is involved.

In *Instagram* pages, the template is limited to displaying a description of its author alongside the profile picture, should he or she choose to provide these. Visitors to *nomadicmatt* will see the same image of Uncle Travelling Matt, of Fraggle Rock fame, that appears on the *Twitter* page for the blog. They will also read a description of Nomadic Matt who is presented here as a bestselling travel book author, an adventurer, a nomad, and a backpacker. Interestingly, the account does not link back to the blog, but instead promotes *Take Flyte*, a non-profit organisation supporting youth travel that was founded by Nomadic Matt. The page thus extends some aspects of the online self of *Nomadic Matt* but also indicates other roles occupied online. While the description refers to a traveller self who is not rooted in any one destination, it also promotes travel as a profession and a commodity to be sold. Nomadic Matt's motives are altruistic and *Take Flyte* is an initiative that supports potential travellers. Yet, the *Instagram* description alludes to a commoditisation of his own travel to promote books and run an organisation, and this commercial undertone may be perceived as touristic.

A number of elements on Eva Rees's *Flickr* page refer to aspects of the self she presents in *Forks and Jets*. A paragraph at the top of the page describes her, much as the blog does, as a Polish-born resident of Los Angeles. The listing of Warsaw as her 'Hometown' and Los Angeles as her current location reiterates this. The paragraph goes on to state: 'Since March 2009 my husband and I have been traveling around the world with our backpacks and a camera. We blog about the trip at *Forks and Jets*. I have a little blog over *here* too' (Rees 2016).

Brief as this may seem, these lines contribute significantly to presenting the blog and its author. First, they draw attention to the link to *Forks and Jets*. In addition to this, reference to travelling 'with our backpacks and a camera' suggests that the *Flickr* album is mainly concerned with the photography of travel experiences, the central theme of the blog whereas in fact, Rees has been a member of *Flickr* since 2006, and her archive displays images on a variety of subjects posted since that time. Although Rees's 'little blog' which is at *LiveJournal*, seems a secondary concern, both in its later mention and the apparent absence of a name, its entries are nevertheless relevant as they describe the lead up to the creation of *Forks and Jets*. In general, the paragraph highlights the *Flickr* album's relevance to the travel blog and Rees's role as a travel blogger.

Although the descriptive paragraph creates the impression that the *Flickr* page is mainly concerned with themes of relevance to *Forks and Jets,* as with Nomadic Matt's *Instagram* page, other elements of the profile present different aspects of Eva Rees – her position as a travel blogger and in particular her professional role as a graphic designer. The 'Website' link leads to *Design Domesticated*, a website where she showcases the work she has done in a professional capacity. She follows *Flickr* members with user names such as 'The Wide Wide World', 'The 10 cent designer', and 'road triper' [sic] (Rees 2016). It has been argued that the connections and associations that users display in an online profile are self-presentational (boyd and Heer 2006; Donath and boyd 2004; Papacharissi 2009). In this context, therefore, linking to such users presents Rees as a member of an online community that similarly views travel as an escape and an exploration of the world. This reinforces the author's self-presentation as a travel blogger and reiterates themes of the blog. It should be noted though, that not all of Rees's contacts have such travel-themed user names.

A similar display of connections is visible in Eva Rees's membership in various *Flickr* groups, which include 'Typography and Lettering', 'Lights and Shadows', 'Your "Postcard" Shot', and 'Lonely Planet' among others (Rees 2016). Here again, Rees's association with communities interested in travel-related photography reinforces her position as a travel blogger. At the same time her interest in typography strengthens her position as a graphic designer. This is not unlike her *Facebook* profile, where links to pages that Rees likes indicate her interest in graphic design as well as themes of relevance to *Forks and Jets*. For readers of the blog who are familiar with these parallels, the *Flickr* profile validates the *Facebook* profile and vice versa. This particular element of the *Flickr* profile presents two different aspects of the blogger, and opens the possibility for other discursive tensions.

This closer look at other aspects of Rees's personal life may also give readers a sense of greater intimacy with the author. On the one hand, such a personal voice suggests a tone in keeping with travel discourse. At the same time, the *Flickr* profile launches the blogger's profession as a graphic designer. This subtle self-promotion, which has little to do with the blog, nonetheless has the commercial overtones common with tourist discourse. Despite these tensions, the *Flickr* page acts as a centralising force for the different strands of Rees's online self. For some readers, therefore, it may seem that Rees's *Flickr* page is the blog.

Eva Rees's membership of the 'Lonely Planet' group is particularly significant. The guidebook publisher's official website, *Lonely Planet*, runs two groups on *Flickr* – the 'Lonely Planet: Photo Challenges' and 'Lonely Planet: Contributor

Pool' – each of which is easily identified with the *Lonely Planet* brand because of the LP logo in the profile picture. However, the 'Lonely Planet' group that Eva Rees belongs to is not endorsed by the company, although it is a community of individuals interested in travel-related photography. Nevertheless, those familiar with the guidebook publisher may well associate the 'Lonely Planet' label and the group itself with the contexts of commercial tourism suggested by the name. Through this association, the group capitalises on the popularity of *Lonely Planet* as a brand, and manipulates tourist discourse to gain visibility. This creates some free publicity for *Lonely Planet*. However, the comparative lack of restrictions governing image submissions for this group (the company-endorsed groups run themed competitions) suggests that this is a community that is more engaged with the kind of spontaneous and personal discourse associated with travel. It is difficult for a casual visitor to establish whether Eva Rees is aware that the group is not associated with *Lonely Planet*, the publisher. Nevertheless, her membership in this group is self-presentational, validating her role as a travel blogger by drawing on the contexts of the name 'Lonely Planet'. Consequently, and perhaps unintentionally, her position as a travel blogger is also situated in discourses of both travel and tourism.

Another principal element of the *Flickr* profile is the thumbnail display of photographs from other *Flickr* users that Rees considers to be her 'Favorites' (Rees 2016). Some of these are travel-related photographs depicting landscapes, aerial snapshots, and tourist destinations. Others include posters and images of various subjects that are notable for their colour and composition. As with the group membership, this wide range of photographs presents two different aspects of Eva Rees – the self as travel blogger as well as the self as graphic designer. Linking to these photographs, and through them to other *Flickr* users, strengthens her association with two different communities, both of whom are essential to her overall online self-presentation.

Ultimately, the *Flickr* profile describes those interests and aspects of her online self that Eva Rees wishes to explicitly present to an online audience. As a result, it is situated in a wide range of discourses, including those of travel and tourism. Although the paragraph description suggests that the album and images contained within are mainly concerned with *Forks and Jets*, this is not necessarily the case. In fact, there is an overlapping of the different online roles that Rees plays. As her website *Design Domesticated* does not link to the travel blog, or vice versa, these are two distinct roles. However, the *Flickr* profile tries to do justice to both aspects of Rees's personality and shifts between a presentation of her professional life and her interest in travel blogging. Although *Forks and Jets* names both Eva and Jeremy Rees as its authors, the *Flickr* profile suggests that the latter plays a secondary role in the creation of the album. The profile contributes a sense of only one author as a travel blogger, and this is Eva Rees. The focus on Eva Rees is to some extent a result of the limitations of the template of *Flickr*'s profiles. There is only room for the name of one user, one person's hometown, or one website link. Rees overcomes some of these limitations by linking to her blogs via the paragraph describing the album. However, the architecture of the platform forces Rees to choose what information she will provide here, and some of these decisions relegate her co-author to the sidelines.

Worth a thousand words...or more

The old saying that a picture is worth a thousand words implies that images are a simpler and more explicit form of expression than words. This chapter began with the argument that there is nothing simple about the discourses that make up travel-related photography. The photographs analysed here suggest that an image in itself combines discourses of both travel and tourism. Furthermore, the accompanying text for these photographs, regardless of whether this is contributed by the author or the audience, plays a significant role in muddying the waters when it comes to determining meaning. Comments, captions, and blog entries that constitute the writing surrounding a photograph may, in fact, make its meanings more ambiguous. This is contrary to Barthes' proposition that accompanying text fixes the meaning of the image (Barthes 1977). In the travel blogs studied here, such text encourages polysemy and situates each image in a variety of discourses including those of travel and tourism.

The chapter additionally argues that the manner in which photographs are displayed and distributed also contributes to the ambiguity of meaning. In particular, sequencing and tagging of photographs – as evidenced by Nomadic Matt's mountain landscape and the Auschwitz photographs in Eva Rees's *Flickr* album and the corresponding blog entry – locates them in various discursive contexts. The meaning of a single image changes with the change in its position from a blog entry to a *Flickr* album to a sequence of random images bearing the same tag. In the process, tensions may be produced between discourses of travel and tourism. The *Forks and Jets* entry on museums, as well as its links to *Flickr* and the hashtags accompanying the image of Torres del Paine suggest that sequencing and tagging are self-presentational in that they can contribute to the idea of the author as a travel blogger and reinforce themes of the travel blog. It is worth noting, however, that describing this as self-presentation implies that the authors can control the way the information is presented, which is not necessarily the case. Quite often the features of the platform play a significant role in determining what will accompany a user's image, contextualise it, and influence how it might be read.

This chapter also supports findings that suggest digital photography and its associated technologies tend to blur the lines between the professionalism and amateurism. As Lo *et al.* point out, photographs are carefully selected and manipulated using appropriate software, before they are shared online (Lo and McKercher 2015, p. 106). In fact, when travel bloggers strive to imitate and adopt the sophisticated techniques of professional photographers, it becomes more difficult to categorise the resulting images as either travel or tourist discourse. This demonstrates the inefficacy of existing frameworks for studying travel-related photography. Although only *Flickr* is analysed in some depth here, there is sufficient indication that techniques such as tagging can locate an amateur image among professional ones. Differences become increasingly indistinct, and this is perhaps best exemplified in the 'Lonely Planet' group.

Finally, the chapter extended the notion that destination is not a key concern for travel bloggers. Most of the travel-related photographs in the blogs as well as in albums on platforms are not concerned with iconic sites of tourist destinations. Even if they do focus on well-known monuments, as is the case with *Traveling Savage*, authors attempt to present a perspective different from the one commonly seen in tourist brochures. Images are contextualised to create the impression that the authors are in most cases travellers seeking experiences off the beaten path. If destination does become a focus, as is obviously the case with geotagging on *Flickr*, this only serves to associate the narrative and the experience described or visualised therein with travel as opposed to tourism. The decision to indicate a destination may therefore be self-presentational and have a specific purpose. Nevertheless, affixing a place name to a photograph only heightens the tensions between the discourses of travel and tourism present in it, as is evidenced by the Eva Rees's geotagged Mayan temple image and Nomadic Matt's Patagonian landscape.

In conclusion, a picture may well be worth a thousand words. However, a picture that is digitally altered may be worth much more than this as it says something about the self that the author wishes to present to the travel blog reader. Furthermore, when words and other images accompany a picture in a travel blog, it is located in a variety of discursive contexts and gains more meaning. Photographs hosted on independent travel blogs contribute to the self-presentation of the blogger. Networked across other online platforms, they gain visibility for the blog and its author. Contextualised within the other texts on these platforms, images have a lot more to say. Thus, for these travel bloggers, a picture is worth a thousand words and more.

Notes

1 This is a common trope in Japanese animator Hayako Miazaki's films. An example of this is Howl's Moving Castle that features in the eponymous animated-film distributed by Disney. Here, the castle is featured atop a green hill against a backdrop of a blue sky and white clouds.

2 Goodchild (2007) defines a geotag as 'a standardized code that can be inserted into information to note its appropriate geographic location' In other words, geotags are metadata that represent the location where an image was captured, generally expressed in terms of latitude and longitude (Yanai and Bingyu 2010).

References

Abarca, B. 2007. Auschwitz I [Online]. *Flickr*. Available: https://www.flickr.com/photos/brunoat/1183264371/in/photostream/ [Accessed 2 May 2016].

Adler, J. 1989. Origins of sightseeing. *Annals of Tourism Research* [Online], 16. Available: http://www.sciencedirect.com/science/article/B6V7Y-460P4F2-33/2/b59a98b7bd314caae047d2c5b4e28852 [Accessed 10 Mar. 2009].

Albers, P. C. and James, W. R. 1988. Travel photography: a methodological Approach. *Annals of Tourism Research* [Online], 15. [Accessed 21 Apr. 2011].

Auschwitz-Birkenau State Museum. 2011. Categories of prisoners [Online]. *Auschwitz-Birkenau State Museum.* Available: http://en.auschwitz.org.pl [Accessed 2 Aug. 2011].

Baerenholdt, J. O., Haldrup, M., Larsen, J. and Urry, J. 2003. *Performing tourist places,* Aldershot, UK: Ashgate.

Bakhtin, M. 1986. *Speech genres and other late essays,* Austin, TX, US: University of Texas Press.

Bamford, W., Coulton, P. and Edwards, R. 2007. Space-time travel blogging using a mobile phone. *Proceedings of the international conference on Advances in computer entertainment technology* [Online]. Available: http://dl.acm.org/citation.cfm?id=1255049 [Accessed 20 Jun. 2011].

Barthes, R. 1977. *Image, music, text,* New York: Noonday.

Barthes, R. 1993. *Camera lucida: reflections on photography,* London: Vintage.

Barton, D. 2015. Tagging on Flickr as a social practice. *In:* Jones, R. H., Chik, A. and Hafner, C. A. (eds.) *Discourse and digital practices: doing discourse analysis in the digital age.* Abingdon, UK: Routledge.

Beech, J. 2009. Genocide Tourism. *In:* Sharpley, R. (ed.) *The darker side of travel the theory and practice of dark tourism.* Bristol, UK: Channel View Publications.

Boyd, d. and Heer, J. 2006. Profiles as conversation: networked identity performance on Friendster. *39th Hawaii International Conference on Systems Sciences* [Online], 3. Available: http://ieeexplore.ieee.org/xpl/articleDetails.jsp?arnumber=1579411 [Accessed 8 Oct. 2010].

Caton, K. and Santos, C. A. 2008. Closing the hermeneutic circle photographic encounters with the other. *Annals of Tourism Research* [Online], 35. Available: http://www.sciencedirect.com/science/article/B6V7Y-4RR8V8X-2/2/5ced5cd41d1abfd6aab42d694abc580b [Accessed 1 Dec. 2009].

Chaplin, E. 2006. The convention of captioning: W. G. Sebald and the release of the captive image. *Visual Studies* [Online], 21. Available: http://www.tandfonline.com/doi/pdf/10.1080/14725860600613212 [Accessed 23 May 2011].

Dann, G. 1996. *The language of tourism: a sociolinguistic perspective,* Wallingford, UK: CAB International.

Dann, G. 1999. Writing out the tourist in space and time. *Annals of Tourism Research* [Online], 26. Available: http://www.sciencedirect.com/science/article/B6V7Y-3VS7VK0-8/2/644ebe6402ad134ca201678b33b3afc4 [Accessed 30 March 2009].

Dann, G. 2003. Noticing notices: tourism to order. *Annals of Tourism Research* [Online], 30. Available: http://www.sciencedirect.com/science/article/B6V7Y-487CRTY-C/2/dc84bfc6ccfbe9d209c9e11f7e7700b6 [Accessed 18 May 2011].

Davies, J. 2007. Display, identity, and the everyday: self-presentation through the online image. *Discourse: Studies in the Cultural Politics of Education* [Online], 28. Available: http://dx.doi.org/10.1030/01596300701625305 [Accessed 22 Sept. 2010].

Donath, J. and boyd, d. 2004. Public displays of connection. *BT Technology Journal* [Online], 22(4), 71–82. Available: http://link.springer.com/article/10.1023/B:BTTJ.0000047585.06264.cc. [Accessed 8 Oct. 2010].

Garrod, B. 2009. Understanding the relationship between tourism destination imagery and tourist photography. *Journal of Travel Research* [Online], 47. Available: http://www.scopus.com/inward/record.url?eid=2-s2.0-58149508293&partnerID=40 [Accessed 1 December 2009].

Golder, S. A. and Huberman, B. A. 2006. Usage patterns of collaborative tagging systems. *Journal of Information Science,* 32, 198–208.

Goldsworthy, P. 2010. Images, ideologies, and commodities: the French colonial postcard industry in Morocco. *Early Popular Visual Culture* [Online], 8. Available: http://www.informaworld.com/10.1080/17460651003693337 [Accessed 23 May 2011].

Goodchild, M. 2007. Citizens as sensors: the world of volunteered geography. *GeoJournal* [Online], 69. Available: http://dx.doi.org/10.1007/s10708-007-9111-y [Accessed 23 Sept. 2011].

Haldrup, M. and Larsen, J. 2009. *Tourism, performance and the everyday: consuming the Orient,* Oxon, UK: Routledge.

Hall, S. 1981. The determinations of news photographs. *In:* Cohen, S. and Young, J. (eds.) *The manufacture of news: social problems, deviance and the mass media.* Rev. ed. London: Constable.

Historic Environment Scotland. 2016. *Edinburgh Castle.* [Online]. Available: http://www.edinburghcastle.gov.uk/ [Accessed 28 Apr. 2016].

Jenkins, O. 2003. Photography and travel brochures: the circle of representation. *Tourism Geographies: An International Journal of Tourism Space, Place, and Environment* [Online], 5. Available: http://www.informaworld.com/10.1080/14616680309715 [Accessed 1 Dec. 2009].

Lennon, J. and Foley, M. 2004. *Dark tourism,* London: Continuum.

Lo, I. S. and McKercher, B. 2015. Ideal image in process: Online tourist photography and impression management. *Annals of Tourism Research,* 52, 104–116.

Lo, I. S., McKercher, B., Lo, A., Cheung, C. and Law, R. 2011. Tourism and online photography. *Tourism Management* [Online], 32. Available: http://www.sciencedirect.com/science/article/pii/S0261517710001123 [Accessed 15 Jul. 2010].

Lonely Planet. 2016a. Edinburgh Castle [Online]. *Lonely Planet.* Available: http://www.lonelyplanet.com/scotland/edinburgh/sights/castles-palaces-mansions/edinburgh-castle [Accessed 28 Apr. 2016].

Lonely Planet. 2016b. Top experiences in Krakow [Online]. *Lonely Planet.* Available: https://www.lonelyplanet.com/poland/malopolska/krakow [Accessed 30 Apr. 2016].

Lonely Planet. 2016c. Top experiences in Warsaw [Online]. *Lonely Planet.* Available: https://www.lonelyplanet.com/poland/malopolska/krakow [Accessed 30 Apr. 2016].

Long, B. 2012. *Complete digital photography,* Boston, MA, US: Course Technology.

MacCannell, D. 1976. *The tourist: a new theory of the leisure class,* New York: Schocken.

MacCannell, D. 2001. Tourist agency. *Tourist Studies* [Online], 1. Available: http://tou.sagepub.com/cgi/content/abstract/1/1/23 [Accessed Jun. 1, 2001].

MacCannell, D. 2008. Why it never really was about authenticity. *Society* [Online], 45. Available: http://dx.doi.org/10.1007/s12115-008-9110-8 [Accessed 25 Jan. 2010].

Marlow, C., Naaman, M., boyd, d. and Davis, M. 2006. HT06, Tagging paper, taxonomy, Flickr, academic article, to read. Hypertext '06, 2006 New York: Association for Computing Machinery, 31–40.

Nelson, M. E. and Hull, G. A. 2008. Self-presentation through multimedia: A Bakhtinian perspective on digital storytelling. *In:* Lundby, K. (ed.) *Digital storytelling, mediatized stories: self-representations in new media.* New York: Peter Lang.

Nomadic Matt. 2015. How to take professional travel photos. *Nomadic Matt* [Online]. Available from: http://www.nomadicmatt.com/travel-blogs/travel-photography-tips/ [Accessed 28 Apr. 2016].

Nomadic Matt. 2016. Nomadicmatt [Online]. *Instagram.* Available: http://www.nomadicmatt.com/ [Accessed 28 Apr. 2016].

Oded, N. and Chen, Y. 2010. Why do people tag?: motivations for photo tagging. *Communications of the ACM* [Online], 53(7). Available: http://dl.acm.org/citation.cfm?doid=1785414.1785450 [Accessed 23 Jun. 2011].

Papacharissi, Z. 2009. The virtual geographies of social networks: a comparative analysis of Facebook, LinkedIn and ASmallWorld. *New Media and Society,* 11, 199–220.

Pinch, T. 2010. The invisible technologies of Goffman's sociology from the merry-go-round to the Internet. *Technology and Culture* [Online], 51(2), 409–425r. [Accessed 19 Jul. 2010].

Rees, E. 2009a. Eva Rees' Photostream [Online]. *Flickr.* Available: http://www.flickr.com/people/evarees/ [Accessed 30 Apr. 2016].

Rees, E. 2009b. Temple of the Inscriptions [Online]. *Flickr.* Available: https://www.flickr.com/photos/evarees/3398064974/in/album-72157615671195779/ [Accessed 2 May 2016].

Rees, E. 2016. Eva Rees [Online]. *Flickr.* Available: http://www.flickr.com/people/evarees/ [Accessed 30 Apr. 2016].

Rees, E. and Rees, J. 2008. About us [Online]. N.p. *Forks and Jets.* Available: http://forksandjets.com/about/ [Accessed 24 Mar. 2016].

Rees, E. and Rees, J. 2009. Culture vulture [Online]. *Forks and Jets.* Available: http://forksandjets.com/2009/12/16/culture-vulture/ [Accessed 13 Jul. 2011].

Richter, R. and Schadler, C. 2009. See my virtual self? dissemination as a characteristic of digital photography – the example of Flickr.com. *Visual Studies* [Online], 24(2). Available: http://www.tandfonline.com/doi/full/10.1080/14725860903106179 [Accessed 26 May 2011].

Robinson, M. and Picard, D. 2009. Moments, magic, and memories: photographing tourists, tourist photographs, and making worlds. *In:* Robinson, M. and Picard, D. (eds.) *The framed world: tourism, tourists, and photography.* Farnham, UK: Ashgate.

Savage, K. 2011. Picture This: The Castle on the Rock [Online]. *Traveling Savage.* Available: http://www.traveling-savage.com/2011/03/25/picture-this-edinburgh-castle-rock/ [Accessed 28 Apr. 2016].

Serfaty, V. 2004. *The mirror and the veil: an overview of American online diaries and blogs,* Amsterdam: Rodopi.

Sontag, S. 1977. *On photography,* New York: Farrar, Strauss, and Giroux.

Tarlow, P. E. 2005. Dark tourism: The appealing 'dark' side of tourism and more. *In:* Novelli, M. (ed.) *Niche tourism: contemporary issues, trends and cases.* Amsterdam: Elsevier.

Urry, J. and Larsen, J. 2011. *The tourist gaze 3.0,* Los Angeles, CA, US: Sage.

Van Dijck, J. 2008. Digital photography: communication, identity, memory. *Visual Communication* [Online] 7. Available: http://vcj.sagepub.com/content/7/1/57.abstract [Accessed 29 Apr. 2011].

Van Dijck, J. 2010. Flickr and the culture of connectivity: sharing views, experiences, memories. *Memory Studies* [Online]. Available: http://mss.sagepub.com/content/early/2010/10/12/1750698010385215.abstract [Accessed 22 Jul. 2011].

Van House, N. A. 2009. Collocated photo sharing, story-telling, and the performance of self. *International Journal of Human-Computer Studies* [Online], 67. Available: http://www.sciencedirect.com/science/article/B6WGR-4X7GMN5-1/2/ff2cc44feca2c127c270bc4a17c62b83 [Accessed 19 Jul. 2010].

Walker, A. L. and Moulton, R. K. 1989. Photo albums: images of time and reflections of self. *Qualitative Sociology* [Online], 12. Available: http://dx.doi.org/10.1007/BF00988996 [Accessed 9 May 2011].

Westman, S. and Laine-Hernandez, M. 2008. The effect of page context on magazine image categorization. *Proceedings of the American Society for Information Science and Technology* [Online], 45. Available: http://dx.doi.org/10.1002/meet.2008.1450450255 [Accessed 22 Jun. 2011].

Yanai, K. and Bingyu, Q. 2010. Mining regional representative photos from consumer-generated geotagged photos. *Handbook of Social Network Technologies and Applications* [Online]. Available: http://dx.doi.org/10.1007/978-1-4419-7142-5_14 [Accessed 23 May 2012].

7 Mapping the travel blog

Conclusions on the discourses of travel and tourism

Travel and tourism often inspire blogging. The practice of blogging, in its turn, contributes to the promotion of tourism and the dissemination of experiences of travel. The discourses of travel and tourism are interrelated, and each travel blog negotiates the inherent tensions between these discourses differently. Approaching the travel blogs selected for this study as heteroglossic and polyphonic texts, has enabled a better understanding of how this discursive tension informs the presentation of travel experiences, tourist destinations, and the individuals who write about them and about themselves. It has also revealed how this relationship complicates the notion of blogs as personal and social narratives with definitive formal features. This book does not presume to offer a complete picture of how blogs work or indeed predict how these narratives will evolve. However, despite its limitations, this study does reveal something of the lay of the land that is the travel blogosphere and the uncharted territories that lie beyond. First, it has discovered that a travel blog's negotiation of travel and tourist discourses ultimately indicates the need for a more flexible definition of these texts. Furthermore, technology plays a central role in how tensions between these discourses are set up and play out in the self-presentation of travel bloggers. Finally, there is a growing online relationship between *Lonely Planet* and individuals who create travel-related content that merits further consideration. Based on these findings, this chapter ultimately presents the conclusions drawn from this study of how travel blogs negotiate the discursive tensions between travel and tourism.

The discursive relationship between travel and tourism plays out in many ways across the various travel blogs investigated in this study. *Tony Wheeler's Travels*, essentially a text that was, in all likelihood, conceived with a commercial purpose and promoted tourism, is constructed as a personal narrative in which the author assumes the role of a traveller and styles himself as a blogger. Although the blog is no longer hosted on the *Lonely Planet* website, the tensions between the personal travel and commercial tourism still remain. In blogs on travel-specific web hosts, entries that dissociate travel experiences from touristic ones are framed within advertisements from sponsors and web hosts. These sponsors rely on authors to generate travel-related content that underwrites their own promotion of tourism. Similarly, independent blog authors who use the themes and language of travel to position themselves as adventurous nomads publicise their texts and validate their position as experts on travel through the use of touristic narrative techniques. The relationship is therefore largely determined by the constantly changing narratorial positions of travel bloggers and the interaction they have with others. Moreover, discourses of travel and tourism in these blogs, though dissonant, are not mutually exclusive.

Travel blogs are often analysed to gain an understanding of how individuals describe destinations. However, most of the travel blog posts in this study, with the exception of *Tony Wheeler's Travels*, focused on the experience of travelling rather than the destination to be reached. This is understandable, given that many bloggers position themselves as travellers and associate their experiences with travel rather than tourism. In the case of blogs hosted on *TravelBlog*, *TravelPod*, and *BootsnAll*, which do have a touristic focus on destination, this is usually imposed by the web host or sponsor. Viewing travel blogs as forms of self-presentation and as polyphonic texts enables a better understanding of how individuals and destinations are described in these narratives. It also may help explain why some travel blogs may be inadequate as sources of information on destination image.

The multimodality and multivocality of travel blogs support the intertwining of forms of discourse associated with both travel and tourism. This in turn complicates the notion of these texts as personal narratives. If for some readers *Tony Wheeler's Travels* lacks conviction as a personal narrative and a travel blog, this is due in some part to the links and paratextual elements that display its connection with *Lonely Planet* or other commercial entities. Likewise, *TravelBlog* and *TravelPod* frame personal travel narratives in tourist advertising by virtue of platform structures that include third-party advertising and web-hosted content. Faced with a multiplicity of voices, it is sometimes difficult to interpret these travel blogs as texts that are personal in the sense that they express a blogger's views and choices alone. Nevertheless, a number of formal features and paratextual elements are integral to presenting the travel blogger. The design of title banners, the displayed links, embedded photographs and their accompanying captions and tags, and hashtags on *Twitter* all contribute to this self-presentation. While some of these formal elements draw on the contexts of travel to position the blogger as a traveller, others draw on discourses of tourism to validate this position and the narrative. This confirms Papacharissi (2009) and Pinch's (2010) observations on the centrality of the applications and architecture of online platforms in self-presentation. However, it also points for a need for technical definitions of travel blogs to be more expansive.

While this analysis of travel and tourist discourses affirms the social nature of blogging, it finds that that interaction is not limited to conversations within the blog and between bloggers. At the time of writing this chapter, independent travel blogs were comparatively social in nature, exhibiting reciprocal links, reaching out to readers across multiple platforms, and engaging them in conversation. These bloggers also shared content on *Facebook* and used *Twitter* to increase their visibility and keep in touch with audiences. *Lonely Planet* repeatedly featured in this interaction as bloggers commented on its guidebooks, used its hashtags, or displayed its logo on their web pages. Likewise, this publisher engaged with travel bloggers across a variety of platforms and manipulated their personal narratives of travel experiences in order to promote tourism via its own website. This supports Helmond's concept of blogs as distributed self-presentational narratives (2010). It also reiterates the need for examining blogs not as stand-alone texts, but as networked narratives that extend across several online platforms. Again, this suggests that definitions of the blogging need to be more flexible.

Keeping these key issues at the forefront, this concluding chapter reflects on how the discourses of travel and tourism contribute to the complexities of defining the travel blog. The findings of this discursive analysis of travel blogs indicate a need to re-evaluate existing definitions of this form or, as Mary Garden (2011) suggests, to arrive at a definition that is specific to the study of travel blogs instead of importing and applying generic descriptions as previous studies have done. The chapter then considers how the affordances of different platforms influence the discursive tensions in the text. Finally, by outlining the significance of *Lonely Planet* to travel and tourist discourse online, it recognises potential areas and new directions for researchers interested in further explorations of the travel blogosphere.

Where the travel blog lies

Although a case-study-like approach to examining blogs has its limitations, this study does reveal some of the reasons why the definition of travel blogs is difficult and perhaps even problematic. Often, who publishes the blog and how the author wishes to present himself or herself online play a significant role in the construction and structure of these narratives. *Tony Wheeler's Travels* tries very hard to create the impression that it is a travel blog. It is personalised to the extent that photographs of Wheeler are integrated in its title banner – a technique that no other text in this study employs. Furthermore, its claim to being one of the earliest travel blogs ever written underscores the author's reputation as an authority on travel. In the posts, however, the voice of the adventurous traveller often vies with the impersonal tones of the tour guide to describe destinations, many of which are popular tourist attractions. Despite the intimacy suggested by the title and the upper half of the home page, the links at the bottom serve to promote *Lonely Planet* and other initiatives with which Wheeler is involved. So, the intimacy that suggests travel often serves an underlying touristic commercialism. The text is consequently heteroglossic. The website is styled as a blog and structures its contents in reverse-chronological posts, but there is no reciprocal linking with other blogs, no interaction with readers, and therefore no real participation in the blog culture. It is but the hollow shell of a travel blog, and this consequently weakens the credibility of the author's self-presentation as a blogger. In the end, *Tony Wheeler's Travels* indicates that formal features alone cannot define a travel blog.

The relationship between travel and tourism in the blogs found on travel-specific web hosts such as *TravelBlog*, *TravelPod*, and *BootsnAll* is best described as one of dissonance and mutual interdependence. Here, web hosts and their sponsors rely on the narratives of bloggers to promote travel-related services via third-party advertising. That is to say, tourism needs travel to discover and write about places that it can then promote. Conversely, authors who use these services need advertising to underwrite their narratives of travel experiences. The authority of these bloggers and the authenticity of their blogs validates the advertisements that frame the narrative. The relationship between travel and tourism in these texts is therefore one characterised by a polyphony that is exhibited in diverse formal elements such as paratexts (titles, banners, and pseudonyms) and links. Approaching these texts from the perspective of Gérard Genette's theories of paratext (1997) allows for a consideration of features such as advertisements that have been largely ignored in previous analyses of blogs. It also allows for a more expansive definition of travel blogs that accounts for the contribution of these elements and the role of the web host or publisher towards the narrative and the presentation of its author(s).

Some content in *TravelBlog*, *TravelPod*, and *BootsnAll* blogs is generated by the bloggers, and the rest by the web host and advertisers. It is therefore sometimes difficult to determine who should be attributed as the author of the content in these narratives, and this has consequences for definitions of the form. It is difficult to view these texts as personal commentary because there are at least three contributors of content – the blogger, the web-host publisher, and the advertiser. Definitions that emphasise a personal voice as a characteristic quality of blogs therefore need some refining to be applicable to such texts. To consider only the content created by the blogger as comprising the blog is equally problematic, for this would mean ignoring several distinctive features usually regarded as being definitive to blogs. The web hosts often impose a certain format on narrative and locate this within a body of other similar texts. Their role must therefore to be considered, both when defining a blog by its formal elements and when viewing it as a text that gives a sense of its author.

A greater degree of customisation is possible in blogs that are hosted independently, and consequently the author's online self is writ large across these texts. Often, these bloggers position themselves as travellers who go off the beaten path. At other times, they adopt the stance of experts or tour guides. As they occupy a variety of narratorial positions, the discursive style of the blog shifts from the monologic tones associated with tourism to the personal voice associated with travel. The distribution of these blogs across a variety of social media platforms has the effect of engaging a diverse and largely unknown audience in a conversation about journey and the content of the blog, turning what is presented as an intimate and solitary travel experience into one that is shared and whose meaning is negotiated in the conversation between authors and readers. This combination of monologue and dialogue complicates the positioning of the blog, with reference to frameworks such as those suggested by Stine Lomborg (2009).

Clearly, technical features alone do not a blog make. Nevertheless, it does not follow that defining travel blogs by their constituent travel and tourist discourses is more practicable. Each travel blog variously incorporates these discourses and negotiates them differently, making it difficult to arrive at a generic definition of this format. On the whole, travel blogs exhibit multiple narrative styles. Ultimately, discursive tensions are negotiated in a manner that ensures the text has at least a superficial integrity as a blog, while presenting the online self of its blogger, describing experiences, and promoting destinations. A discursive approach to these texts can, however, provide a broader interpretation of what constitutes a travel blog.

Technology and the travel(ler) blogger

Many of the travel bloggers studied here present themselves as travellers and associate their experiences of places with travel as opposed to tourism. How they achieve this is due in part to the affordances of the platform they use, be it the blog itself or the social media it links to. Bloggers generally utilise a variety of formal features – title banners, posts, blogrolls, visual elements, etc. – to present several narratorial positions. However, there are also instances when the platform determines discursive tensions and this is beyond a blogger's control – as indicated by the way tags work with photographs in *Flickr* and *Instagram* or the inclusion of advertisements in *TravelBlog*. Affordances can therefore strengthen a narrative's connection with discourses of either travel or tourism. They may even shape how readers view a travel blog. Thus, technology is a key factor in how travel and tourist discourses inform this self-presentation.

In a similar manner, the negotiation of travel and tourist discourses is predicated on the technology of the web hosting service. For the most part, authors blogging on *TravelPod*, *TravelBlog*, and *BootsnAll* attempt to style themselves as wanderers, adventurers, and nomads. Accordingly, they narrate experiences of travel as opposed to tourism. Regardless of an author's effort to present this as being off the beaten path, the technology inscribes a route. In general, these travel-specific web hosts gather entries from across a number of blogs, categorise them by destination, and package them in a uniform template. These platforms restrict how authors create texts, in this sense guiding their blogging experience and prescribing a structure for their narratives. Also, such is their design that they usually accentuate destinations. *TravelBlog* and *TravelPod* in particular locate the place described in the post in its town or city, state, country, and continent. The way these platforms organise content creation and distribution and impose conformity parallels touristic practices. In addition to this, hosting a blog on these services hardly constitutes going off the beaten path.

Technology also plays a twofold role in deciding how tourist discourse in the form of advertisements forms a part of these travel blogs, and the implications this has for discourses of travel in the text. On the one hand, the structure of the platform decides how these appear alongside blog entries on *TravelBlog*, *TravelPod*, and *BootsnAll*. This is something that authors cannot control, although what they write in their posts does determine the content of advertisements generated by Google's AdSense. On the other hand, a more technically adept reader can choose to view the text free of advertising by using suitable ad-blocking software. These advertisements authenticate the destination and validate the entry by promoting travel-related services available at or near the places mentioned in the post. In effect, they encourage readers to visit these places themselves – to book a flight, rent a room, or sign up for a tour. The dissonance lies in the fact that a place described as being off the beaten path by the blogger is made easily approachable or accessible by the advertiser. In this sense, travel paves the way for tourism while the latter underwrites the narrative of a travel experience.

It is also worth noting that the technology of these platforms also guides readers' reception and response to the narrative. Perhaps symbolically, blogs on *TravelBlog* and *TravelPod* are restricted to linking with other texts within the same website. Individuals using this service cannot distribute their content, via their travel blogs, across other social media in the manner of independent travel bloggers. Consequently, readers are also 'guided' to other *TravelBlog* or *TravelPod* content, which includes other blogs using the same web hosts. In this sense, both the blogs and their readers are not allowed to wander or be spontaneous. The presentation and reading of this narrative is managed to a large extent by the web host for the purpose of promoting tourism to audiences.

This is not to suggest, however, that technology is wholly deterministic. Bloggers such as Steve Nakano work around the limitations of *BootsnAll* to ensure that the text looks like a blog. Their inclusion of an 'About' post in his blog, makes up for the absence of an 'About' page in the web host's template. Both the act of creating this post and its content indicate a singularity (in comparison with other *BootsnAll* blogs) that enhances this author's position as a traveller. Therefore, while technology is important to self-presentation, how authors utilise the tools available is also significant.

Independently hosting a travel blog facilitates the presentation of travel in a number of ways. In the first place, a greater degree of customisation is possible, so authors have greater freedom of self-expression. For bloggers like Eva Rees and Laura Walker, it is an opportunity to demonstrate their competence as designers. For others like Keith Savage, it enables a more controlled presentation of the self as a travel writer – he is the sole author of all content in *Travelling Savage*. Each of these authors strives to create a sophisticated text, both in terms of visual appeal and informative content, which reflects their individuality. At the same time, the more polish these texts acquire, the more they slip into the superficial perfection of tourist discourse, which these authors are keen to avoid. Formal elements are therefore self-presentational elements that indicate a blogger's narratorial position, and are consequently integral to the negotiation of travel and tourist discourses. A second point worth noting is that by not following the crowd regarding choice of web hosting service, authors' enhance their position in the blog as travellers or adventurers.

Indeed, the individualistic website design and personalised titles, banners, and logos of these blogs complement the presentation of a self that seeks experiences that are far from commonplace. The display of technological competence supports this self-presentation. The way in which travel blogs network their narratives across a variety of online platforms also has implications for the relationship between travel and tourism. Most independent travel blogs link to *Facebook* and *Twitter*. The majority also link to each other. Some even have similar titles. Here again is the 'enclave culture' of blogs that Geert Lovink talks about (2008, p. 252). As this community grows, the travel experiences they describe become increasingly distributed and publicised, and thus less unique. Over time, multiple narratives about a single destination accumulate in the travel blogging community. From the point of view of a reader faced with a wealth of information about the same place, there may appear to be few travel experiences left to discover. The more a destination is written about, the less off the beaten path it can seem.

It is worth noting the significance of a travel blog's interactivity for a convincing presentation of the self as travel blogger. Blogs that best impress on their audience the position of their authors and the nature of the text are often those that facilitate conversations between bloggers and readers and linking to other similar blogs. In this way, these blogs become a 'dialogical space' to borrow a phrase from Serfaty (2004, p. 53), which allows the manifestation of multiple voices and discourses. In such a space authors interact with readers and in the process define their role as travel bloggers and their texts as blogs. The presence of a dialogical space is therefore integral to the interplay between travel and tourist discourses that inform a blogger's self-presentation. Still, the extent to which this influences a reader's perception of a blog and its author as authentic and credible can only be determined by further research and by applying different methodologies.

The blogs studied here confirm findings that technical features of online platforms are self-presentational elements. Bloggers manipulate a number of available online tools to present themselves as best as they can, but it is necessary to recognise that at times they can go only as far as the technology permits. This bears out Papacharissi's (2009) and Pinch's (2010) observations on the importance of technology in mediating online behaviour. On the other hand, the polyphony of these blogs makes it difficult to describe blogging, as Trammell and Keshelashvili (2005) do, as a deliberate self-presentational process in a virtual environment controlled by the author. Digital technologies in particular can change a text in ways that bloggers often cannot foresee. As a result, the impression that authors think they are creating is not necessarily the one that readers see. However, it is beyond the scope of this study to ascertain whether these travel bloggers have experienced this with their readers.

Ultimately, a blogger's choice of platform plays a significant part in how discourses of travel and tourism inform their blogs. Specific features of a platform often play a crucial role in how discursive tensions are set up, displayed, or managed. On the one hand, contextualisation of a narrative in discourses of travel and tourism is in some part decided by its underlying technologies. On the other hand, the way authors, web hosts, or sponsors utilise these technologies also has some influence on the presentation of the self as a traveller or the touristic promotion of a destination. Therefore, the chosen platform's intrinsic structure and the affordances it offers to users are important factors in how these narratives manage discursive tensions.

Going everywhere with *Lonely Planet*

This research project began with an analysis of *Tony Wheeler's Travels*, and therefore it seems only appropriate to conclude with a discussion of *Lonely Planet*'s relationship with travel bloggers. By interacting with individuals who create travel-related texts online, this publisher has reinforced its own reputation and online presence. A large number of individuals, including travel bloggers, are constantly creating a vast store of travel-related content online including blog entries, microblog posts, and photographs. Through its website and its own pages on websites such as *Flickr* and *Twitter*, *Lonely Planet* curates this information and facilitates access to it. This process links themes and ideas usually associated with travel to places that are generally acknowledged as being touristic destinations. This has implications for self-presentation – *Lonely Planet* positions itself as an arbiter of taste, picking out content that is genuine and proving itself capable of recognising the unique and extraordinary, that is to say what is travel-like, in destinations that have become clichéd or touristic. *Lonely Planet*'s mobilisation of travel and tourist discourses can offer a wider perspective on how similar tourism organisations position themselves online to promote their services.

The *Lonely Planet* website promotes the organisation as being part of a community of individuals committed to travelling responsibly, describing their travels accurately, and providing reliable advice and information to potential travellers. Its purpose is to fulfil the publisher's commitment to providing readers with credible, carefully researched information about destinations, including maps for places for which no maps exist. This is neatly summed up in the promise that its 'Thorn Tree Travel Forum' will cover all places on the planet including those they do not have guidebooks for (*Lonely Planet* 2016). The statement refers to *Lonely Planet*'s intention to map real places, but is equally applicable to the company's online presence. There are two networks of connections at work here. The first is at a textual level and consists of travel-related content drawn together, in the case of *Twitter* and *Instagram*, by tags such as '#lp' or '#LonelyPlanet' respectively. The other involves the relationship between the organisation and a vast number of individuals who author travel-related online texts, including travel bloggers whose blogs and images are featured on *Lonely Planet*. The publisher's vast network of web pages across a variety of social media suggests that it certainly tries to 'cover every place' (*Lonely Planet* 2016) in the online world, and its relationship with travel bloggers across multiple online platforms contributes significantly towards achieving this goal.

Through both networks, *Lonely Planet* creates an association with travel that enhances its own self-presentation. The company positions itself alongside travellers and sells the idea of travel. When bloggers create travel-related content on various platforms and appropriately tag this to make it easily accessible to *Lonely Planet*, they help the publisher discover this new information for its readers and to collate firsthand information on destinations across the world. *Lonely Planet* repurposes this material, distributing it across its own web pages, thus enhancing its credibility as a producer of authentic content. It also encourages individuals to produce a certain type of content, as is the case with themed competitions on *Flickr*, and thus organises narratives of travel experiences for consumption by potential tourists. This places *Lonely Planet* in the role of facilitator. In this manner, the publisher initiates a potential circle of representation of destinations and travel-related concepts as described by Urry and Larsen (2011). For bloggers, such competitions are an opportunity to enhance their reputation as authors and to publicise their travel blogs. By amassing a wealth of user-generated travel-related content through these connections across various online platforms, *Lonely Planet* manages to cover both well-known and remote destinations across the world. Yet, covering everything everywhere makes 'real' travel and writing about 'real' travel increasingly impossible.

Through the 'Lonely Planet Pathfinders' page, the publisher also regularly promotes certain blog posts as a 'Featured Blog', thus increasing the travel blog's visibility. Here, content that comes straight from the pages of independent and amateur travel blogs enhances *Lonely Planet*'s reputation. At the same time it potentially sells travel-related products and services, and thus paves the way for tourism to the places described therein. This is by no means a one-sided relationship as bloggers benefit from this link as well. Such recognition from *Lonely Planet* reinforces an author's position as an expert on travel. In this sense, discourses of travel and tourism complement each other. It is possible that content created subsequent to this recognition is influenced by this corporate association, and that a 'featured' blogger may therefore appear less genuine. While it is difficult to establish this, given the approach that this study takes, there is room for further research into how readers perceive travel narratives that receive the stamp of approval from corporate tourism.

Not surprisingly, *Lonely Planet* itself figures in several blog entries. Some travel bloggers consult its guidebooks, assess their reliability, and measure their own experiences against them. Darryl and Sarah Howells frequently refer to *Lonely Planet*'s guidebook on Australia, and mention this in their posts in *Wallaby Wanderers*. Some of these analyse the accuracy of its descriptions while others focus on places that deserve mention principally because they are not mentioned in the *Lonely Planet* guidebook and are therefore not on a 'tourist's radar' (Howell and Howell 2010). While there is a touristic aspect to using a guidebook that is at odds with these bloggers' position as wanderers, mentioning *Lonely Planet*, an organisation that associates itself with offbeat travel, is also self-presentational, serving to define experiences as travel as opposed to tourism. Also paradoxically, in this particular instance, destinations acquire the distinction of being travel as opposed to tourism, simply because they do not figure in the guidebook.

Brian Thacker's eponymous blog (2008) is probably one of the best examples of a travel blog inspired by a *Lonely Planet* guidebook. Using the original 1975 edition of *South East Asia on a Shoestring* as a guide, Thacker travelled through East Timor, Indonesia, and Malaysia, retracing Tony and Maureen Wheeler's journey through this region. His blog about his experiences describes his rediscovery of places mentioned in the guidebook. Tony Wheeler accompanied Thacker during part of this journey, and this inspired the writing of an entry in

Tony Wheeler's Travels, which promotes both the latest edition of the South East Asia guidebook as well as Thacker's own blog on the journey (Wheeler 2011). Thacker's trip subsequently inspired the writing of his own travel book *Tell Them to Get Lost* (2011).

This is admittedly an exceptional case – not all blogs are based on *Lonely Planet*'s guidebooks, and even Thacker's blog describes other journeys not based on *South East Asia on a Shoestring*. Still, the links between *Brian Thacker* and *Tony Wheeler's Travels* reveal how discourses of travel and tourism are constantly collapsing into each other. Guidebooks are generally regarded as touristic objects and the author is clearly retracing a well-beaten path. Yet, his take on *South East Asia on a Shoestring* turns an itinerary originally planned for potential tourists into a travel experience based on the adventure of rediscovering what still remains of the places first visited in 1975. *Brian Thacker*, with its themes of travel, in its turn becomes a self-presentational tool for *Tony Wheeler's Travels*, enhancing the latter's association with travel as opposed to tourism. At the same time, it promotes *Lonely Planet*'s more recent publications on the region and potentially encourages a new wave of tourism to the places described in the guidebook. What all of this points to is the centrality of *Lonely Planet* and its discourse to the narration of contemporary travel experiences and the presentation of authors as travellers in the blogs studied here. Blogs that focus on descriptions of travel as opposed to tourism are equally important to the online presentation and the reputation of *Lonely Planet*. The relationship between the publisher and travel bloggers has mutual benefits. Ultimately, this is an association established through the negotiation of both travel and tourist discourses.

Of travel, tourism, and blogging

Like journeys, narratives have a beginning, middle, and end. However, while there are some structural parallels between the serial narrative that is the travel blog and the journey it describes, many of these narratives seem to have no clear ending. This is not to say that a conclusion is not possible. Indeed, the *Wallaby Wanderers* blog has a definite conclusion, although there is a suggestion that the authors may continue the narrative sometime in the future. However, many of the other travel blogs here describe successive trips and there appears to be no imminent closure. Also, many of the independently hosted travel blogs analysed here distribute content across several platforms and this too makes for a narrative that seems infinite. Furthermore, readers can enter the narrative at a number of different points, none of which may be the travel blog entry, which implies that it is they, and not the author, who decide where the narrative begins and ends.

It is also often difficult to achieve a balance between travel and blogging, and this is a dilemma that is discussed at some length in the blogs of Nomadic Matt and Laura Walker. Both authors agree that it is hard to keep up with blog updates while travelling. Certainly, the idea of travel as being a journey of exploration and discovery suggests that real travel should be to destinations that are so remote that an Internet connection may be difficult to find. Consequently, there must be a gap between the experience of real travel and its narration in a blog. Conversely, as Nomadic Matt points out, the demands of maintaining a website make it difficult to travel spontaneously (2011). Still, it is increasingly possible that mobile phone technology will compress the time difference between travelling and blogging. With the appropriate applications, travelling while blogging or vice versa may become a real possibility.

The downside to advances in technology is that 'real' travel becomes hard to achieve. Already, Eva Rees's *Flickr* album demonstrates how the effects of geotagging and mapping make it difficult to find places that are off the beaten path. Indeed, the very existence of travel blogs and their associated media shows that travel is intricately bound up with the use of various technologies of the Internet. This too is a matter that occupies Nomadic Matt who wonders whether we have become 'too wired in our travels' (2010). He points out that the Internet enables travellers to find places, stay in touch with each other and the rest of the world, and to keep themselves occupied during the journey. Consequently, he argues, travellers spend more time exploring the digital world than the place they are in. This suggests a touristic lack of involvement or investment in the visited destination. Real travel, according to this blogger, is only possible when technology is turned off.

This research monograph has examined various travel blogs, particularly those that are hosted independently, as a centralising force for different threads of an individual's online self-presentation that is networked across multiple platforms. However, it is equally possible that a different online platform acts as the focal point. Eva Rees's *Flickr* page is an example of this. For others, the travel blog may form one part of a networked presentation of self that centres on their *Facebook* page or profile. Furthermore, as individuals explore and develop content on new applications that are constantly emerging, the centre of their networked self may shift from their travel blog to a different online platform. For example, many travel blogs that did not use *Pinterest* or *Instagram* now link to content on these platforms via widgets.

Over the course of its journey through the travel blogosphere, this study has encountered and analysed three aspects of discourse – the utterances that make up the narrative, the manner in which narrative techniques are used, and the practices of travel and tourism that shape the blog. The outcomes of this analysis have determined that travel blogs negotiate the discourses of travel and tourism on all three levels. First, each element of a blog draws together utterances associated with both discourses into a presentation of travel blogger and the narrative of what is usually described as a travel experience. An utterance associated with travel can, however, be strategically employed to promote tourism or be associated with a touristic concept and vice versa. This is exemplified in Tony Wheeler's London taxi image, in the title of Ross Pringle's 'Life on the Fringe' and in Keith Savage's photograph of Edinburgh Castle. These findings support Goffman's theory that a single self-presentational cue can be meaningfully employed in different contexts. Travel blogs negotiate discursive tensions by combining narrative forms and techniques – cues – that best indicate narratorial positions and themes within the text.

Travel blogs also manage discursive tensions through a manipulation of both the narrative as a whole and relating this to other texts. This is best demonstrated in the way sponsors of travel-specific web hosts frame their advertisements on blog posts that describe travel in order to promote touristic services. It is also indicated in the way independent travel bloggers link to *Lonely Planet* to support their own presentation of travel experiences. The use of particular affordances such as hashtags on *Twitter* allows bloggers to draw on discourses of tourism to establish and promote the blog as a whole and the traveller self that is presented within.

Finally, concepts and practices associated with travel and tourism play an important role in shaping travel blogs to some extent. Tourism's focus on destination finds expression in the content provided by the sponsors and web hosts of *TravelBlog*, *TravelPod*, and *BootsnAll* blogs. Yet, the content of these advertisements and links is based on blog posts that usually describe experiences of travel. Conversely, where travel's focus on experience is often expressed in the content of photographs and blog posts these are equally framed in, or contain discourses of, tourism. Therefore, travel blogs negotiate discursive tensions through the narrative forms and techniques that present and promote authors, destinations, and experiences. How they do this depends largely on what is being presented and the technologies available for this self-presentation.

This study contributes to research into travel blogs in several ways. A discursive examination of the same categories of blogs suggested by Schmallegger and Carson (2008), for the purpose of marketing research, reveals a different aspect to how individuals present their travel experiences. Tourism marketing researchers who regard these texts as accounts of consumer experience may gain a better understanding of how travel bloggers position themselves in their narratives and describe destinations. In particular, the theoretical approach outlined here reveals a self-presentational aspect to the narration of travel in several online platforms and indicates that this heteroglossic. As mentioned in the introduction, this conceptual approach develops out of Hevern's analysis of blogs and has, it is hoped, provided a better understanding of discourse in travel blogs. A juxtaposition of the theories of Bakhtin and Goffman may be similarly useful to the study of other travel-related texts as forms of self-presentation as well as discursive tensions in other genres of blogs – corporate or political blogs, for example. This book also outlines a conceptual approach to the analysis of travel-related images and folksonomies. This is particularly relevant at the time of concluding this study as image-oriented platforms such as *Instagram* and *Vine* become increasingly popular as do practices such as moblogging and tagging. Given the rapid rate of change of such technologies, the approach outlined can by no means be a definitive model. However, it could be developed further and adapted to the study of discourse and meaning in images on other such platforms.

Ultimately, the blog itself travels. It is sometimes distributed across many, many online platforms. It continuously evolves in form and content. Its narrative is generally continuous, heteroglossic, and polyphonic. It is constituted in discourses of travel as it is in discourses of tourism. It escapes definition. It is therefore difficult to establish exactly where a travel blog lies. Although there is much more to discover about these texts and their authors, this exploration of the travel blogosphere must end here. The journey of the travel blog through time is, however, one marked by constant transformation as new forms of travel-related communication emerge online. It is, therefore, a narrative that is constantly evolving and never-ending.

References

Garden, M. 2011. Defining blog: a fool's errand or a necessary undertaking. *Journalism* [Online]. Available: http://jou.sagepub.com/content/early/2011/09/14/1464884911421700.abstract [Accessed 20 Sept. 2011].

Genette, G. 1997. *Paratexts: thresholds of interpretation,* Cambridge, UK: Cambridge University Press.

Helmond, A. 2010. Identity 2.0: Constructing identity with cultural software. Digital Methods Initiative. *Anne Helmond* [Online]. Available: http://www.annehelmond.nl/wordpress/wp-content/uploads/2010/01/helmond_identity20_dmiconference.pdf [Accessed 22 Jun. 2010].

Howell, D. and Howell, S. 2010. If paradise is half as nice [Online]. *TravelBlog*. Available: http://www.travelblog.org/Oceania/Australia/Tasmania/Mole-Creek/blog-475478.html [Accessed 12 Feb. 2011].

Lomborg, S. 2009. Navigating the blogosphere: towards a genre-based typology of weblogs. *First Monday* [Online], 14. Available: http://www.uic.edu/htbin/cgiwrap/bin/ojs/index.php/fm/article/view/2329/2178 [Accessed 28 Jan. 2010].

Lonely Planet. 2016. Thorn tree travel forum [Online]. *Lonely Planet*. Available: https://www.lonelyplanet.com/thorntree [Accessed 5 May 2016].

Lovink, G. 2008. *Zero comments: blogging and critical Internet culture,* New York: Routledge.

Nomadic Matt. 2010. Are we too wired while traveling? [Online]. *Nomadic Matt*. N.p. Available: http://www.nomadicmatt.com/travel-blogs/are-we-too-wired-while-traveling/ [Accessed 4 Aug. 2010].

Nomadic Matt. 2011. Learning to go with the flow [Online]. *Nomadic Matt*. Available: http://www.nomadicmatt.com/travel-blogs/going-with-the-flow/ [Accessed 15 Mar. 2011].

Papacharissi, Z. 2009. The virtual geographies of social networks: a comparative analysis of Facebook, LinkedIn and ASmallWorld. *New Media and Society,* 11, 199–220.

Pinch, T. 2010. The Invisible Technologies of Goffman's Sociology From the Merry-Go-Round to the Internet. *Technology and Culture* [Online], 51(2) 409–425r. [Accessed 19 Jul. 2010].

Schmallegger, D. and Carson, D. 2008. Blogs in tourism: changing approaches to information exchange. *Journal of Vacation Marketing* [Online], 14. Available: http://jvm.sagepub.com/cgi/content/abstract/14/2/99 [Accessed 15 May 2009].

Serfaty, V. 2004. *The mirror and the veil: an overview of American online diaries and blogs,* Amsterdam: Rodopi.

Thacker, B. 2008. *Brian on a shoestring* [Online]. Available: http://www.brianthacker.tv/blog/brian-on-a-shoestring/ [Accessed 29 Nov. 2011].

Thacker, B. 2011. *Tell them to get lost: travels with the Lonely Planet guide book that started it all.* Melbourne, Australia: William Heinemann.

Trammell, K. D. and Keshelashvili, A. 2005. Examining the new influencers: a self-presentation study of A-list blogs. *Journalism and Mass Communication Quarterly* [Online], 82. Available: http://jmq.sagepub.com/content/82/4/968 [Accessed 11 Sept. 2010].

Urry, J. and Larsen, J. 2011. *The tourist gaze 3.0,* Los Angeles, US: Sage.

Wheeler, T. 2011. Tell them to get lost. *Tony Wheeler's Travels* [Online]. Lonely Planet. Available: http://tonywheeler.com.au/tell-them-to-get-lost/ [Accessed 17 May 2016].

Index